# The Moral Economy
# of the Peasant

## REBELLION AND SUBSISTENCE
## IN SOUTHEAST ASIA

James C. Scott

New Haven and London, Yale University Press

Library of Congress catalog card number 75-43334
International standard book number: 0-300-02190-9 (paperbound)

Designed by John O. C. McCrillis and set in Baskerville Roman types. Printed in the
United States of America.

The paper in this book meets the guidelines for permanence and durability of the
Committee on Production Guidelines for Book Longevity of the Council on Library
Resources.

23   22   21   20   19   18   17

For Mia, Aaron, and Noah

# Contents

# Preface

This study of the basis of peasant politics and rebellion begins with Tawney's metaphor describing "the position of the rural population" as "that of a man standing permanently up to the neck in water, so that even a ripple might drown him." It places the critical problem of the peasant family—a secure subsistence—at the center of the study of peasant politics, where I believe it belongs. I try to show how the fear of dearth explains many otherwise anomalous technical, social, and moral arrangements in peasant society.

The fact that subsistence-oriented peasants typically prefer to avoid economic disaster rather than take risks to maximize their average income has enormous implications for the problem of exploitation. On the basis of this principle, it is possible to deduce those systems of tenancy and taxation that are likely to have the most crushing impact on peasant life. The critical problem is not the average surplus extracted by elites and the state, but rather whose income is stabilized at the expense of whom. The theory is examined in the light of the historical development of agrarian society in Lower Burma and Vietnam. Both the commercialization of agriculture and the growth of bureaucratic states produced systems of tenancy and taxation that increasingly undermined the stability of peasant income and provoked fierce resistance. Two notable episodes of such resistance, the Saya San Rebellion in Burma and the Nghe-Tinh Soviets in Vietnam, are analyzed in some detail.

Throughout the volume, I have taken pains to emphasize the *moral* content of the subsistence ethic. The problem of exploitation and rebellion is thus not just a problem of calories and income but is a question of peasant conceptions of social justice, of rights and obligations, of reciprocity.

Since proofreading the final version of this manuscript I have come across a good many economic studies of Third World agriculture as well as archival material on rebellion which might have strengthened the argument and added a few nuances. In particular, I regret that Keith Griffin's *The Political Economy of Agrarian Change* and Jeffrey Paige's *Agrarian Revolution* were not available to me in the course of writing.

Readers will note that the study of the moral economy of the peasantry, while it begins in the domain of economics, must end in the study of peasant culture and religion. I have tried to indicate, especially when discussing the problem of false consciousness, the lines along which such an inquiry might proceed but I have only scratched the surface here. In subsequent work I hope to explore more fully the cultural basis, within the peasantry's "little tradition," of moral dissent and resistance.

The contents of this book were drafted in 1973-74 when I had the good luck to land a National Science Foundation Grant and to accompany Louise Scott to Paris where she settled in to study nineteenth-century art. I took advantage of the year in Paris to read more widely the work of what is loosely known as the *Annales* school of historiography, particularly Marc Bloch and Emmanuel Le Roy Ladurie, as well as that of Robert Mandrou and R. C. Cobb on *mentalités populaires*. Something of the spirit of these works has found its way into this volume, although I would not want to tarnish their schools of thought by claiming membership in their fraternity. My appreciation of Marxist thought was considerably enhanced by occasional visits to the stimulating seminars of Nicos Poulantzas and Alain Touraine of the Ecole Pratique des Hautes Etudes. Georges Condominas also welcomed me to his exciting weekly seminars for Southeast Asian specialists. Like many scholars before me, I profited from the facilities and atmosphere of the library of the Maison des Sciences de l'Homme to whose staff I am very grateful. The intellectual companionship I found there from scholars like Serafina Salkoff, Ezra Suleiman, and Yanne Barbé provided a welcome diversion from the essentially lonely task of writing. The Archives d'Outre Mer in Paris and the India Office Library in London, whose staff I should like to thank, were the sources for the case studies of Vietnam and Burma in this volume.

I would not have been in a position to write had it not been for a semester grant from the Southeast Asian Development Advisory Group of the Asia Society in the spring of 1973 which allowed me to organize thoughts that had been brewing for some time.

The intellectual debts I have amassed in thinking through this argument defy accounting and, for all I know, many of my silent partners would prefer to remain anonymous. Nevertheless I would like to thank James Roumasset, Barrington Moore, and Sydel Silverman, whose work was formative in structuring my own thought. Without the criticism and help of Gail Paradise Kelly, Sam Popkin, Ben Kerkvliet, and Alex Woodside I would undoubtedly have fallen into more errors of fact and analysis than I have. On the subject of deference and false consciousness, a treacherous ground under any circumstances, I have chosen to resist many of the criticisms of Ronald Herring, Thomas Bossert, Charles Whitmore, and Michael Leiserson. Their assaults on my argument have served to sharpen it considerably, though they may well regret that I went seeking reinforcements rather than abandon the position altogether. Some of that reinforcement came from the work of the brilliant Dutch scholar W. F. Wertheim, many of whose values and perspectives I have come to share.

Of all my prepublication critics, none were so searching as Clifford Geertz, Michael Adas, and an anonymous reader for Yale Press. Many arguments were rethought and reformulated as a consequence of their careful reading and although I have certainly not laid all the problems they raised to rest, whatever quality the final product has is due to their detailed comments. The Land Tenure Center at the University of Wisconsin, which is largely responsible for my education in peasant studies, was kind enough to provide summer support so that I might redraft the manuscript in line with the many helpful criticisms I had received.

My colleagues at the University of Wisconsin, particularly Don Emmerson, Murray Edelman, and Fred Hayward have stimulated me in ways too diverse to pin down precisely. Above all, Edward Friedman, with whom I have given courses on peasant politics and revolution, has taught me more about demystifying scholarship, about Marx, and about the peasantry than I can ever repay. I only hope this volume does justice to his friendship and instruction.

Jenny Mittnacht did more than just type the manuscript; she repaired much of the damage caused by my early inattention to grammar and spelling bees.

At this point in the standard preface it is customary for the author to claim total responsibility for error and wrongheadedness and to absolve others of blame. I am not so sure I want to do that. While I am happy to stand or fall with what I have written, it is also clear that I have learned so much from so many scholars that a great many of us are implicated in this enterprise. If it should turn out that I am on the wrong track, I suspect that many of them are on the same errant train with me!

I wish also to report that my wife and children, who have their own scholarly and other concerns, had virtually nothing to do with this volume. They were not particularly understanding or helpful when it came to research and writing but called me away as often as possible to the many pleasures of a life in common. May it always remain so.

*Madison, Wisconsin*
*May 26, 1976*

J.C.S.

# Introduction

> There are districts in which the position of the rural population is
> that of a man standing permanently up to the neck in water, so that
> even a ripple is sufficient to drown him.[1]

Tawney was writing about China in 1931 but it would not stretch his
graphic description much to apply it to the peasantry of Upper Burma,
Tonkin and Annam in Indochina, or East and Central Java in the early
twentieth century. Here too, lilliputian plots, traditional techniques, the
vagaries of weather and the tribute in cash, labor, and kind exacted by
the state brought the specter of hunger and dearth, and occasionally
famine, to the gates of every village.

The particular ecological niche occupied by some sectors of the
peasantry in Southeast Asia exposed them, more than most, to subsistence risks. Upper Burma's Dry Zone, always at the mercy of a capricious
rainfall, suffered a catastrophic famine in 1856–57, shortly after Brit-
ain's conquest of Lower Burma. "The rains failed and the rice withered
in the fields . . . and the people died. They died in the fields gnawing
the bark of trees; they died on the highways while wandering in search
of food; they died in their homes."[2] In Annam, in northeast Thailand,
and elsewhere where nature is unkind, most adults must have experienced, within living memory, one or more times of great scarcity when
the weak and very young died and when others were reduced to eating
their livestock and seed paddy, to subsisting on millet, root crops,
bran—on what they might normally feed their animals.

The great famine of 1944–45 experienced by the peasantry of North
Vietnam, however, was of such magnitude as to dwarf other twentieth-
century subsistence crises in the region. In the best of times, the cultivated land in Tonkin barely sufficed to feed its own population. The
Japanese and their Vichy allies, nevertheless, converted much paddy
land to jute and other war-machine crops. After the October 1943
harvest, the occupation forces literally scoured the countryside in armed
bands, confiscating much of the crop. A near-famine became a total
famine when a series of typhoons from May to September broke dikes
and flooded much of Tonkin's paddy land, destroying the tenth-month

---

1. R. H. Tawney, *Land and Labor in China* (Boston: Beacon Press, 1966), p. 77.

2. From the *Government of Burma Report on the Famine in Burma 1896–97*, quoted by
Michael Adas in *Agrarian Development and the Plural Society in Lower Burma* (Madison:
University of Wisconsin Press, 1974), p. 45.

harvest in 1944. Even millet, potatoes, and rice bran were exhausted; potato leaves, banana roots, grasses, and the bark of trees remained. Those who tried to plant a few potatoes might find that they had been pulled out and eaten during the night. Starvation began in October 1944 and before the spring harvest in 1945 as many as two million Vietnamese had perished.[3]

Subsistence crises and periods of dearth for most Southeast Asians have typically been on a smaller scale: local droughts or floods, epidemics that destroyed plow animals, winds or rains at harvest that beat down or spoiled much of the grain, or birds, rats, or crabs that ravaged the crop. Often the shortage might be confined to a single family whose land was either too high and dry or too low and wet, whose working head fell ill at transplanting or harvest time, whose children were too many for its small patch of land. Even if the crop was sufficient, the claims on it by outsiders—rent, taxes—might make it insufficient.

If the Great Depression left an indelible mark on the fears, values, and habits of a whole generation of Americans, can we imagine the impact of periodic food crises on the fears, values, and habits of rice farmers in monsoon Asia?

The fear of food shortages has, in most precapitalist peasant societies, given rise to what might appropriately be termed a "subsistence ethic." This ethic, which Southeast Asian peasants shared with their counterparts in nineteenth-century France, Russia, and Italy, was a consequence of living so close to the margin. A bad crop would not only mean short rations; the price of eating might be the humiliation of an onerous dependence or the sale of some land or livestock which reduced the odds of achieving an adequate subsistence the following year. The peasant family's problem, put starkly, was to produce enough rice to feed the household, buy a few necessities such as salt and cloth, and meet the irreducible claims of outsiders. The amount of rice a family could produce was partly in the hands of fate, but the local tradition of seed varieties, planting techniques, and timing was designed over centuries of trial and error to produce the most stable and reliable yield possible under the circumstances. These were the *technical arrangements* evolved

---

3. For a description of this incredible winter, see Ngo Vinh Long's translation of Tran Van Mai, *Who Committed This Crime?*, in Ngo Vinh Long, *Before the Revolution: The Vietnamese Peasants Under the French* (Cambridge, Mass.: M.I.T. Press, 1973). Many peasants experienced the Viet Minh in this period as an organization that helped organize attacks on official granaries or on Japanese rice shipments and brought available grain from the periphery of the Delta. For a brief discussion of Vietnamese politics in this period, see Huynh Kim Khanh, "The Vietnamese August Revolution Reinterpreted," *Journal of Asian Studies* 30:4 (August 1971), 761–81.

by the peasantry to iron out the "ripples that might drown a man." Many social arrangements served the same purpose. Patterns of reciprocity, forced generosity, communal land, and work-sharing helped to even out the inevitable troughs in a family's resources which might otherwise have thrown them below subsistence. The proven value of these techniques and social patterns is perhaps what has given peasants a Brechtian tenacity in the face of agronomists and social workers who come from the capital to improve them.

The purpose of the argument which follows is to place the subsistence ethic at the center of the analysis of peasant politics. The argument itself grows out of a prolonged effort on my part to understand some of the major peasant rebellions which swept much of Southeast Asia during the Great Depression of the 1930s. Two of those insurrections, the Saya San Rebellion in Burma and what has been called the Nghe-Tinh Soviets in central Vietnam, are analyzed in some detail.

In a broad view of colonial history in Southeast Asia, these rebellions and others like them might be considered epiphenomena, though they were hardly trivial for the men and women who fought and died in them. Both uprisings were ultimately crushed; both failed to achieve any of the peasants' goals; both are considered minor subplots in a political drama that was to be increasingly dominated by the struggle between nationalists and colonizers. In still another and more profound historical sense, these movements were marginal. They looked to a closed and autonomous peasant utopia in a world in which centralization and commercialization were irresistible. They were more or less spontaneous uprisings displaying all the trademarks of peasant localism in a world in which the big battalions of secular nationalism were the only effective opposition to the colonial state. Along with other backward-looking movements of peasants or artisans, they were, in Hobsbawm's phrase, "inevitable victims" inasmuch as they ran "dead against the current of history."[4]

Viewing from another perspective, however, we can learn a great deal from rebels who were defeated nearly a half-century ago. If we understand the indignation and rage which prompted them to risk everything, we can grasp what I have chosen to call their moral economy: their notion of economic justice and their working definition of exploitation—their view of which claims on their product were tolerable and which intolerable. Insofar as their moral economy is representative of peasants elsewhere, and I believe I can show that it is, we may move

4. E. J. Hobsbawm, "Class Consciousness in History," in Istvan Mezaros, ed., *Aspects of History and Class Consciousness* (London, 1971), pp. 11–12.

toward a fuller appreciation of the normative roots of peasant politics. If we understand, further, how the central economic and political transformations of the colonial era served to systematically violate the peasantry's vision of social equity, we may realize how a class "of low classness"[5] came to provide, far more often than the proletariat, the shock troops of rebellion and revolution.

One cautionary note is in order. This study is not primarily an analysis of the *causes* of peasant revolution. That task has been attempted, and with notable success, by Barrington Moore Jr. and Eric R. Wolf.[6] A study of the moral economy of peasants can tell us what makes them angry and what is likely, other things being equal, to generate an explosive situation. But if anger born of exploitation were sufficient to spark a rebellion, most of the Third World (and not only the Third World) would be in flames. Whether peasants who perceive themselves to be exploited actually rebel depends on a host of intervening factors—such as alliances with other classes, the repressive capacity of dominant elites, and the social organization of the peasantry itself—which are not treated except in passing here. Instead, I deal with the nature of exploitation in peasant society as its victims are likely to see it, and what one might call the creation of social dynamite rather than its detonation. (I limit myself to this terrain not only out of respect for the fine work done on revolution by Moore and Wolf and a sense of the division of academic labor, but because exploitation without rebellion seems to me a far more ordinary state of affairs than revolutionary war.) In the final chapter, I try to indicate what the tragic options are for an exploited peasantry in the absence of rebellion.

The basic idea upon which my argument rests is both simple and, I believe, powerful. It arises from the central economic dilemma of most peasant households. Living close to the subsistence margin and subject to the vagaries of weather and the claims of outsiders, the peasant household has little scope for the profit maximization calculus of traditional neoclassical economics. Typically, the peasant cultivator seeks to avoid the failure that will ruin him rather than attempting a big, but risky, killing. In decision-making parlance his behavior is risk-averse; he minimizes the subjective probability of the maximum loss. If treating the peasant as a would-be Schumpeterian entrepreneur misses his key existential dilemma, so do the normal power-maximizing assumptions fail to

5. Theodor Shanin, "The Peasantry as a Political Factor," *Sociological Review* 14:1 (1966), 5.

6. See *Social Origins of Dictatorship and Democracy* (Boston: Beacon Press, 1966), and *Peasant Wars of the Twentieth Century* (New York: Harper and Row, 1969), respectively.

do justice to his political behavior. To begin instead with the need for a reliable subsistence as the primordial goal of the peasant cultivator and then to examine his relationships to his neighbors, to elites, and to the state in terms of whether they aid or hinder him in meeting that need, is to recast many issues.

It is this "safety-first" principle which lies behind a great many of the technical, social, and moral arrangements of a precapitalist agrarian order. The use of more than one seed variety, the European traditional farming on scattered strips, to mention only two, are classical techniques for avoiding undue risks often at the cost of a reduction in average return. Within the village context, a wide array of social arrangements typically operated to assure a minimum income to inhabitants. The existence of communal land that was periodically redistributed, in part on the basis of need, or the commons in European villages functioned in this way. In addition, social pressures within the precapitalist village had a certain redistributive effect: rich peasants were expected to be charitable, to sponsor more lavish celebrations, to help out temporarily indigent kin and neighbors, to give generously to local shrines and temples. As Michael Lipton has noted, "many superficially odd village practices make sense as disguised forms of insurance."[7]

It is all too easy, and a serious mistake, to romanticize these social arrangements that distinguish much of peasant society. They are not radically egalitarian. Rather, they imply only that all are entitled to a *living* out of the resources within the village, and that living is attained often at the cost of a loss of status and autonomy. They work, moreover, in large measure through the abrasive force of gossip and envy and the knowledge that the abandoned poor are likely to be a real and present danger to better-off villagers. These modest but critical redistributive mechanisms nonetheless do provide a minimal subsistence insurance for villagers. Polanyi claims on the basis of historical and anthropological evidence that such practices were nearly universal in traditional society and served to mark it off from the modern market economy. He concludes, "It is the absence of the threat of *individual* starvation which makes primitive society, in a sense, more human than market economy, and at the same time less economic."[8]

7. Michael Lipton, "The Theory of the Optimizing Peasant," *Journal of Development Studies* 4 (1969), 341, cited in Wolf, *Peasant Wars of the Twentieth Century*, p. 279.

8. Karl Polanyi, *The Great Transformation* (Boston: Beacon Press, 1957), pp. 163–64. Even the term seminal, applied as it is without discretion, is too weak a tribute for this book. His analysis of premarket and market economies has been formative for my own work. The emphasis in this quote has been added.

The provision of subsistence insurance was not confined to the village sphere; it also structured the moral economy of relations to outside elites. As Eric Wolf observed,

> It is significant, however, that before the advent of capitalism . . . social equilibrium depended in both the long and short run on a balance of transfers of peasant surpluses to the rulers and the provision of minimal security for the cultivator. Sharing resources within communal organizations and reliance on ties with powerful patrons were recurrent ways in which peasants strove to reduce risks and to improve their stability, and both were condoned and frequently supported by the state.[9]

Again, we must guard against the impulse to idealize these arrangements. Where they worked, and they did not always work, they were not so much a product of altruism as of necessity. Where land was abundant and labor scarce, subsistence insurance was virtually the only way to attach a labor force; where the means of coercion at the disposal of elites and the state was sharply limited, it was prudent to show some respect for the needs of the subordinate population.

Although the desire for subsistence security grew out of the needs of cultivators—out of peasant economics—it was socially experienced as a pattern of moral rights or expectations. Barrington Moore has captured the normative tone of these expectations:

> This experience [of sharing risks within the community] provides the soil out of which grow peasant mores and the moral standards by which they judge their own behavior and that of others. The essence of these standards is a crude notion of equality, stressing the justice and necessity of a minimum of land [resources] for the performance of essential social tasks. These standards usually have some sort of religious sanction, and it is likely to be in their stress on these points that the religion of peasants differs from that of other social classes.[10]

The violation of these standards could be expected to provoke resentment and resistance—not only because needs were unmet, but because rights were violated.

The subsistence ethic, then, is rooted in the economic practices and social exchanges of peasant society. As a moral principle, as a right to

9. Wolf, *Peasant Wars,* p. 279.

10. Moore, *Social Origins,* pp. 497–98. I believe the emphasis in most peasant societies is not so much on land per se as on the right to a share of the product of land; hence I have added "resources" in brackets.

subsistence, I believe I can show that it forms the standard against which claims to the surplus by landlords and the state are evaluated. The essential question is who stabilizes his income at whose expense. Since the tenant prefers to minimize the probability of a disaster rather than to maximize his average return, the stability and security of his subsistence income are more critical to his evaluation of the tenure system than either his average return or the amount of the crop taken by the landlord. A tenure system which provides the tenant with a minimal guaranteed return is likely to be experienced as less exploitative than a system which, while it may take less from him on the average, does not rate his needs as a consumer as primary. The same reasoning may be applied to the claim of the state. To the extent that that claim is a fixed charge which does not vary with the peasant's capacity to pay in any given year, it is likely to be viewed as more exploitative than a fiscal burden which varies with his income. The test for the peasant is more likely to be "What is left?" than "How much is taken?" The subsistence test offers a very different perspective on exploitation than theories which rely only on the criterion of surplus value expropriated. While the latter may be useful in classifying modes of expropriation, it is my contention that they are less likely to be an adequate guide to the phenomenology of peasant experience than the subsistence test. For it is the question of subsistence that is most directly related to the ultimate needs and fears of peasant life.

Two major transformations during the colonial period in Southeast Asia served to undermine radically the preexisting social insurance patterns and to violate the moral economy of the subsistence ethic. These were, first, the imposition of what Eric Wolf has called "a particular cultural system, that of North Atlantic capitalism"[11] and, second, the related development of the modern state under a colonial aegis. The transformation of land and labor (that is, nature and human work) into commodities for sale had the most profound impact. Control of land increasingly passed out of the hands of villagers; cultivators progressively lost free usufruct rights and became tenants or agrarian wage laborers; the value of what was produced was increasingly gauged by the fluctuations of an impersonal market. In a sense, what was happening in Southeast Asia was nothing more than a parochial recapitulation of what Marx had observed in Europe. "But on the other hand, these new freedmen became sellers of themselves only after they had been robbed of all their own means of production and of all the guarantees of existence afforded by the old feudal arrangements. And the history of

11. Wolf, *Peasant Wars*, p. 276.

this, their expropriation, is written in the annals of mankind in letters of blood and fire."[12] On the land in Lower Burma and in the Mekong Delta these "new freedmen" faced an increasingly implacable class of land-owners whose claims on the harvest varied less with the needs of their tenants than with what the market would bear. What had been a worsen-ing situation throughout the early twentieth century became, with the onset of the world depression, a zero-sum struggle based as much on coercion as on the market. Peasants resisted as best they could and, where circumstances permitted, they rebelled.

The state was as much an actor in this drama as were the owners of the scarce factors of production. Not only did it provide the legal and coercive machinery necessary to ensure that contracts were honored and the market economy retained, but the state was itself a claimant on peasant resources. Much of its administrative effort had been bent to enumerating and recording its subjects and their land for tax purposes. Its fiscal advisors reasoned much as landlords: a stable income was preferable to a fluctuating income and therefore fixed head taxes and fixed land rates were preferable to a tax on actual income. When the economic crisis came, the state's receipts from customs duties and other variable sources of income fell dramatically and it accordingly bore down more heavily on its most steady revenue producer, the head tax. This claim, further burdening an already hard-pressed peasantry, also provoked resistance and rebellion.

It is possible to discern in all of this a strong parallel with the earlier creation of nation-states and the development of a market economy in Europe which produced similar resistance.[13] There too the problem of subsistence income was exacerbated by market forces and by a more intrusive state. R. C. Cobb, in his masterful study of popular protest in eighteenth-century France, maintains that it can be understood only in terms of the problem of food supply, the danger of shortages, and their political meaning.

> Attitudes to dearth conditioned popular attitudes to everything else: government, the countryside, life and death, inequality, depri-vation, morality, pride, humiliation, self-esteem. It is the central theme in all forms of popular expression. Nor were the common

12. *Capital*, vol. 1 (New York: New World Paperbacks, 1966), p. 715.

13. See, for example, Polanyi, and Roland Mousnier, *Peasant Uprisings in Seventeenth-Century France, Russia, and China*, trans. Brian Pearce (New York: Harper and Row, 1970), and E. P. Thompson, "The Moral Economy of the English Crowd in the Eighteenth Century," *Past and Present* 50 (February 1971).

people living in a world of myth and panic fear: for dearth and famine were in fact the biggest single threat to their existence.[14]

Despite the striking parallels, a good case can be made that the process of transformation was, if anything, more traumatic for colonial peoples. For one thing, it telescoped a process which had taken as much as three centuries in England or France into a forced march of mere decades. In Europe, moreover, as Polanyi eloquently shows, the indigenous forces which had much to lose from a full market economy (including, at times, the crown, portions of the aristocracy, artisans, peasants, and workers) were occasionally able to impede or at least restrict the play of market forces by invoking the older moral economy. In Germany and Japan the creation of strong conservative states allowed what Moore has called "a revolution from above" which kept as much of the original social structure intact as possible while still modernizing the economy. The results, while laying the ground for fascism and militarism at a later date, were somewhat less traumatic in the short run for the peasantry. But in the colonial world the political forces which would have opposed or moderated the full impact of the market economy had little or no capacity to make themselves felt except at the level of insurrection.

The problem for the peasantry during the capitalist transformation of the Third World, viewed from this perspective, is that of providing for a minimum income.[15] While a minimum income has solid physiological dimensions, we must not overlook its social and cultural implications. In order to be a fully functioning member of village society, a household needs a certain level of resources to discharge its necessary ceremonial and social obligations as well as to feed itself adequately and continue to cultivate. To fall below this level is not only to risk starvation, it is to suffer a profound loss of standing within the community and perhaps to fall into a permanent situation of dependence.

The precapitalist community was, in a sense, organized around this problem of the minimum income—organized to minimize the risk to which its members were exposed by virtue of its limited techniques and the caprice of nature. Traditional forms of patron-client relationships, reciprocity, and redistributive mechanisms may be seen from this perspective. While precapitalist society was singularly ill-equipped to provide for its members in the event of collective disaster, it did provide household social insurance against the "normal" risks of agriculture through an elaborate system of social exchange.

14. R. C. Cobb, *The Police and the People: French Popular Protest Movements 1789–1820* (London: Oxford University Press, 1970), p. xviii.

15. I am grateful to Van Ooms for suggesting this.

In more recent times, of course, the state itself has assumed the role of providing for a minimum income with such devices as countercyclical fiscal policy, unemployment compensation, welfare programs, social medicine, and the negative income tax. One effect of these guarantees, incidentally, has been to make it more rational for individuals to engage in profit-maximizing behavior.

The colonial period in Southeast Asia, and elsewhere for that matter, was marked by an almost total absence of any provision for the maintenance of a minimal income while, at the same time, the commercialization of the agrarian economy was steadily stripping away most of the traditional forms of social insurance.[16] Far from shielding the peasantry against the fluctuations of the market, colonial regimes were likely to press even harder in a slump so as to maintain their own revenue. The result was something of a paradox. In the midst of a booming export economy, new fortunes for indigenous landowners, officeholders, and moneylenders and, occasionally, rising average per capita income, there was also growing concern with rural indebtedness and poverty and an increasing tempo of peasant unrest. It was not unlike the discovery of pauperism in the midst of England's industrial revolution.[17] The explanation for this paradox is to be sought in the new insecurities of subsistence income to which the poorer sector of the population was exposed. Although the average wage rate might be adequate, employment was highly uncertain; although the average prices for peasant produce might be buoyant, they fluctuated dramatically; although taxes might be modest, they were a steady charge against a highly variable peasant income; although the export economy created new opportunities, it also concentrated the ownership of productive resources and eroded the leveling mechanisms of the older village economy.

The moral economy of the subsistence ethic can be clearly seen in the themes of peasant protest throughout this period. Two themes prevailed; first, claims on peasant incomes by landlords, moneylenders, or the state were never legitimate when they infringed on what was judged to be the minimal culturally defined subsistence level; and second, the product of the land should be distributed in such a way that all were guaranteed a subsistence niche. The appeal was in almost every case to the past—to traditional practices—and the revolts I discuss are best seen as defensive reactions. Such backward-looking intentions are by now a

16. A possible exception to this rule was the Dutch East Indies where, at least on Java, colonial policy was bent to extracting a marketable surplus while at the same time preserving—not to say fossilizing—as much of rural society as possible.

17. See Wolfram Fischer, "Social Tensions at the Early Stages of Industrialization," *Comparative Studies in Society and History* 9 (1966–67), 64–83.

commonplace in the analysis of peasant movements. As Moore, citing Tawney, puts it, "the peasant radical would be astonished to hear that he is undermining the foundations of society; he is merely trying to get back what has long been rightfully his."[18] The revolts were, by the same token, essentially the revolts of consumers rather than producers. Except where communal land had been appropriated by local notables, the demand for the redistribution of land itself was strikingly absent. Protests against taxes and rents were couched in terms of their effect on consumption; what was an admissible tax or rent in a good year was inadmissible in a bad year. It was the smallness of what was left rather than the amount taken (the two are obviously related, but by no means are they identical) that moved peasants to rebel.

The initial chapter, which borrows shamelessly from economists and anthropologists, describes what the "subsistence ethic" means analytically for peasant economics. The applicability of what has been called the "safety first" principle of decision-making to the peasantry in Southeast Asia is explained and illustrated.

*ch. 1*

In the second chapter I attempt to show that the subsistence ethic is not only a given of peasant economics, but that it has a normative or moral dimension as well. This can be seen in the structure of village reciprocity, in social choices, in preferred systems of tenancy, and in attitudes toward taxes. On this basis, I try to distinguish which systems of tenancy or taxes are most exploitative from the perspective of subsistence security and to demonstrate that this perspective is in accord with peasant values.

Chapters 3, 4 and 5 represent an effort to apply this argument to the development of the colonial economy and peasant politics in Southeast Asia, particularly in Burma and Vietnam. Chapter 3 is devoted to an analysis of how structural change in the colonial economy not only narrowed the subsistence margin of many peasants but exposed them to new and greater risks of subsistence crises. The effect of the fiscal claim of the colonial state on the peasantry is analyzed in much the same way in Chapter 4. In Chapter 5, two major rebellions in Vietnam and Burma are examined in the light of the subsistence ethic and the "safety-first" principle.

Chapter 6 is a more general effort to apply the political economy of the subsistence ethic to peasant politics (I argue that the peasant's notion of social justice can be derived from the *norm of reciprocity* and the *right to subsistence*) and to formulate an *operational* concept of exploitation which asks two questions: What is the balance of exchange between peasants

18. Moore, *Social Origins,* p. 498.

and elites? What are the effects of this balance on peasant subsistence security?

Chapter 7 addresses the question of peasant rebellion. First, the conditions that, when joined with exploitation, seem to make for rebellion are discussed. This leads inevitably to a consideration of why rebellion is not the characteristic expression of peasant politics. What are the alternatives to rebellion? Finally we turn to the age-old question of false consciousness: How can we know if peasants feel unjustly exploited when the power of the state makes rebellion a mortal risk? This question, I believe, may be answered by looking at levels of coercion and especially at the development of peasant culture, which can tell us whether peasants accept or reject the key values of the agrarian order in which they live.

# 1 The Economics and Sociology of the Subsistence Ethic

The distinctive economic behavior of the subsistence-oriented peasant family results from the fact that, unlike a capitalist enterprise, it is a unit of consumption as well as a unit of production. The family begins with a more or less irreducible subsistence consumer demand, based on its size, which it must meet in order to continue as a unit. Meeting those minimal human needs in a reliable and stable way is the central criterion which knits together choices of seed, technique, timing, rotation, and so forth. The cost of failure for those near the subsistence margin is such that safety and reliability take precedence over long-run profit.

Many of the seeming anomalies of peasant economics arise from the fact that the struggle for a subsistence minimum is carried out in the context of a shortage of land, capital, and outside employment opportunities. This restricted context has at times driven peasants, as A. V. Chayanov has shown in his classic study of Russian smallholders, to choices that defy standard bookkeeping measures of profitability.[1] Peasant families which must feed themselves from small plots in overpopulated regions will (if there are no alternatives) work unimaginably hard and long for the smallest increments in production—long after a prudent capitalist would move on. Chayanov calls this "self-exploitation." When this pattern becomes characteristic of an entire agrarian system, as it did in Tonkin and Java, it represents what Clifford Geertz has called "agricultural involution."[2] That the marginal return on his additional labor is miniscule matters little to the capital-poor, land-short peasant who must wring the family's food out of what he has.

Because labor is often the only factor of production the peasant possesses in relative abundance, he may have to move into labor-absorbing activities with extremely low returns until subsistence demands are met. This may mean switching crops or techniques of cultivation (for example, switching from broadcasting to transplanting rice) or filling the slack agricultural season with petty crafts, trades, or marketing which return very little but are virtually the only outlets for surplus

1. A. V. Chayanov, *The Theory of Peasant Economy,* ed. Daniel Thorner, Basile Kerblay, and R. E. F. Smith (Homewood, Ill.: Richard D. Irwin, for the American Economic Association, 1966; originally published in 1926).

2. Clifford Geertz, *Agricultural Involution* (Berkeley: University of California Press, 1963).

labor.[3] Chayanov shows how, holding the family size constant, the proportion of the year spent in crafts and trades increases as the land available to the peasant family diminishes. The strong traditional role of crafts and trades in land-starved areas such as Upper Burma, Annam, and Tonkin, and the pattern of small-scale peasant marketing in Java are in keeping with this relationship.[4]

Guaranteeing themselves a basic subsistence, an orientation that focuses unavoidably on the here and now, occasionally forces peasants to mortgage their own future. A crop failure may force them to sell some or all of their scarce land or their plow animals. If the failure is widespread they must sell in a panic at extremely low prices. The result may be both tragic and preposterous: "It is well known, for example, that in the famine year of 1921 in the lower Volga area, meat was cheaper than bread."[5]

The overriding importance of meeting family subsistence demands frequently obliges peasants not only to sell for whatever return they can get but also to pay more to buy or rent land than capitalist investment criteria would indicate. A land-poor peasant with a large family and few labor outlets is often willing to pay huge prices for land, or "hunger rents," as Chayanov calls them, so long as the additional land will add *something* to the family larder. In fact, the less land a family has, the *more* it will be willing to pay for an additional piece: a competitive process that may drive out capitalist agriculture which cannot compete on such terms.[6]

It seemed to Chayanov some fifty years ago that the peculiarities of peasant economics invalidated the assumptions of classical economics about rational behavior. Today, however, such peasant economics is better understood as a special case of what standard microeconomic theory would predict.[7] The continued application of labor to poorly compensated farming or handicrafts, for example, is a product of the low opportunity cost of labor for the peasant (that is, few outside employment possibilities) and the high marginal utility of income for those

3. Cf. Ester Boserup, *The Conditions of Agricultural Growth: The Economics of Agrarian Change under Population Pressure* (Chicago: Aldine Atherton, 1965), whose theory of agrarian change treats population pressure as the central independent variable.

4. See, for example, Pierre Gourou, *The Peasants of the Tonkin Delta,* vol. 2, trans. the Human Relations Area Files (New Haven: HRAF Press, 1955), pp. 503–15, and Alice Dewey, *Peasant Marketing in Java* (Glencoe, Ill.: The Free Press, 1962).

5. Chayanov, *Peasant Economy,* p. 171.

6. Ibid., pp. 10, 28. Most such peasants, of course, are unable to buy additional land because they lack the funds, although they would be willing to pay inflated prices.

7. I wish to thank Van Ooms and Ronald Herring for showing me the applicability of microeconomic theory to peasant behavior.

near the subsistence level. It makes sense, in this context, for the peasant to continue to apply labor until its marginal product is quite low—perhaps even zero. Microeconomic theory thus provides for the "self-exploitation" which Chayanov observed. The phenomenon of "hunger-rents" is explicable in much the same fashion. The larger the family (more mouths to feed and more hands to work), the larger the marginal product of any additional land and, hence, the larger the maximum rent the family is willing to pay. Because of its near-zero opportunity cost and its need to reach an adequate subsistence, the peasant household will work for very low implicit wages.

The supposed anomalies of "self-exploitation" and "hunger-rents" are thus a special case in microeconomic theory where land-hunger and no employment outlets conspire to drive peasants to tragic choices and allow others, in turn, to extract high returns from their predicament.

## "SAFETY-FIRST":[8] THE ECONOMICS OF SUBSISTENCE

It is perfectly reasonable that the peasant who each season courts hunger and all its consequences should hold a somewhat different opinion of risk-taking than the investor who is gambling "off the top." To illustrate more clearly what the nature of that difference is, I turn now to an explicitly economic formulation of peasant risk-avoiding behavior. This economic model has great substantive value for understanding patterns of innovation such as investing in tube wells, changing cultivation techniques, or planting high-yielding rice. Learning how peasants shape their economic life to ensure a stable subsistence will help us appreciate how the same concern unifies much of their social and political life.

If we begin with the core dilemma of the consumption demands of the farm family and the fluctuation in the yield of the crop(s) it grows, the hypothetical example in Figure 1 will serve to illustrate the problem. The vertical axis represents net yields in baskets of rice with a total of 80 baskets defined as a subsistence level.

Let us assume that line T represents thirty years of net crop yield figures for the traditionally planted variety of rice on a typical holding in a given area. The amplitude of the fluctuations is not out of line with actual rice-yield variability in areas where there is irrigation or dependable rainfall. Most peasant cultivators might also be expected to have an approximate notion of yields over the past thirty years, if not longer.

8. The term is borrowed from James Roumasset, as is the "green revolution" example that follows. "Risk and Choice of Technique for Peasant Agriculture: Safety First and Rice Production in the Philippines" Social Systems Research Institute, University of Wisconsin, Economic Development and International Economics, No. 7118 (August 1971).

Figure 1. Crop Yields and Subsistence for a Peasant Household

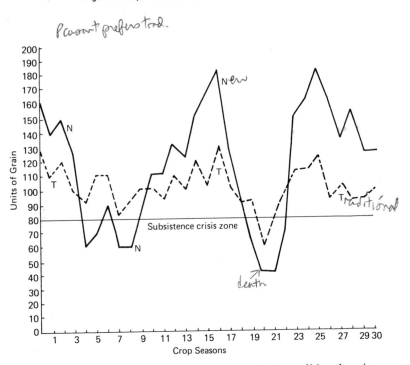

*Peasant prefers food.*

The important thing to note about the yield of the traditional variety, however, is its reliability; it only once plunges below the subsistence level, though it hovers near it for much of the time. The risk of a disaster with the traditional variety could be calculated from past experience (assuming it is representative) as one in thirty.

The notion of subsistence level and disaster level as used here requires some elaboration since it combines objective and subjective features.[9] A *minimum* disaster level is objective in the sense that it represents a food supply close enough to the physiological minimum that further reductions will lead to malnutrition and early death. Here one might begin with the estimates by French geographers of Indochina of the minimal number of kilos of rice (approximately 300) required annually by each

9. Clifton R. Wharton, "The Economic Meaning of Subsistence," *The Malayan Economic Review* 8:2 (October 1963), 46–58.

adult.[10] Beyond these brute physiological needs there is clearly an historical dimension to subsistence levels in which minimum standards bear
some relation to previous experience. Thus, the poor Thai peasant's
notion of the bare essentials in food would probably be slightly more
generous than what a North Vietnamese or a Javanese peasant would
consider rock-bottom. Recognizing the historical and cultural dimensions of subsistence levels, we might want to take that level of income
below which nothing is saved, or below which ceremonial expenses are
pared to the bone, as an empirical point of departure. Peasant living
standards in most of Southeast Asia, however, have remained close
enough to the basics so that the historical experience does not diverge
far from what goes to make up the traditional standard diet, clothing,
and shelter, and the minimum costs of rice cultivation.

The setting of a subsistence crisis level does not, of course, mean that
those peasant families whose crop falls short of that level automatically
starve. In practice, peasants may turn to millet or root crops, children in
the family may be sent to live with relatives, a plow animal or piece of
land may have to be sold, the whole family may migrate. If the crisis
affects a wide area or if a family has two or three consecutive bad years,
then it may actually become a question of sheer survival. The subsistence
crisis level—perhaps a "danger zone" rather than "level" would be more
accurate—is a threshold below which the qualitative deterioration in
subsistence, security, status, and family social cohesion is massive and
painful.[11] It is the difference between the "normal" penury of peasant
life and a literally "hand-to-mouth" existence.[12]

Given the social reality of the subsistence crisis level for most peasant
cultivators, it makes eminent sense for them to follow what Roumasset
calls the "safety first" principle.[13] In the choice of seeds and techniques

10. This is a subsistence level which assumes a pattern of food preferences and is itself
therefore culturally determined. Nutritionists have often suggested even cheaper diets
which provide the necessary nutrition at a cost in taste which only the very desperate would
be willing to pay. Cf. Wharton, p. 51, and George Orwell, The Road to Wigan Pier (New
York: Harcourt, Brace, 1958), pp. 85–100.

11. The significance of this "disaster level" obviously depends on the structure of
opportunity in the economy at large. If alternative employment is readily available, secure,
and relatively well-paid, the costs of a bad crop are far less than if outside opportunities are
few. The modest level of economic alternatives and, above all, their insecurity served to
make the risks of crop failure very severe in colonial Southeast Asia.

12. The Malays have an expression nearly equivalent to "hand-to-mouth" to describe
this situation: Kais pagi, makan pagi; kais petang, makan petang ("Scratch in the morning, eat
in the morning; scratch in the afternoon, eat in the afternoon").

13. For the mathematical elaboration of this principle and its application to the adop-

*peasants will oppose shift to riskier but potentially more profitable methods*

of cultivation, it means simply that the cultivator prefers to minimize the probability of having a disaster rather than maximizing his average return.[14] This strategy generally rules out choices which, while they promise a higher net return on the average, carry with them any substantial risk of losses that would jeopardize subsistence.

In one form or another, this risk avoidance principle has been noted by most economists who study low-income agriculture in the Third World. The four statements that follow are taken from the major work on the economics of subsistence farming and express the basic accord on this point.

> For near-subsistence peasants, risk aversion may be quite strong because the returns above expected values may not offset the severe penalties for returns below the expected values.[15]

> Special value tends to be attached to survival and maintenance of position as opposed to change and the improvement of position. . . . The economic basis for an attitude which is conservative . . . lies with the high risks associated with change in traditional agriculture and the potentially high penalties for failure in change.[16]

Risk avoidance is also invoked to explain the preference for subsistence crops over nonedible cash crops:

> It is quite rational for peasants in "overpopulated" countries with very little margin for taking risks above their subsistence level to be

--------

tion or nonadoption of "green revolution" techniques in the Philippines, I am indebted to James Roumasset, "Risk and Choice of Technique for Peasant Agriculture."

14. There are a number of knotty operational problems in applying this predictive model. What does the peasant regard as an unacceptable risk? Roumasset puts it at .025 or one failure in forty crops. I suspect it is generally a bit higher. How much additional risk will peasants run for what increment in expected return? How do peasants judge the risks of techniques with which they have little experience? One expects that they inflate the riskiness of a given technique in proportion to their ignorance about its performance. Each of these questions is answerable in quantitative terms only for specific categories of peasants whose situation is known. For our purposes it is enough to know that the marginal peasant has a high relative preference for security over profitability. If the two coincide, so much the better—that is a technocrat's dream—but they are more likely to diverge, as we shall see.

15. Jere R. Behrman, "Supply Responses and the Modernization of Peasant Agriculture: A Study of the Major Annual Crops in Thailand," in Clifton R. Wharton, Jr., ed., *Subsistence Agriculture and Economic Development* (Chicago: Aldine, 1969), p. 236.

16. John W. Mellor, "The Subsistence Farmer in Traditional Economies," in Wharton, ibid., p. 214.

content with a lower return for subsistence production than to choose the higher but riskier returns from cash production.[17]

The most careful formulation of the principle of decision-making involved, however, is that of Leonard Joy:

We might postulate that farmers' willingness to innovate for an increase in long-run average net return is subject to the condition that the risk of reducing the net return in any one year not exceed some given value. Further, we might postulate that the degree of risk that farmers are willing to incur is related to their nearness, in some sense, to "biological subsistence." . . . We thus have a hypothesis that subsistence farmers may resist innovation because it means departing from a system that is efficient in minimizing the risk of a catastrophe for one that significantly increases this risk.[18]

Even with the steadiest traditional technique, as in Figure 1, there is an irreducible element of risk each year. The peasant who has managed with this technique in the past will not ordinarily exchange it for a substantially more risky technique whose average returns may be much higher. What the peasant seeks, as Chayanov notes, are those crops and cultivation techniques "which will give the highest *and most stable* payment for labor."[19] Where these twin goals clash he will normally prefer the less risky crops and techniques if he is close to the margin.

A hypothetical contrast of this kind is illustrated in Figure 1, comparing the performance of technique N to technique T. Technique N (relative to crop, seed, manner of cultivation) has a higher average return than technique T, and the farmer who used it thirty years running would have a higher average income. The trouble is that peasants using technique N would rarely survive intact past year five to enjoy their bumper crops. In practice the years of poor yield might mean having to sell the land or acquiring costly debts and, for a tenant, they might mean dismissal in favor of another prospect who could pay the costs of the next crop. Technique N plunges a family into the subsistence crisis zone not for one year but for eight years; the probability of going

17. Hla Myint, "The Peasant Economies of Today's Underdeveloped Areas," in ibid., p. 103.

18. J. Leonard Joy, "Diagnosis, Prediction, and Policy Formulation," in ibid., pp. 377–78. Joy refers to data from the Punjab that confirm this hypothesis. See also Irma Adelman, "Social and Economic Development at the Micro Level—A Tentative Hypothesis," chap. 1 in Eliezar B. Ayal, ed., *Micro Aspects of Development* (New York: Praeger, 1973), pp. 3–12.

19. Chayanov, *Peasant Economy,* p. 134, emphasis added.

under with N is over 25 percent while the comparable figure for T is less than 4 percent.

Our hypothetical example is not far removed from the real world of peasant choice. In an attempt to apply the "safety-first" principle to the choice of technique in the Philippines, Roumasset developed four representative examples of risks and returns which compared three varieties of high-yielding rice to traditional cultivation. The *average* yield of the new seeds was in every case more than twice that of old techniques. In one case, it was nearly triple. The problem, however, was that the new seeds were far more sensitive to variations in water supply so that, particularly in rain-fed areas, yields per hectare could be expected to fluctuate dramatically. All of the new seed varieties, moreover, required much larger investments of cash for fertilizer and for nonfamily labor at transplanting and harvest time. The average cash cost per hectare of the old method was 100 pesos while the cash requirements of the new methods varied between 320 and 435 pesos per hectare.[20] In a bad year the impact of these fixed costs was enormous for the new varieties since a larger yield was required merely to meet production expenses.

Setting a disaster level of 200 pesos (cash equivalent of yield) per hectare and a desire to avoid probabilities larger than .025 of slipping below that line, Roumasset calculates that peasants would, under these assumptions, rationally prefer traditional techniques in spite of their poor yields. This theory of peasant choice predicts the actual pattern of adoption of high-yielding rice varieties in parts of Central Luzon. In irrigated areas where the reliable water supply lowers the risk of the new seed considerably, smallholders have switched to the new techniques far more readily than in rain-fed regions where their adopion courts disaster.

In deciding whether or not to grow cash crops, it appears that cultivators near the subsistence margin apply essentially the same test. There is almost always some increment of risk in shifting from subsistence production to cash cropping. A successful subsistence crop more or less guarantees the family food supply, while the value of a nonedible cash crop depends on its market price and on the price of consumer necessities. Quite apart from the frequently higher costs of growing and harvesting cash crops, a bumper cash crop does not, by itself, assure a family's food supply.

The amount of risk such a shift entails and the capacity of the cultivators in question to assess and bear that risk are typically the key

20. Quite apart from the risk involved, such high input costs simply exclude poorer peasants, who lack the savings or access to credit, from growing new varieties.

variables in the decision. In C. M. Elliott's study of the adoption of cotton in East Africa, risk factors were decisive.[21] Cultivators in Buganda switched to cotton readily because it did not compete with their food crop of plantain and because the reliable rainfall in their area meant that the risk of losing the crop was negligible. For the Luo of Kenya, however, the risks were prohibitive. The labor requirements for cotton growing there competed directly with the labor needs for the major food crop, maize, and the variation in rainfall was such that the risk of crop failure was quite high. Comparable variations in risk to subsistence appear to explain why cocoa growing spread rapidly in Ghana and Nigeria but not in Sierra Leone. The colonial governments in each of these cases did what they could to encourage cash-cropping by imposing hut taxes and other levies that would increase the need for cash production. "But whenever a substantial increase in risk was involved in this transformation, as with cotton in Kenya and cocoa in Sierra Leone, agricultural development proved impossible."[22]

The argument about the nature of peasant caution so far has been made for subsistence cultivators in some abstract sense. It should be clear, however, that the tolerance for risk of peasant families varies according to how closely their resources skirt basic subsistence needs. For two families farming the same way on comparable small plots, the larger the family, the more disadvantageous its position, since the minimal yields which will keep it going (its subsistence-crisis level) are that much higher. This is true even if the extra members of the family can work (because of diminishing marginal returns to labor), but it is excruciatingly true for big families with a large proportion of nonproducing consumers. There is a period of maximum dependency in the natural history of most families, when the children are too young to add much labor but must be fed, and during which, other things being equal, the family is particularly vulnerable to subsistence crises.

Similarly, holding family size constant, the family with the smaller plot of land to work is obviously in a more tenuous situation. With additional land a family can tolerate occasional low yields per acre that would ruin a marginal smallholder. Savings operate in the same manner; they pro-

21. C. M. Elliott, "Agriculture and Economic Development in Africa: Theory and Experience 1880–1914," pp. 123–50 in E. L. Jones and S. J. Woolf, eds., *Agrarian Change and Economic Development: The Historical Problems* (London: Methuen, 1974).

22. Ibid., p. 147. Eric Wolf goes so far as to build into the definition of the term "peasant" a desire to reduce market risks: "the peasant most often keeps the market at arm's length, for unlimited involvement in the market threatens his hold on his source of livelihood. . . . Moreover, *he favors production for sale only within the context of an assured production for subsistence.*" Wolf, *Peasant Wars of the Twentieth Century*, p. xiv, emphasis added.

vide a protective margin for risk-taking. The closer to the line a family is—provided it is still above it—the less its tolerance for risk and the more rational and binding the "safety-first" formula becomes.

To say that safety-first principles are particularly applicable to marginal smallholders and tenants who "are up to the neck in water" is to describe, in the same breath, much of the agrarian population of Southeast Asia. Studies of peasant economic life in the region have emphasized, in one form or another, the subsistence orientation which structures economic decisions. In his landmark study of cultivation patterns in Indochina, Pierre Gourou put the matter succinctly: "Agriculture in Tonkin and Annam is not an economic enterprise looking to do business and assure profits, but an agriculture of subsistence which is limited exclusively to feeding those who practice it."[23] A more recent study of agriculture in the Mekong Delta of southern Vietnam has emphasized the caution typical of safety-first concerns. "A natural conservatism leads to a preference for that which is more assured and more predictable than an alternative which has a greater element of risk."[24] In this connection, Lucien Hanks stresses that the operational goal of Thai peasant farmers is to have, at the end of the year, enough rice in their bins to carry them through till the next harvest. Questions of profitability of investment, yield per unit of land, the productivity of labor are *in themselves* of secondary concern.[25] The distinctive traces of the safety-first rule are also to be found in common observations that Southeast Asian peasants are reluctant to strike out for profits when to do so might mean upsetting subsistence routines which had proved adequate in the past.[26] Finally, the goal of a secure subsistence is expressed in a wide

23. Pierre Gourou, *L'Utilisation du sol en Indochine Française*, Centre D'Études de Politique Étrangère, Travaux des Groupes d'études—Publication No. 14 (Paris: Paul Hartmann, 1940), p. 240. All translations mine unless otherwise noted.

24. James B. Hendry, *The Small World of Khanh Hau* (Chicago: University of Chicago Press, 1964), p. 54.

25. Lucien Hanks. *Rice and Man: Agricultural Ecology in Southeast Asia* (New York: Aldine Atherton, 1972), p. 48.

26. See, for example, M. G. Swift, *Malay Peasant Society in Jelebu*, London School of Economics Monographs in Social Anthropology (London: Athlone Press, 1965), chap. 3; Kamol Odd Janlekha, *A Study of the Economy of a Rice Growing Village in Central Thailand* (Bangkok: Division of Agricultural Economics, Office of the Under Secretary of State, Ministry of Agriculture, 1960), pp. 43, 173; and J. H. Boeke, *The Structure of the Netherlands Indian Economy* (New York: Institute of Pacific Relations, 1942), pp. 30–31. A more recent case from Kelantan, Malaysia, analyzes the introduction of tobacco planting there and shows that those who had stable wet rice fields thought tobacco growing much too risky. See Guus W. von Liebenstein and B. Gunawan, "Poverty in Kelantan: Some Recent Findings in the Bachok District," in M. A. Jaspan, ed., *The Sociology of Poverty in Southeast Asia* (forthcoming, 1976).

array of choices in the production process: a preference for crops that can be eaten over crops that must be sold, an inclination to employ several seed varieties in order to spread risks, a preference for varieties with stable if modest yields.

Michael Moerman's fine study of peasant agriculture in a northern Thai village provides one of the most convincing demonstrations of the priority of subsistence concerns over profitability.[27] The villagers of Ban Ping were something of a textbook case simply because their lives as cultivators were divided largely between two rice fields, one of which was devoted to subsistence needs, while at the other "the desire for profit dominate[d]."

On the Great Field near the village, the subsistence crop was grown exclusively. The glutinous rice favored by villagers was called "eating rice" and each family had an allocation within the Great Field that would normally yield the family's annual requirements. Only traditional plow techniques were used in the Great Field and this meant that the cash needs of cultivation (212 baht compared to 1,892 baht for cultivation in the Central Plain) were low enough for every family to meet.

At the new Thunglor field, however, many of these villagers were transformed into untrammeled Schumpeterian entrepreneurs and "price and profit became the major standards for crop selection."[28] Here the villagers grew "selling rice," a nonglutinous variety which they would not think of eating. This field, quite far from the village, was plowed by tractor and harvested with the help of outside wage labor, thus involving the cultivator in considerable capital costs which he had to recover by marketing his crop.

The critical finding of Moerman's study is that there is no question about the priority of subsistence cultivation on the Great Field, despite the fact that the cultivation of "selling rice" is far more profitable by most measures. The villager only attends to his "selling rice" field *after* his subsistence field tasks are completed. Ban Ping peasants have not "gone commercial," growing exclusively "selling rice" and then buying glutinous rice for food—one resident, forced by debt to do this, was seen as demented by his neighbors. Unless villagers were certain of having enough glutinous rice to eat and to meet customary entertainment and religious needs, they did not plant "selling rice." "However, acute the peasant's entrepreneurial ambitions, peasant rationality precludes planting commercial crops that threaten subsistence."[29]

27. Michael Moerman, *Agricultural Change and Peasant Choice in a Thai Village* (Berkeley and Los Angeles: University of California Press, 1968).

28. Ibid., p. 68.

29. Ibid., p. 69.

Relatively prosperous though they are by Southeast Asian standards, these Thai peasants are chary of commercial risks unless they have a solid subsistence foundation under them. The field at Thunglor is potentially very profitable; but the route to profit is strewn with pitfalls. The yields are far more erratic, cash is needed to hire tractors and outside labor, legal title must be secured, carts must be built or borrowed to haul the harvest home and, finally, success depends heavily on capricious strangers—tractormen—who plow a peasant's plot at their convenience. Plow cultivation in the Great Field is, by contrast, labor intensive and its yields are modest; its virtue is that it is a cheap and communally guaranteed form of food production that has reliably fed villagers for decades.

The safety-first principle thus does not imply that peasants are creatures of custom who never take risks they can avoid. When innovations such as dry season crops, new seeds, planting techniques, or production for market offer clear and substantial gains at little or no risk to subsistence security, one is likely to find peasants plunging ahead. What safety-first does imply, however, is that there is a defensive perimeter around subsistence routines within which risks are avoided as potentially catastrophic and outside of which a more bourgeois calculus of profit prevails.

Such risk-spreading techniques are not the monopoly of peasants. Fishermen and petty traders living close to the margin also spread risks to help ensure a steady income. A small trader will, for example, try to develop a number of steady customers to whom he gives small advantages in order to maintain their patronage.[30] He will avoid selling all his goods to one customer, preferring to disperse his risks. Such risk dispersal has also been observed among poor ex-peasants who may respond to the risk of unemployment by pursuing several minor occupations to minimize the danger of ever being entirely out of work.[31]

In fact, it is not at all clear that capitalist firms do not often choose stability and steady growth over profit maximization. Baumol has suggested that corporations maximize profits subject to a minimal profit or cash-flow constraint.[32] This comes very close indeed to the safety-first formula as it has been applied to cultivators: "Farmers maximize their

30. See Sidney Mintz, "Pratik: Haitian Personal Economic Relationships," in Jack M. Potter et al., eds., *Peasant Society: A Reader* (Boston: Little, Brown, 1967), pp. 98–110, and especially Maria Cristina Blanc Szanton, *A Right to Survive: Subsistence Marketing in a Lowland Philippine Town* (University Park, Pa.: Pennsylvania State University Press, 1972).

31. S. Greenfield, "Stocks, Bonds, and Peasant Canes in Barbados," in G. K. Zollschan and W. Hirsch, eds., *Explorations in Social Change* (Boston: Houghton Mifflin, 1964).

32. William J. Baumol, *Business Behavior: Value and Growth*, rev. ed. (New York: Harcourt, Brace, 1967).

net income under the constraint that the possibility is very small in any given year of having an income below a fixed minimum."[33] Capitalist firms pursue a wide array of strategies such as diversifying to spread risks, agreeing on prices and shares of the market with competitors, integrating vertically to ensure supply, and so forth—all of which do not necessarily maximize net income. The specter of recession or the downswing of the business cycle is for the firm, perhaps, the functional equivalent of crop failure for the peasant, providing an incentive to a guaranteed and steady return over larger, but uncertain, profits. For the firm as well as for the peasant, Simon's theory of "satisficing" may be a more powerful predictor of behavior than profit maximization.[34]

We are not therefore confronted with a dichotomy between swashbuckling capitalist risk-taking on the one hand and immovable peasant conservatism on the other. The subsistence peasant is more accurately seen as something of a limiting case in risk-management. He works close enough to the margin that he has a great deal to lose by miscalculating; his limited techniques and the whims of weather expose him, more than most producers, to unavoidable risks; the relative absence of alternatives for gainful employment offer him precious little in the way of economic insurance. If he is even more cautious about endangering his livelihood, he has a rational basis for his reluctance.

The argument I am making about the economics of subsistence is meant to apply in its full force, then, only to those cultivators who share a common existential dilemma. For those peasants with very low incomes, little land, large families, highly variable yields, and few outside opportunities, the pattern of safety-first, and the social patterns to be described later, should hold quite consistently. For peasants with high incomes, abundant land, small families, reliable crop yields, and outside employment opportunities, the argument probably is not applicable. In general terms, it will apply to the poor peasant or tenant and not the rich peasant who regularly hires labor and has ample acreage and savings. It is not possible, or necessary in this context, to fix the upper threshold of income and security beyond which risks are far more rational. On the basis of the Thai example, among others, I am persuaded that safety-first behavior characterizes not only the poorest peasants but much of what is known as the middle-peasantry as well.[35]

33. Jean-Marc Boussard and Michel Petit, "Representation of Farmers' Behavior under Uncertainty with a Focus-Loss Constraint," *Journal of Farm Economics* 49:1 (November 1967), 869–80. Again, I am grateful to Ronald Herring and Van Ooms for calling the recent work on the theory of the firm to my attention.

34. Herbert Simon, *Models of Man: Social and Rational* (New York: Wiley, 1957).

35. I should add perhaps that safety-first behavior hardly rules out all innovation, but rather those innovations with high risks. It is possible to imagine a rate of return high

A critical assumption of the safety-first rule is that subsistence routines are producing satisfactory results. What if they are not? Here the rationale of safety-first breaks down. To continue the same routines means to go under in any case and it once again makes sense to take risks; such risks are in the interest of subsistence.[36] Peasants whose subsistence formulas are disintegrating due to climate, land shortage, or rising rents do what they can to stay afloat—this may mean switching to cash crops, taking on new debts and planting risky miracle rice, or it may mean banditry. Much of peasant innovation has this last-gasp quality to it. The economic context in which it makes sense for peasants to strike out for the unknown has social and political implications as portentous as their usual skeptical caution.[37]

## THE SOCIOLOGY OF THE SUBSISTENCE ETHIC

The peasant cultivator of rice will always find himself at the mercy of a capricious nature. From among the array of techniques available to him, he can choose that routine which minimizes the chance of a failure but, as his margin is small, even the best technique leaves him vulnerable. Where water supply is assured, the variation in the harvest is modest but tangible; in rain-fed areas or flood-prone regions, the risk is enormous.

Even after the wisest technical precautions, the peasant family must somehow survive those years when the net yield or resources fall below basic needs. How do they make do? In part, they may tighten their belts further by eating only one meal each day and switching to poorer foods. Peasant belts have precious little slack, however, and if the crisis is an extended one this is not a viable strategy. Second, at the family level, there are a variety of subsistence alternatives which we may group under the heading "self-help." This may include petty trade, small crafts,

enough to discount risk altogether but such situations are exceptional. In addition, in a socialist state, or any state which insures a minimal income to all, the risk associated with innovation is socially insured although bureaucratic obstacles may more than offset this effect.

36. One such case of risk-taking under threat of ruin was the introduction of motor-driven water pumps in the Mekong Delta in the early 1960s. A drought threatened the entire crop of smallholders and tenants, and unless they acted many would have nothing but debts after harvest. They had little to lose by borrowing for the rental or purchase of a water pump which could save the crop. Cf. Robert L. Sansom, *The Economics of Insurgency in the Mekong Delta* (Cambridge, Mass.: M.I.T. Press, 1970), chaps. 7 and 8.

37. This seems to be similar to what Eric Wolf has in mind when he writes: "Perhaps it is precisely when the peasant can no longer rely on his accustomed institutional context to reduce his risks, but when alternative institutions are either too chaotic or too restrictive to guarantee a viable commitment to new ways, that the psychological, economic, social, and political tensions all mount toward peasant rebellion." *Peasant Wars,* p. xv.

casual wage labor, or even migration.[38] For many Southeast Asian peasants whose net yields (after rent and interest) are below subsistence, these "sidelines" have now become a regular and necessary part of the subsistence package.

Finally, there is an entire range of networks and institutions outside the immediate family which may, and often do, act as shock absorbers during economic crises in peasant life. A man's kinsmen, his friends, his village, a powerful patron, and even—though rarely—the state, may help tide him over a difficult period of illness or crop failure. We will examine the performance and availability of these subsistence options in much greater detail later. For our immediate purposes, however, it is important to note that the more *reliable* each of these options is, the more resource-poor it tends to be. Self-help is perhaps the most reliable strategy inasmuch as it is not contingent on someone else's assistance but, by the same token, it only yields up what a man can lay his own hands on. Kinsmen normally feel obliged to do what they can for a close relative in trouble, but they can offer no more than the pool of resources at their command.

As we move to reciprocity among friends and to the village, we move to social units which may control more subsistence resources than kinsmen and are still a part of the intimate world of the peasantry where shared values and social controls combine to reinforce mutual assistance. In most cases, however, a man cannot count with as much certainty or for as much help from fellow villagers as he can from near relatives and close neighbors.[39]

Patron-client ties, a ubiquitous form of social insurance among Southeast Asian peasants, represents yet another large step in social and often moral distance, particularly if the patron is not a villager. Whether a landowner, petty official, or trader, the patron is by definition a man who is in a position to help his clients. Although clients often do what they can to cast the relationship in moral terms—since their sheer bargaining power is often minimal—patronage is more to be recommended for its resources than for its reliability.[40]

The last social unit, the state, fits strangely in this company. It is often

38. Collecting firewood, making charcoal, and engaging in petty trade have been traditional ways of making ends meet in slack seasons or after crop failures in Southeast Asia.

39. The reciprocities of kinship, particularly among bilateral kindred, diminish perceptibly the more distant the bond; at the periphery of a kin network, performance may be less reliable than among unrelated neighboring villagers.

40. There are large variations in the reliability of patron-client ties. For a discussion of this variance, see James C. Scott, "Patron-Client Politics and Political Change in Southeast Asia," *American Political Science Review* 66:1 (March 1972), 91–113.

distinguished more by what it takes from peasants than what it gives, and its social distance from the peasantry, especially in the colonial era, was measured in light years.[41] Nevertheless, both the traditional state— through regional granaries, public works employment paid in kind, famine relief—and the modern state, through employment, welfare, and relief, may help peasants survive. The state's assistance, if it arrives at all, however, is hardly reliable.

This inverse relationship of reliability and resources presents the peasant, on the one hand, with a brother who would give him the shirt off his back but is more likely than not to be as destitute as he and, on the other hand, with a state which could more easily help but is far less likely to recognize his need as its responsibility.[42] Given the choice, peasants would probably prefer to meet their needs on their own or with the help of reliable kinsmen and villagers, but the choice may not be theirs if the protection afforded by their immediate circle does not suffice.

It is also evident that as soon as a peasant leans on his kin or his patron rather than on his own resources, he gives them a reciprocal claim to his own labor and resources. The kin and friends who bail him out will expect the same consideration when they are in trouble and he has something to spare. In fact, they aid him, one might say, because there is a tacit consensus about reciprocity, and their assistance is as good as money in the bank against the time when the situation is reversed. Similarly, in the village context, the village norms which may assure a poor man a patch of communal land and food also require him to provide labor when village officials or notables call for it. The client who relies on a more powerful patron for protection is obliged, at the same time, to serve him as a loyal member of his entourage and to be at his beck and call for many services. The claims of the state (taxes, corvée, conscription) speak for themselves and it is questionable whether the peasant ever sees these claims as a repayment for services received (law and order? peace? religious functions?).

41. The normative order of the traditional Southeast Asian state did assume a responsibility on the part of the ruler to provide for his subjects in time of distress. Not only was the ruler responsible in some cosmological and magical sense for the prosperity of his kingdom, but he was expected to help in more material ways as well as by charity, reducing taxes, and so forth. See, among others, Somersaid Moertono, *State and Statecraft in Early Java* (Ithaca: Cornell University Southeast Asian Program, 1968).

42. Again, the traditional Southeast Asian state with its paternalist moral order was perhaps more likely to recognize its responsibilities in this respect, but its capacity to store and move grain any distance from the capital was sharply limited. It must not be imagined, moreover, that the storage of grain was undertaken solely in the interest of public relief. Just as often it served as a means for the capital and its officials to withstand sieges and rebellions by would-be usurpers.

All of these institutions, then, have an ambivalent role in peasant life. They may provide vital social insurance against a time of dearth, but they also make claims on a peasant's resources—claims which he may be strapped to meet. *The timing, size, and scope of their contributions and claims to peasant resources are the key to their legitimacy*—to their place in peasant values. How these claims and contributions are judged by peasants can, in turn, best be understood in terms of the subsistence ethic examined above.

## THE DISTRIBUTION OF RISK IN PEASANT SOCIETY

The safety-first maxim, a logical consequence of the ecological dependence of peasant livelihood, embodies a relative preference for subsistence security over high average income. Not only does this security-mindedness make abstract economic sense but, as I hope to show below, it finds expression in a wide array of actual choices, institutions, and values in peasant society. Before describing these concrete patterns, however, it is necessary to sketch briefly the implications the subsistence ethic has for the relationship of peasants to the institutions around them and for their notions of justice and equity.

What the subsistence ethic provides is a perspective from which the typical peasant views the inevitable claims made upon his resources by fellow villagers, landowners, or officials. It implies, above all, that such claims are evaluated less in terms of their absolute level than in terms of how they complicate or ease his problem of staying above the subsistence crisis level. It implies that a rent of 40 percent of the crop in a good year is likely to meet less explosive resistance than a rent of 20 percent after a particularly poor year. The peasant's criterion will be what is left after outside claims have been met—whether it is enough to maintain his basic requirements—rather than the level of the claims per se.

At the risk of laboring the obvious, Figure 2 illustrates two ideal-typical claims by outsiders on peasant resources. Line A represents the same hypothetical crop yields as in Figure 1, while the line at 80 units of rice again represents the subsistence crisis level. Lines B and C reflect the impact of two vastly different kinds of claims on peasant income, which may be thought of as varying forms of land rent or taxation. Line B represents the effect on peasant subsistence resources of an unremittingly fixed, absolute tax or rental claim. Year in, year out, a steady twenty units of rice is exacted from the net yield; the effect on household resources is simply to maintain the shape of the yield line but lower it twenty units. Its effect on peasant life is massive. The net remaining for consumption plunges not once but thirteen times below the subsistence crisis line, and for four successive years (18–21) it remains below that

Figure 2. Crop Yields and Claims on Peasant Income

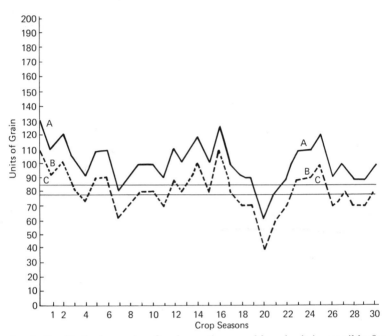

level. Qualitatively, such a fixed exaction would make it impossible for the peasant family to maintain its already tenuous position and some major and painful adaptation would be necessary (for example, sell land, migrate, resist). The risks of agriculture, in this case, are still fully borne by the cultivator, but at a level which is increasingly insupportable. By contrast, the state or landlord has stabilized its (his) income at the expense of the peasant.

Line C represents the polar opposite of a fixed claim on peasant resources. Each year, grain is exacted so that the peasant family is left five units above the subsistence crisis line. On three occasions where the yield line drops below eighty-five, this implies an *actual subsidy* of some form to the peasant to raise him to that level. Here the qualitative changes in the character of peasant life are enormously reduced as the subsistence crisis threshold is never reached. In fact, it is conceivable that the peasant might actually prefer C to a situation without rents, inasmuch as he may be willing to pay a large income premium in order to guarantee himself a subsidy in a bad year. The risks of agriculture, in this situation, are borne by the state or landlord, whose income fluctuates to steady the net resources left for the peasant household.

The key element for the peasant in judging the exactions that are an inevitable part of his life is whether they increase or reduce the chance of a disaster. This is not necessarily identical, by any means, with what might be considered the average extraction of surplus from the peasantry by elites. The total resources squeezed from the countryside under a variable claim (C) that stabilizes peasant income are actually, in this example, greater than with a fixed levy (B). If we were to use as a standard of exploitation the average "take" of elites from peasants, then the stabilizing claim would qualify as the most exploitative. Given the subsistence precipice along which the peasant treads, however, the stabilizing claim (though it may end by taking more) is less resented, stirs less ferocious resistance, and is experienced as less "exploitative," inasmuch as it avoids outcomes that peasants fear most.

I am proposing a fundamentally different concept of exploitation than is normally used—a definition that seems far more in accord with the major existential problems of peasant life. The usual procedure is to ask how much elites expropriate from the peasantry and to use the proportion of the product expropriated as a measure of the level of exploitation. This is quite in keeping with both the Marxist notion of surplus value and with common sense. But if we wish a measure of exploitation that accords with peasant perceptions, this definition is not adequate. There are radically different ways for elites to expropriate an average of, say, 25 percent from peasant incomes. Although the peasant may resent any such claim, it is the claim that most often threatens the central elements of his subsistence arrangements, that most often exposes him to subsistence crises, that is naturally perceived as the most exploitative. He asks how much is left before he asks how much is taken; he asks whether the agrarian system respects his basic needs as a consumer.

So there is no misunderstanding about the normative standing of my argument, it should be clear that my analysis is essentially phenomenological. Although I may have deduced the safety-first logic from the material basis of peasant life, the persuasiveness of my analysis depends ultimately on demonstrating that this logic is reflected in peasant values and experience. It is *not* necessary for my argument, nor would I necessarily claim, that the peasant's view of relative equity is to be preferred on normative grounds to any other standard of exploitation. In fact, the argument is in no way inconsistent with a view that would label this peasant notion of exploitation a form of false-consciousness. From an outside global view, after all, the context in which peasant needs arise is in part a social artifact; presumably the cultivator needs security largely because his land has been taken from him and a small elite controls most scarce values.[43] Be this as it may, a phenomenological approach has at least two advantages over purely deductive theories of exploitation. Beginning as it does with the values of real actors, it offers a more reliable guide to behavior than abstract standards which offer no conceptual link between the theory of exploitation and the feelings of the exploited. Second, to the extent that the actor has his own durable moral economy which continues to define the situation for him, I believe that a study of such real values may help sharpen and clarify the moral underpinnings of even abstract theories of justice.

As peasants experience it, then, the *manner* of exploitation may well make all the difference in the world. Forms of exploitation that tend to offer built-in subsistence security and which, in this sense, adapt themselves to the central dilemma of peasant economics are, and are seen to be, far less malign than claims which are heedless of minimum peasant standards.

The argument also implies that fixed claims on peasant resources usually are far more painful in areas where yields are most variable. A hypothetical peasant on utopian land which regularly yields him a ten-basket surplus of paddy each season may well resent a five-basket impost, but it will never throw him below the disaster line. Another peasant with an *average* surplus of ten baskets which is, however, achieved through wide oscillations, will more often be thrown below subsistence by a five-basket levy. The explosive potential of fixed rents or taxes in the nonirrigated area of Upper Burma, in Northeast Thailand, or in Northern Annam is thus likely to be greater than in areas where yields are far more steady.[44]

SUBSISTENCE AS A MORAL CLAIM

The peasant's perspective as drawn here is very much in keeping with "the moral economy of the poor" as it has appeared historically in other

43. Relevant in this context is Lukács's distinction between "the real psychological thoughts of men about their lives" (class psychology) and "the thoughts and feelings which men *would have if they were able to assess* both it and the interests arising from it in their impact on immediate action and on the whole structure of society" (i.e., "objective economic totality"). The distance between the two is, for Marxists, a measure of the level of false consciousness. Georg Lukács, "Class Consciousness," in *History and Class Consciousness: Studies in Marxist Dialectics,* trans. Rodney Livingstone (Cambridge, Mass.: M.I.T. Press, 1971), pp. 50–51.

44. Of course, if the steady yield in question is already at the subsistence level, any claim at all will spell disaster.

contexts.[45] At the core of popular protest movements of urban and rural poor in eighteenth- and nineteenth-century Europe was not so much a radical belief in equality of wealth and landholding but the more modest claim of a "right to subsistence"—a claim that became increasingly self-conscious as it was increasingly threatened.[46] Its central assumption was simply that, whatever their civil and political disabilities, the poor had the social right of subsistence. Hence, any claim on peasants by elites or the state could have no justice when it infringed on subsistence needs. This notion took many forms and was of course interpreted elastically when it suited, but in various guises it provided the moral indignation that fueled countless rebellions and *jacqueries*. The *"droit de subsistance"* was what galvanized many of the poor in the French Revolution; it was behind *"taxation populaire"* when the public seized grain and sold it at a popularly determined just price; it was also behind the "Jacobin maximum" which tied the price of basic necessities to wage levels.[47] In England it can equally be seen in bread riots and in the ill-fated Speenhamland relief system.[48] The minimal formulation was that elites must not invade the subsistence reserve of poor people; its maximal formulation was that elites had a positive moral obligation to provide for the maintenance needs of their subjects in time of dearth.[49] For the

45. The term is E. P. Thompson's. See his classic *The Making of the English Working Class* (New York: Vintage Books, 1966), p. 203.

46. For a discussion which notes the difference between the claim to subsistence and the more comprehensive Marxist notion of "the right to the whole produce of labour" and treats each historically, see Anton Menger, *The Right to the Whole Produce of Labour: The Origin and Development of the Theory of Labour's Claim to the Whole Product of Industry*, trans. M. E. Tanner (New York: Augustus M. Kelley, 1962; originally published 1899).

47. See, for example, Richard C. Cobb, *The Police and the People*, part 3 (New York: Oxford, 1970); and Richard B. Rose, "Eighteenth-Century Price Riots and the Jacobin Maximum," *International Review of Social History* 4:3 (1959), 432–33; and "Food Supply and Public Order in Modern Europe," in Charles Tilly, ed., *The Building of States in Western Europe* (Princeton: Princeton University Press, 1974).

48. For England, see E. P. Thompson, "The Moral Economy of the English Crowd in the Eighteenth Century," *Past and Present* 50 (February 1971); Karl Polanyi, *The Great Transformation, passim;* and E. Hobsbawm and G. Rudé, *Captain Swing* (New York: Pantheon, 1968).

49. From a normative perspective there is some reason to believe that the "right to subsistence" as a political claim constitutes the first and primary criterion of justice. W. G. Runciman, drawing on Rawls's theory of justice, asks what rules of justice or criteria of distribution would men agree to in principle before they knew what their actual place in society would be. The first rule he deduces is based on need—the notion that one man's right to subsistence supersedes another man's right to a surplus. "This priority may be initially summarized in the dictum that in a society where anyone was starving it is a crime to have more than enough." "If in the state of nature, I know that I may in due course find myself starving, even though willing to work, while others have the wherewithal to keep me alive, I shall want to ensure not only that I have a claim recognized as just on the basis of need, but that I have a claim which overrides claims made on the basis of either merit or

Southeast Asian peasant also, this ethos provided a standard of equity against which the moral performance of elites might be judged.

Finally, the notion that, for those at the margin, an *insecure* poverty is far more painful and explosive than poverty alone, receives strong confirmation from research linking insecurity to radicalism. In contexts as divergent as Cuba, the United States, England, and Germany, the experience of economic insecurity, particularly unemployment, predisposed workers to militant politics.[50] The comparative history of mineworker protest in England and Germany is representative here. In England where miners were at the mercy of the trade cycle and had no accident protection, labor was a tumultuous affair of "bargaining-by-riot" and machine-breaking. In Germany, by contrast, where mineworkers were employees of the state covered by an umbrella of paternalist regulations insuring them medical benefits and employment security despite very low pay, protest was replaced by deferential and submissive petitions for assistance.[51] Summarizing much of the research in this area, Leggett claims that "in all parts of the world, occupational groups subject to great fluctuations in income have traditionally thrown their support behind leftist parties."[52] This evidence, though hardly conclusive, is suggestive. It indicates that the stabilization of real income for those close to subsistence may be a more powerful goal than achieving a higher *average* income; it indicates that we may learn more about the politics of peasants by asking not merely how poor they are but also how precarious their livelihood is.

---

contribution to the common advantage." *Relative Deprivation and Social Justice* (Berkeley and Los Angeles: University of California Press, 1966), p. 264. That this right was not without some practical effect in traditional societies we may see, for example, in E. E. Evans-Pritchard's statement that "no one in a Nuer village starves unless all are starving." *Kinship and Marriage Among the Nuer* (Oxford: Oxford University Press, 1951), p. 58.

50. See Maurice Zeitlin, "Economic Insecurity and the Political Attitudes of Cuban Workers," *American Sociological Review* 31:1 (February 1966), 35–51; John C. Leggett, "Economic Insecurity and Working-Class Consciousness," *American Sociological Review* 29:2 (April 1964), 226–34; and Gaston Rimlinger, "The Legitimation of Protest: A Comparative Study in Labor History," *Comparative Studies in Society and History* 2:3 (April 1960), 329–43.

51. Rimlinger, passim.

52. John C. Leggett, *Class, Race, and Labor* (New York: Oxford University Press, 1968), p. 78. I should add that in the case of shopkeepers and rural smallholders, economic insecurity can just as easily lead to right-wing radicalism as to left-wing movements.

# 2 Subsistence Security in Peasant Choice and Values

We have seen how the narrowness of the peasant's economic margin leads him to choose techniques that are safe even if they give away something in average yield. Socially as well, the peasant in principle seeks to transfer as much of his economic risk as possible to other institutions—to give income as ransom for safety.

If subsistence security is a more active principle of peasant choice and values than maximizing average return, this fact should be reflected in a whole series of shared preferences. In four major areas—stratification, village reciprocity, tenancy, and taxation—asking what one would anticipate those preferences to be on the basis of safety-first considerations, I attempt to show that evidence of actual preferences is substantially in accord with what one would deductively expect. The safety-first concept thus helps to unify a structure of real preferences which might otherwise seem anomalous. While the evidence presented here is largely taken from Southeast Asia, I believe it may be representative of many peasant societies.

## RISK AND STRATIFICATION

If income were the active principle of occupational preference, it would be sufficient to rank occupations by average income to obtain a schedule of preferences. If, on the other hand, subsistence security were the determining factor, one would expect that increments in economic security would be as important as increments in income in structuring preferences. Just such considerations, judging from the ethnographic literature on Southeast Asia, appear to account for many preferences which do not make sense in terms of income alone.

The conventional hierarchy of status among the rural poor is usually smallholder, tenant, wage-laborer. These are not, of course, mutually exclusive categories, since it is common to find cultivators who simultaneously own some land and farm additional land as tenants, as well as wage laborers who have a plot of their own. Yet, through much of colonial and contemporary Southeast Asia, these categories have had a social reality in preferences and in status in the countryside despite the fact that the categories could and did overlap considerably in terms of income. Marginal smallholders, for instance, were often poorer than tenants who could rent large plots; marginal tenants, in turn, were often poorer in a good labor market than wage workers. The social sticking-power of this hierarchy—even when it seemed anomalous in income terms—can be explained, I believe, by the sharp drop in security which each of these descending statuses ordinarily implied.

The key advantage of the smallholder was that he possessed, in his own hands, the means of his subsistence. This access to subsistence, unlike that of most tenants, is not as contingent on the good will of another man. Although he may not do quite so well as a large-scale tenant in a given season, his claim to the product of the land he holds is far stronger and therefore his subsistence is generally more secure. "The value of owning land lies in the owner's immunity from involuntary loss of land or its product."[1] Actual title, then, assumes significance *only* insofar as it symbolizes a more *secure access* to the means of subsistence. In portions of Tonkin, Upper Burma, and Java, some forms of tenancy have traditionally been so secure that the social significance of legal title was minimal. Where tenancy was less secure, the significance of ownership was consequently larger.[2]

In the commercializing economies of colonial Southeast Asia, a secure claim to the product of the land had another critical advantage. The direct consumption of food crops insulated a peasant from the fluctuations of market prices. Again, the smallholder or subsistence tenant might live more frugally than a laborer in a boom market, but his living was steadier; he preferred "the long-run stability of land derived income compared with the uncertainties of the labor market."[3] The wisdom of this course was only too evident to the peasantry of Southeast Asia in the Great Depression when the Vietnamese, Javanese, Burmese, and Filipino peasants who had been forced onto the labor market had to retreat in disarray back to the subsistence economy.[4]

Similar considerations of subsistence security impel peasants generally to choose a bare subsistence as a tenant over wage labor. A tenant not only avoided the full impact of market fluctuations but he often gained

1. Moerman, *Agricultural Change and Peasant Choice,* p. 99.

2. Where land is plentiful and cheap, of course, the social significance of ownership per se may all but disappear. In fact it is possible to imagine a situation of abundant land and scarce labor, where to be a tenant or laborer was more advantageous in terms of income *and* security than landownership. The importance of control over land is thus based on the assumption that it is the scarce factor of production; where it is not the scarce factor, as in many traditional states, control over men rather than land was the secure basis of power and income.

3. Sansom, *The Economics of Insurgency,* p. 199.

4. The best account of this retreat is Clifford Geertz's description of the Javanese economy where the sugar system was an explicit and institutionalized arrangement of having the traditional economy bear the welfare costs of commercialized agriculture. Geertz, *Agricultural Involution.*

access to the resources of the owner who had an interest in his subsistence, at least until the crop was harvested. Insofar as tenancy involves a link to a patron who will help in a crisis, it may be rationally preferred by those close to subsistence over labor for cash at a higher average rate of return. In parts of Central Luzon, according to Takehashi, peasants continued as tenants on small patches of land that returned them much less than wage labor only because of the economic insurance the landlord provided. "So long as they remain tenants, they can expect to borrow living expenses from their landlords, in other words, the minimum level of livelihood of tenants is ensured by landlords."[5] James Anderson, discussing tenancy in Pangasinan, Central Luzon, explains the preference there for tenancy in identical terms:

> Even under the traditional tenancy system . . . tenants are somewhat better off than agricultural laborers. . . . Tenants under the traditional system *seem willing to put up with its injustices for this compensating security.* They may not readily give up these advantages without a significant gain in income which could compensate them for their loss of security.[6]

In the Mekong Delta of Vietnam as well, where tenancy was less stable than in Pangasinan, it often included the same valuable fringe benefits:

> Small tenants are not much better off than simple coolies; the land they rent provides them only an average of 73 Piastres or 48% of their total resources. . . . But the great superiority of the small tenant over the coolie is his certainty of getting advances if he needs them. While the coolie does not inspire the confidence of the moneylender, the tenant has an assured credit source in his landlord. . . . *The life of the small tenant is not much more brilliant than that of the coolie, but he is better protected against the blackest misery.*[7]

Colonial officials in Lower Burma, attempting to explain why the preference for tenancy prevailed despite a buoyant labor market in the 1920s, found that easy access to landlord credit was the motive. "But people will seek to secure a tenancy because of the ability to borrow money."[8]

5. Akira Takahashi, *Land and Peasants in Central Luzon* (Honolulu: East-West Center Press, 1969), p. 137. See also Jorge Prion, "Land Tenure and Level of Living in Central Luzon," *Philippine Studies* 4:3 (September 1956), 393.

6. J. H. Anderson, "Some Aspects of Land and Society in a Pangasinan Community," *Philippine Sociological Review* 10:1–2 (January-April 1966), 58. Emphasis added.

7. Pierre Gourou, *L'utilisation du sol*, pp. 404–5.

8. *Maubin Settlement Report, Season 1925–1928,* Settlement Officer U. Tin Gyi (Rangoon:

Ownership was prized over tenancy and tenancy over casual labor because, even though they might overlap in terms of income, each represented a quantum leap in the reliability of subsistence. Crisis security was, therefore, a more active principle of stratification in the peasant's view than income. Distinctions *within* the categories of tenant and laborer were, moreover, largely predicated on the security of tenure or work and the degree of social insurance the owner or employer customarily gave.

Perhaps the best example anywhere of a labor system which depended traditionally for its cohesion on subsistence guarantees was the *jajmani* relationship between landed and landless castes in India. This system provided a fixed annual payment in kind to the landless clients of a peasant cultivator in return for their caste-specified services. Its effect was precisely to guarantee a minimum subsistence level to the poorer castes in an agrarian system fraught with risks. As Scarlett Epstein notes, "untouchables were prepared to accept the system of fixed rewards because it provided them with security even in bad years."[9] Since the return to the lower castes varied little from year to year, the profits of a bumper crop accrued almost entirely to the landowning class. Following a poor harvest, however, the owner-cultivators had no more grain to eat than did their low-caste dependents. The exploitative features of the system are obvious, inasmuch as it is based on a caste monopoly of land and transfers most, if not all, of the surplus beyond subsistence needs to the dominant caste. Its social tenacity, though, is to be explained by the fact that it gave a crisis subsistence guarantee to subordinate castes in all but the most catastrophic harvests.

The same pattern of social choice holds among Javanese rural workers. Van der Kolff has reported that Javanese laborers near Kediri would choose one form of labor contract (the *pakehan*) over another (the *ngrampijang*) even though it involved more work, because they "were assured of a long period of reaping or of a definite amount of paddy, while, for the *ngram* reapers, the time of work and therefore the amount that they would get was uncertain."[10] Generally, agricultural labor by

Government of Burma, 1929), p. 68. See also the *Report on the Revision Settlement of Bassein District, Season 1935–39,* Settlement Officer Maung Maung Gyi (Rangoon: Government of Burma, 1940), p. 54, which notes, "Some labourers become tenants chiefly to acquire the status which gives them greater independence and the power to borrow money."

9. Scarlett Epstein, "Productive Efficiency and Customary System of Rewards in Rural South India," in Raymond Firth, ed., *Themes in Economic Anthropology* (London: Tavistock, 1967), pp. 229–52, esp. p. 244.

10. G. H. Van der Kolff, *The Historical Development of the Labour Relationships in a Remote Corner of Java as They Apply to the Cultivation of Rice: Provisional Results of Local Investigations* (Report C, International Research Series of the Institute of Pacific Relations, issued under

the year or season with meals provided, though it paid less, was preferable to daily wage labor without meals; a secure tenancy with traditional crisis assistance was favored over unstable tenancy with impersonal landlords.[11] Just as the shepherd, the permanent farm laborer, or the domestic servant in rural Europe paid for his relative security with low wages,[12] so also did subsistence guarantees come at a premium for Southeast Asian peasants. Where a capitalist labor market existed, one might even measure the relative preference for security over income by the wage premium sacrificed for successively more secure situations, as employers could take full economic advantage of the subsistence ethic.

The central role of security for the peasantry suggests that interpretations of peasant politics based on their deprivation in income terms may fail to do their circumstances justice. It implies, for example, that downwardly mobile peasants may resist *most* bitterly at those thresholds where they risk losing much of their previous security. One such threshold occurs at the point where self-sufficient smallholders lose the land that gives them their fairly autonomous subsistence.[13] The means of subsistence passes out of their hands and they face having to become more or less permanently dependent clients whose security is contingent on their relations with those who have the resources to help them.[14] As the

the auspices of the National Council for the Netherlands and the Netherlands Indies, May 2, 1936, chap. 3. See also H. ten Dam, "Cooperation and Scoial Structure in the Village of Chibodas," in *Selected Studies of Indonesia by Dutch Scholars*, vol. 6, *Indonesian Economics: The Concept of Dualism in Theory and Policy* (The Hague: W. van Hoeve, 1961).

11. In all these cases we are speaking of preferences within a highly constrained, not to say exploitative, environment. The choice is socially structured and between alternatives neither of which may be attractive. I by no means wish to imply that peasants necessarily accept as legitimate the circumstances which force such choices upon them, only that, within this context, security is preferred to short-run income gains.

12. For shepherds and permanent farm laborers, see J. A. Pitt-Rivers's fine study of Andalusia, *The People of the Sierra* (Chicago: University of Chicago Press, 1961). For domestics, see, for example, F. M. L. Thompson, *English Landed Society in the Nineteenth Century* (London: Routledge and Kegan Paul, 1963), p. 194.

13. Dependence was common in precolonial Southeast Asia but it was for the most part based on the need for physical protection rather than the need for land.

14. My impression is that the loss of a more or less autonomous subsistence is frequently found at the root of many forms of anarchism. Small peasants about to lose their land, artisans pushed to the brink by the factory system, may seek, in their political reaction, a means to restore their freedom to live and work independently.

The desire to maintain a viable independence is illustrated in Java by the fact that villagers "at all costs avoid entering sharecropping relationships with landowners or working for a wage, since income from ownership of land and income from selling one's labor power produced a basic status division among villagers, expressed in practice by relationships of patronage and dependency." Victor T. King, "Some Observations on the Samin Movement of North Central Java," *Bijdragen tot de Taal-, Land-, en Volkenkunde* 129:4 (1973), 466–67. King is citing fieldwork by Robert Jay, *Javanese Villagers* (Cambridge, Mass.: M.I.T. Press, 1969).

land/man ratio worsened in colonial Southeast Asia, the land holding of an ever-growing proportion of the peasantry was inadequate for its subsistence. The result might be termed a "crisis of dependence" involving a painful choice between an economically precarious independence and a more secure situation of dependence.[15]

A second threshold—one far more characteristic of such areas as Lower Burma and Cochinchina where capitalist agriculture was strongest—occurs when the subsistence guarantees *within dependency* collapse. At this point, a landowning elite is stripping away the last more or less feudal guarantees shielding the peasantry from the full impact of market fluctuations. Here we can expect—and have seen historically—a ferocious resistance. Without secure tenancies, pre-harvest loans, lower rents in bad years, and help at times of sickness, the peasant shoulders the full risk not only of crop yield fluctuations but of the labor and commodity markets as well. As we shall see later, the impact of both commercial agriculture and the growth of the state was to steadily reduce the reliability of subsistence guarantees to a point where peasants had hardly any other alternative but resistance.

RISK INSURANCE IN THE VILLAGE

If the need for a guaranteed minimum is a powerful motive in peasant life, one would expect to find institutionalized patterns in peasant communities which provide for this need. And, in fact, it is above all within the village—in the patterns of social control and reciprocity that structure daily conduct—where the subsistence ethic finds social expression. The principle which appears to unify a wide array of behavior is this: "All village families will be guaranteed a minimal subsistence niche insofar as the resources controlled by villagers make this possible." Village egalitarianism in this sense is conservative not radical; it claims that all should have a place, a living, not that all should be equal.

The social strength of this ethic, its protective power for the village poor, varied from village to village and from region to region. It was, on balance, strongest in areas where traditional village forms were well developed and not shattered by colonialism—Tonkin, Annam, Java, Upper Burma—and weakest in more recently settled pioneer areas like Lower Burma and Cochinchina. This variation is instructive, however, for it is in precisely those areas where the village is most autonomous and

15. An equivalent threshold may occur in agrarian systems where the common village land and communal economic rights which made it possible for the poorest to eke out an independent living are disappearing. See Marc Bloch, *French Rural History: An Essay on Its Basic Characteristics*, trans. Janet Sondheimer (Berkeley: University of California Press, 1970), p. 224, and also J. L. Hammond and Barbara Hammond, *The Village Labourer, 1760–1832* (New York: Harper Torchbooks, 1970).

cohesive that subsistence guarantees are strongest. Given control over their local affairs, then, peasants choose to create an institution that normally insures the weakest against ruin by making certain demands on better-off villagers.

An understanding of the informal social guarantees of village life is crucial to our argument because, as they are sustained by local opinion, they represent something of a living normative model of equity and justice. They represent the peasant view of decent social relations. Embodying the right of all to a subsistence niche and the pooling of risks, they are standards of moral judgment which will reappear later in the peasant view of the state and of landlords. Given a choice, the peasant preferred a system of tenancy or dependency in which the landlord/patron protected his tenant/client against ruin in bad years and an officialdom which, at the very least, made allowances in periods of dearth. These elites should, ideally, assume a protective role akin to village patterns of sharing. To the extent that the peasant could actually structure his relations with landowners and with the state, we shall see that he did move the relationship in this direction.

Few village studies of Southeast Asia fail to remark on the informal social controls which act to provide for the minimal needs of the village poor.[16] The position of the better-off appears to be legitimized only to the extent that their resources are employed in ways which meet the broadly defined welfare needs of villagers. Most studies repeatedly emphasize the informal social controls which tend either to redistribute the wealth or to impose specific obligations on its owners. The prosaic, even banal, character of these social controls belies their importance. Well-to-do villagers avoid malicious gossip only at the price of an exaggerated generosity. They are expected to sponsor more conspicuously lavish celebrations at weddings, to show greater charity to kin and neighbors, to sponsor local religious activity, and to take on more dependents and employees than the average household. The generosity enjoined on the rich is not without its compensations. It redounds to their growing prestige and serves to surround them with a grateful clientele which helps validate their position in the community.[17] In addition, it repre-

16. See, for example, Pierre Gourou, *Peasants of the Tonkin Delta*, vol. 1, p. 379; William F. and Corinne Nydegger, *Tarong: An Ilocos Barrio in the Philippines*, vol. 6, Six Cultures Series (New York: John Wiley, 1966), chap. 5; M. G. Swift, *Malay Peasant Society in Jelebu* (London: Athlone Press, 1965), chap. 2; Manning Nash, *The Golden Road to Modernity* (New York: John Wiley, 1965); Robert R. Jay, *Religion and Politics in Rural Central Java* (New Haven: Yale University, Southeast Asian Studies, Cultural Report Series, 1963), pp. 44, 52–55.

17. It should also be recalled that, where strong outside guarantees for wealth and position did not exist, the standing of local elites depended ultimately on the following they

sents a set of social debts which can be converted into goods and services if need be.

What is notable is that the normative order of the village imposes certain standards of performance on its better-off members. There is a particular rule of reciprocity—a set of moral expectations—which applies to their exchanges with other villagers. Whether or not the wealthy actually live up to these minimal moral requirements of reciprocity is another question, but there can be little doubt that they exist. Their normative character is apparent in the reaction provoked by their violation. In village Thailand, for example,

> A farmer with money is in a position to exert pressure on many other farmers. He is the *phujaj* [big man] in the *phujaj-phunauj* [big man-little man] relationship. It is to him that others must often turn in order to borrow and to rent tools, to obtain cash loans and land to farm. Once the transaction is made, the debtor is obligated in many small ways throughout the year. However, wealth without the proper behavior results in contempt and malicious gossip, and receives only token respect in the poor farmer's moment of need.[18]

A wealthy man who presses his tactical advantage does so at the cost of his reputation and moral standing in the community. The same reaction was noted by Firth in his study of a Malay fishing village.

> These two features [small and ephemeral differences in wealth], combined with the practice of charity enjoined on the rich, probably account to a considerable extent for the absence of any marked feeling of resentment towards the wealthy on the part of the poorer elements in the community. . . . Where resentment and criticism do enter is when the rich man does not show himself generous, when "his liver is thin," when he does not practice charity to the poor, build wayside shelters, or prayer houses, or entertain liberally.[19]

Where such social controls survived with some vigor in the colonial period they tended to block the growth of sharp class cleavage within the village. In East and Central Java this has meant villages of "just-enoughs" and "not-quite-enoughs" in which a Byzantine maze of land,

---

could muster in a showdown. There are thus very good reasons for local powerholders to build sizable clienteles in such circumstances.

18. Howard Keva Kaufman, *Banghuad, A Community Study in Thailand*, Monographs of the Association of Asian Studies, No. 10 (Locust Valley, N.Y.: J. J. Augustin, 1960), p. 36.

19. Raymond Firth, *Malay Fishermen: Their Peasant Economy* (London: Routledge and Kegan Paul, 1966), p. 295.

sharecropping, and labor rights have tended, until recently, to provide villagers a minimal niche, albeit at declining levels of welfare for all.[20] The crisis value of such leveling pressures is most dramatically evident for a famine-stricken village in Tonkin where Gourou reported that only the equal distribution of hunger throughout the commune prevented anyone from starving.[21] Guarantees were less ironclad elsewhere, but they generally helped "poor families to manage through periods of difficulty."[22]

Occasionally, where the communitarian tradition was strongest, most notably in Tonkin, Annam, and Java, the subsistence ethic took the form of village rights over land. An average of roughly 25 percent of the land in Tonkin and Annam was communal land, and in Quang Tri and Quang Binh provinces the figure was over 50 percent of paddy land.[23] Some of this land was allotted more or less on the basis of need to poor villagers. The rent from communal land was deployed in part to help the poor pay taxes and to support noncultivating widows and orphans. Elsewhere, rights to cultivate local wasteland within the village domain, grazing rights, gleaning rights, and the customary rule that no outside tenants or laborers be engaged if a needy villager could be found, all served the same end of enabling the village poor to scrape by.[24]

Village redistribution worked unevenly and, even at its best, produced no egalitarian utopia. We may suppose that there was always some tension in the village between the better-off who hoped to minimize their obligations and the poor who had most to gain from communal social guarantees. The poor, for their part, got "a place," not an equal income, and must have suffered a loss of status as a result of their permanent dependence. Nevertheless, this pattern did represent the minimal moral requirements of village mutuality. It worked through the support or acquiescence of most villagers and, above all, in normal times it assured the "survival of the weakest." What moral solidarity the village

20. Geertz, *Agricultural Involution,* chap. 5. For the argument that the pattern has reached its protective limits, see Margo Lyon, *Bases of Conflict in Rural Java,* Research Monograph No. 3 (Berkeley: University of California Center for South and Southeast Asian Studies, December 1970), and W. F. Wertheim, "From Aliran Towards Class Struggle in the Countryside of Java," *Pacific Viewpoint* 10:2 (September 1969), 1–17.

21. Gourou, *Peasants of the Tonkin Delta,* 2, p. 659.

22. Swift, *Malay Peasant Society in Jelebu,* p. 153.

23. Yves Henry, *Economie agricole de l'Indochine* (Hanoi: Government Générale de l'Indochine, 1932), pp. 43–44. This massive volume contains, as far as I can tell, the aggregate data from which virtually all conclusions about rural landholding, tenure, and living conditions in Vietnam were drawn. It is a monument.

24. For the striking parallels between these patterns and those of the traditional French commune, see Marc Bloch, *French Rural History.*

possessed *as a village* was in fact based ultimately on its capacity to protect and feed its inhabitants. So long as village membership was valuable in a pinch, the "little tradition" of village norms and customs would command a broad acceptance.

## RISK IN TENANCY AND SHARECROPPING

Virtually everywhere in lowland Southeast Asia the colonial introduction of capitalist forms of landownership, coupled with population growth, fostered the development of a large class of tenants and sharecroppers whose livelihood was contingent on their arrangements with a landowner. Village sharing and casual wage labor were not unimportant for members of this class, but their subsistence security or insecurity derived largely from the system of land tenure under which they cultivated.

The same moral criteria which suffused village redistributive norms, the same emphasis on subsistence security, may be used as a basis for evaluating tenancy arrangements. Implicitly, the peasant would ask, "Does this institution safeguard my minimal social rights; does it provide me with a living regardless of what the land may yield this season?" To the extent that it did, we would expect the institution of landownership to retain at least a modicum of legitimacy though it might claim a large share of the harvest. To the extent that it failed to guarantee even the minimal needs of cultivators, we would expect landlords to lose whatever moral claim to legitimacy they might once have had.

Land tenure systems can be located along a continuum according to how they distribute the risk of fluctuating yields between the landowner and cultivator. In Table 1 three simplified systems of tenure are ranked along such a continuum for purposes of illustration. The continuum portrays the extent to which a tenure system insulates the cultivator from crop losses that will ruin him. Toward the "A" end of the continuum, the landlord protects the tenant's living, while at the "C" end, the tenant, in effect, guarantees the income of the landlord, come what may. Peasants, under most circumstances, have naturally preferred tenures that provide subsistence crisis insurance. This preference should be most strongly present where plots are small, yields highly variable, peasants poor, and where few alternative subsistence opportunities exist. It is weaker where large tenancies, stable yields, a well-off peasantry, and ample outside employment opportunities greatly reduce the likelihood of ruin. The conditions of tenancy in colonial Southeast Asia have far more closely approximated the first set of conditions.

The relative legitimacy of tenure systems that embody subsistence guarantees would spring from the fact that the cultivator's needs are

Table 1. Distribution of Risk in Tenancy Systems[25]

| Landlord assumes risk (A) | Risk shared (B) | Tenant assumes risk (C) |
|---|---|---|
| e.g., Traditional (feudal) systems of tenure | e.g., Equal shares sharecropping | e.g., Fixed rent tenancy |
| Cultivator's minimal return fixed and guaranteed | Cultivator's return a fixed proportion of crop | Cultivator assumes risk—and profit—of enterprise |
| Landowner assumes risk—and profit—of enterprise | Landowner's return a fixed proportion of crop | Landowner's return fixed and guaranteed |

taken as the first legitimate claim on the harvest. Such arrangements protect his livelihood and shift the risk of the enterprise to the shoulders of the owner who is normally better able to absorb it. A full subsistence guarantee must, of course, go beyond the tenant's prior claim to the crop: for what if the total crop will not supply his minimal needs? Here the subsistence guarantee involves a subsidy to carry the tenant through a disastrous season. Thus, complete subsistence crisis insurance implies a personal commitment of the landowner to the minimum welfare needs of his tenant. The terms "patron" and "patronage" in their classical use become applicable here inasmuch as the relationship is ultimately focused upon the landowner's responsibility for the tenant and his family as consumers rather than upon an impersonal economic bargain.[26] The beneficiary of these services is often more than a mere tenant; he is usually a "client" tied to his landlord by personal deference and a sense of obligation. Elements of the patron-client bond are evident in most traditional tenancy systems in Southeast Asia, but they were probably best represented in the late nineteenth-century hacienda system in the Philippines.[27]

25. In this illustration I have focused primarily on the provisions for dividing the crop. A more accurate scheme for the distribution of risk would also have to include the distribution of production costs. If the landowner provides all equipment, seed, plow animals, and other cash costs, he assumes this risk, while if these costs are shifted to the tenant, the tenant assumes an even greater risk than the arrangements for dividing the harvest would indicate.

26. This despite the fact that the "patron" probably takes the entire surplus above the tenant's minimal needs in good years. In surplus value terms, the system may be strikingly exploitative.

27. A brilliant portrayal of this system in the early twentieth century in Nueva Ecija may

In keeping with the safety-first principle, the first thing a peasant would want to know about a tenancy system is what it will do for him in a bad year. The traditional system, barring a total disaster, will support him; 50–50 sharecropping may or may not support him. Although the tenant and landowner equally share the risks of yield fluctuations, there is no guarantee that 50 percent of the yield in any given season will meet his basic requirements.

The labels "sharecropping" or "fixed rent" are often only indifferent guides to the actual tenancy relation. The traditional "kasama" tenancy system in Philippine rice cultivation, for example, nominally describes 50–50 sharecropping. In practice, however, in some areas, "An owner, particularly a medium owner, is obliged, in a manner of speaking, to help a tenant when he is able,"[28] while in other regions no mercy is shown. The key is the actual content of the relationship—the actual pattern of reciprocity—and not its formal descriptive terms. Sharecroppers who can count on interest-free food loans prior to harvest, who are allowed more than their nominal share of the crop in a bad year, who get help in case of illness, who enjoy perpetual tenure, and who can count on petty favors from the landowner have a substantially stronger subsistence insurance than one would infer from the usual division of the crop.

Fixed rents—in cash or in kind—would, in safety-first terms, be the most onerous. The amplitude of crop-yield fluctuations are reflected in full in the tenant's income, and while the sharecropping system claims no rent if there is no harvest, the fixed rent system demands its inexorable due even if not a single stalk matures. A simple hypothetical case will illustrate what happens in good and bad years under both systems (see Table 2). In this example, shares are divided 50-50, and the fixed rent is set at half the yield in an average year. Let us assume that 40 baskets of rice are the minimal subsistence needs of a cultivator's family. In an average year both systems yield the tenant 50 baskets of rice, a small margin over basic needs. In a bumper year, of course, the tenant does well under both systems, but exceptionally well under fixed rent.[29] Let

be found in Benedict J. Kerkvliet, "Peasant Unrest Prior to the Huk Revolution in the Philippines," *Asian Studies* 9 (August 1971), 164–213.

28. Anderson, "Some Aspects of Land and Society," p. 50.

29. One might ask why the fixed rent tenant does not use the surplus of the good years to tide him over the bad years. There are several reasons. First, unless the initial years are good, there is no surplus. Second, there is an inevitable storage loss for rice which is kept any length of time. More important, however, is that within a peasant community much of a man's surplus is siphoned off to aid his less fortunate kin and neighbors or for ceremonial obligations that he avoids only at his peril. Finally, of course, peasants *do* store up some wealth in plow animals, pigs, gold—all of which are thrown into the breach in a poor year—but their savings are typically meager.

Table 2. Comparison of Crop Division under
Sharecropping and Fixed Rent

| *50-50 Sharecropping* | | | |
|---|---|---|---|
| Yield | 100 | 200 | 50 |
| Landlord's share | 50 | 100 | 25 |
| Sharecroppers share | 50 | 100 | 25 |
| *Fixed-rent (fixed at 50% of average year)* | | | |
| Yield | 100 | 200 | 50 |
| Landlord's rent | 50 | 50 | 50 |
| Tenant's return | 50 | 150 | 0 |

the yield under fixed-rent fall below 90, however, and every subsequent basket lost comes out of the tenant's subsistence needs. In a poor season, when the total yield is only 50 baskets, the tenant is left with absolutely nothing, while he must deliver to the landowner, who is probably well-off, the baskets of rice that would otherwise feed his family. While fixed rent may maximize a tenant's profit, it also minimizes his security; it is a relentless claim that takes no heed of his fundamental needs.[30]

There is ample evidence that peasants in many parts of lowland Southeast Asia judged the fairness of tenure systems according to how reliable they were in subsistence terms. The very measure of land in Vietnam, the *mau*, was fixed not as a unit of area but as a constant product; thus the *mau* was smaller in Tonkin, where land was more fertile, and larger for the poorer soils of Annam. Vietnamese measured land in subsistence units much as the Irish would speak of "a farm of three cows" to indicate its fodder capacity.[31] In a tenancy arrangement, similarly, a man first asked what his pile of rice would look like after the crop was divided, not what the landowner's cut might be. Inquiries into tenancy in Lower Burma in the 1920s showed that cultivators regarded it as reasonable to pay a *higher percentage share* of their yield to the owner where the land was more fertile or where they could cultivate larger plots.[32] In either case, the landowner could take a larger share and they would still end the season with an ample subsistence ration. On poor lands, with high production costs, they might regard even a smaller percentage as insupportable. And, of course, in a bad year they expected

30. A nominal system of fixed rents might, of course, approximate sharecropping to the extent that the landlord gave remissions in bad years.

31. Ngo Vinh Long, *Before the Revolution*, chap. 1. For a comparable system in traditional Bali, see Clifford Geertz's article in Koentjaraningrat, ed., *Villages in Indonesia* (Ithaca: Cornell University Modern Indonesia Project, 1967).

32. *Report of Inquiry into the Condition of Agricultural Tenants and Labourers*, by T. Couper, Indian Civil Service (Rangoon: Superintendent of Government Printing, 1924), p. 23. Hereafter referred to as *The Couper Report*.

leniency. Vietnamese landlords also received an expanding share of the crop on more fertile lands.[33] It does not follow, therefore, that a landlord who takes half the crop is regarded as 10 percent more exploitative than the landlord who takes 40 percent. The reverse may be the case and the major criterion, as always, is how much is left on the tenant's threshing floor when rent and production costs are paid. While the landlord's share and what remains for the tenant are hardly unrelated, the latter cannot be directly inferred from the former.

Where tenants had sufficient bargaining strength, the conditions of sharecropping tended to approximate their view of what was tolerable. Henry reports that customary sharecropping terms in Tonkin were, by custom, waived when they threatened the sharecropper's subsistence stock: "the owner leaves the entire harvest to the sharecropper in the event of a poor harvest."[34] Early rubber share-tapping practices reflected the same concern for the subsistence claim of the share-tenant. Under the *bagi dua* (roughly, "partners" or "half-shares") system in Indonesia, the tapper got less than half the proceeds when the price of latex was high and a good deal more than half when the price was low.[35] The owner thus assumed the bulk of market risks while the tapper's income was steadied. Generally, tenants could count more on such protection where landlord and cultivator were linked by kinship or lived in the same village or where a labor shortage made it prudent to consider their wishes. Where the tide ran against the tenant, he was more likely to resist both the switch from sharecropping to fixed-rent tenancy and the denial of the special consideration once shown him in hard times.[36]

The importance of subsistence concerns to landlord-tenant relationships is remarkably illustrated in Luzon where the Philippine government has recently attempted to transform rice sharecroppers into fixed-rent tenants.[37] In an effort to make the switch attractive, rents were to be fixed at a figure that corresponded to one-quarter of the average net yield (after subtracting seed, harvesting, threshing, loading, hauling, and milling costs) prior to the date of the change. Sharecropping rents had been one-half of the gross harvest, with the landlord and tenant typically splitting production costs 50-50. Under the new system the tenant could thus expect to realize roughly double his previous

33. Ngo Vinh Long, *Before the Revolution*, chap. 2.

34. Yves Henry, *Economie agricole de l'Indochine*, p. 35.

35. Boeke, *The Structure of the Netherlands Indian Economy*, p. 114. See, for rice areas in Java, Van der Kolff, *Labour Relations in a Remote Corner of Java*, p. 45.

36. See, for example, Takahashi, *Land and Peasants in Central Luzon*, p. 73.

37. See the articles in the *Philippine Sociological Review*, 20:1–2 (January-April 1972).

income in an average year and, with the use of new seed strains, perhaps more than that. Despite the considerable gain in average income that the new system promised, many peasants were reluctant to switch. The reasons for this reluctance were the new subsistence risks inherent in tenancy reform. First, there was the risk of a fixed rent after a meager crop.

> For while under share tenancy he paid a percentage of whatever he managed to reap in a particular year, good or bad, under leasehold he must pay the same amount whether the harvest is abundant or not, and what he cannot pay at harvest time will accrue as debt to be paid at the next crop harvest.[38]

While the tenant might do far better in a good year, the new leasehold arrangements shielded him less against disaster.

Second, and most important, leasehold frequently meant the end of a wide array of landlord services that were critical to tenants' subsistence security. These included the landlord's share of production costs, low interest production loans, food loans, help in time of illness, access to bamboo, wood, and water from the owner's holding, and the right to plant hillside and vegetable crops. On the one hand, the tenant could choose leasehold with a low, legal rent and greater autonomy but at the cost of most previous landlord services and an unvarying charge on his harvest. On the other hand, he could remain a sharecropper paying a high, nonlegal rent which nevertheless varied with his yield and could expect a continuation of landlord credit and assistance.[39] The options were agonizing for peasants and many preferred to remain sharecroppers or to sign "compromise leases" which retained much of the security of the old system. Actual patterns of choice, moreover, reflected the subsistence concerns of tenants. Those moving to leasehold were precisely those for whom the shift was least threatening; they farmed in areas where yields were steadiest, they rented larger and more profitable tenancies which reduced their need for credit, they tended *already* to have landlords who were strict and who granted them few customary

38. Brian Fegan, "Between the Lord and the Law; Tenants' Dilemmas," *Philippine Sociological Review* 20:1–2 (January-April 1972).

39. Ibid., p. 119. Landlords were also wary of the switch, for they feared losing the profits of new high-yielding varieties under the fixed rent system. For this reason they often severely penalized those who made the change. The crop yields that were to be used to calculate the fixed rent were often the subject of prolonged litigation, thereby adding to the tenant's problems. Finally, the success of the reform hinged on the provision of state credit to replace landlord funding. From the tenants' comments it is evident that state credit was too meager and too late, if it arrived at all, thus jeopardizing the financial stability of the new leaseholders.

rights, and they were more likely to have outside employment to fall back upon. For these tenants the risks were minimized. Sharecroppers with small plots, variable yields, no savings or steady outside employment, and lenient landlords, by contrast, had most to lose in terms of subsistence security and were most reluctant to change. As one tenant explained, "I will have to pay higher rent all my' life [under sharecropping] but I can at least get food to live on now."[40]

Both the patterns of choice and the values peasants brought to bear on that choice betray a constant preoccupation with subsistence risks. The overriding goal was "security" and "food and money for subsistence."[41] When leasehold involved no greater risks it was naturally very attractive, but where it threatened to undercut the existing subsistence guarantees of share tenancy, its potential rewards seemed, and were, a dangerous gamble.

There is some independent support for this interpretation from a recent opinion survey of cultivators in the same province.[42] The results suggest that there is a shared normative conception among tenants of what constitutes a "good landlord" and that the provision of minimum welfare needs is a central part of this conception. When asked what qualities the "good landlord" should have, respondents said they would expect him to help with production costs, provide "fringe benefits," and supply liberal credit. The importance of production expenses is obvious in light of the inability of the typical tenant to pay for such inputs himself. The term "fringe benefits," however, is something of a misnomer, given the critical nature of such services. Included in this category were medicine and doctor bills, free housing and house lot, a subsistence food ration (*rasyions, abasto,* or *bugnós*), and pre-threshing rice allowances (*agad*). Finally, share tenants demanded "credit," including lenient terms following a poor harvest. Taken together, fringe benefits and credit represent the belief that share tenancy should provide a guaranteed food supply and make allowances for the tenant's needs and capacity to pay in any given year. Subsistence preoccupations are also reflected in the major complaint against landlords and overseers (*katiwala*): namely, that they were often too strict, enforcing the contract terms regardless of the yield or the difficulties of the cultivator.

The standard moral expectation is nowhere more clearly expressed than in this statement by a tenant in that area: "A man of his [landlord's]

40. Ibid., p. 124.

41. Romana Pahilanga-de los Reyes and Frank Lynch, "Reluctant Rebels: Leasehold Converts in Nueva Ecija," *Philippine Sociological Review* 20:1–2 (January-April 1972), 37, 46.

42. Ibid., passim.

means was *supposed* to loan his tenants rice and help when times were hard. *That's part of being a landlord."* [43] A landlord who fails to honor his obligations becomes a "bad" landlord. So long as the failure is an isolated case, this judgment reflects only on the legitimacy of that particular landlord. Once the failure becomes general, however, the collective legitimacy of landlords as a class may be called into question. "If share-cropping arrangements are such that subsistence is assured, then it is seen as a good system. For the major complaint about share tenancy is not the dependency which it implies, but that often the share is insufficient to meet subsistence needs." [44]

The control of land became, in colonial Southeast Asia, the basis of rural power. Our knowledge of the priorities and needs of peasant cultivators suggests that they had criteria of performance by which to judge the legitimacy of landed power and of those who exercised it. Landlords were acceptable to the extent that they acted as patrons—to the extent, that is, that they used their surplus to provide crisis subsistence insurance to their clients. The peasant held a set of concrete role expectations about the legitimate use of economic power, as expressed by Pitt-Rivers with reference to the Spanish peasant's view of patronage:

> The resentment aims not so much at the existence of economic inequality as at the failure of the rich man to care for those who are less fortunate; at his lack of charity. It is not so much the system which is wrong, it is the rich who are evil. . . . Patronage is good when the patron is good, but like the friendship upon which it is based, it has two faces. It can either confirm the superiority of the *senorito* or it can be exploited by the rich man to gain a nefarious advantage over poor people. It covers a range of relationships from noble protection of dependents in accordance with the moral solidarity of the pueblo to the scurrilous coercions of the later period of *caciquismo. The system is, clearly, only to be judged good insofar as it ensures that people do not go hungry, that injustice is not done.* Where the majority of the community can look to a patron in time of need, such a system reinforces the integration of the pueblo as a whole. Where those who enjoy the advantages of patronage are a minority,

43. Benedict J. Kerkvliet, "Peasant Rebellion in the Philippines: The Origins and Growth of the H.M.B." (forthcoming, University of California Press, 1976), chap. 1, p. 12. It is worth noting that the share tenant defines the social duty of the landlord by reference to his "means" much as the social duty of wealthy villagers is defined by their means and the needs of their fellow villagers.

44. David Christenson, "Reflections on the IPC/BA Economic Study," *Philippine Sociological Review* 20:1–2 (January-April 1972), 169.

then they and their patrons are likely to be resented by the remainder.[45]

The only justification for economic inequality is the benign, community-serving use of power; elites, to validate their power, must do their duty.

RISK AND THE STATE

Following the logic of the subsistence ethic, the peasant would minimally ask of the state what he asks of the patron—that it adjust its claim on his yield to his capacity to pay. The best "real world" state is accordingly one that only taxes the surplus of the good years and, as the patron does, actually subsidizes him in bad years through, say, public works employment and state granaries. A less than ideal situation, comparable to sharecropping in tenure systems, is one which takes a fixed proportion of his annual resources. Even though the tax in this case varies somewhat with his ability to pay, it may nonetheless throw him below the disaster level in a bad year. The worst situation, of course, comparable to the landlord's fixed rent, is an unvarying annual tax which he must pay, fair weather or foul. A brief illustrative example, Table 3, shows the relative impact of proportional and fixed taxes on peasant welfare. Assuming a tax on net yields of 20 percent, a figure well below that used by British settlement officers to fix taxes in Burma, even the proportional tax precipitates a subsistence crisis at yields of 30 or 25 baskets which would, without the tax, be sufficient for minimal needs. The fixed tax, however, increases the peasant's return in a good year but it crushes him far more in a bad season when his survival is at stake. The fixed tax is, in effect, an *expanding* proportional claim on his diminishing resources.

In an instance of rare colonial thoughtfulness, the settlement officer for Shwebo, Burma, a Mr. Williams, actually went so far as to ask smallholders what they thought of fixed taxes. The ferociousness of their response seems to have struck him.

> I have broached [fixed assessments] with many cultivators in connection with the proposals for lump-sum assessments. These, of course, introduce further complications, but on the main issue that in good and bad years the demand should be the same, hostility to the proposal was uncompromising and almost universal.[46]

45. Pitt-Rivers, *The People of the Sierra*, p. 204.
46. *Report of the Committee Appointed to Examine the Land Revenue System of Burma*, vol. 2, *Evidence* (Rangoon: Superintendent of Government Printing, 1922), p. 129. Hereafter referred to as *Report on Land Revenue System, Burma*.

Table 3. Comparative Effect of Proportional and
Fixed Assessments on Peasant Income

| | Net yield (baskets) | | | | | |
| | 50 | 40 | 35 | 30 | 25 | 20 |
|---|---|---|---|---|---|---|
| Proportional tax | | | | | | |
| 20% | 10 | 8 | 7 | 6 | 5 | 4 |
| Remaining | 40 | 32 | 28 | 24 | 20 | 16 |
| Surplus (deficit) over | | | | | | |
| subsistence figure of 25 | +15 | +7 | +3 | −1 | −5 | −9 |
| baskets | | | | | | |
| Fixed tax | | | | | | |
| 8 baskets (20% of average | 8 | 8 | 8 | 8 | 8 | 8 |
| yield of 40) | | | | | | |
| Remaining | 42 | 32 | 27 | 22 | 17 | 12 |
| Surplus (deficit) over | | | | | | |
| subsistence figure of 25 | +17 | +7 | +2 | −3 | −8 | −13 |
| baskets | | | | | | |

As with tenure systems, the nominal forms of taxation are often less
meaningful than their operation on the ground. In this respect, the bark
of the traditional Southeast Asian kingdom was far worse than its bite. In
bad years the collection of taxes fell off substantially and, reluctantly,
remissions were granted for whole districts hit by floods, pests, or
drought. This lenience may in part have been due to a symbolic alignment of the traditional court with the welfare of its subjects but it was
also surely a reflection of the traditional state's inability to reliably control much of its hinterland. We may imagine that the central court would
have preferred, if it could, to steady its income at the expense of the
peasantry. Outside the immediate environs of the court to which the
king's writ did extend, however, the problems of collecting revenue were
enormous. Hard-pressed peasants in one region would move into the
forest or seek the protection of another local chief. Since the basis of
power in the traditional state was control of population (the source of
the surplus) rather than land, local leaders were happy to accept ref-
ugees and to expand their clientele. The resistance to payment of taxes
by those who stayed in place must have also grown after a bad season
and helped reduce the tax-collecting capacity of the state. Traditional
states were, in Myrdal's terms, "soft states" in the classical sense.

Ngo Vinh Long calculates that the actual tax take under the Nguyen
dynasty preceding colonization was between 3 and 4 percent of average
yields in Tonkin and 3.9 to 5.5 percent in Cochinchina.[47] What matters,

47. Ngo Vinh Long, *Before the Revolution,* Chap. 3. The actual percentages are appar-

of course, is how year-to-year taxes varied with the capacity of the
cultivator to pay. In this connection, Long mentions occasional famine
relief, and there appears to have been a traditional decree providing that
taxes be lowered by a percentage nearly equal to the percentage of the
harvest lost and for a complete suspension of taxes if more than 70
percent of the harvest was ruined.[48] The burden of the traditional head
tax was further softened in two ways. First, each village systematically
underreported its population in order to minimize its assessment. Second, since villages and not individuals were taxed, one might expect the
better-off to pay something more than an equal share. Thus there was
some flexibility, however unintended, in what was nominally a fixed-tax
system.

In Thailand, too, a major dilemma of traditional statecraft was to raise
enough revenue in corvée and kind to maintain the court, but not so
much as to drive the cultivating population out of range. During good
crop seasons and where yields were most stable, the problem may have
been manageable, but during hard times the revenue could be squeezed
out, if at all, only at a risk of losing much of the kingdom's future tax
base. The natural limits to what the nobility and the state could extract
from commoners were fixed by the abundance of land and the rudimen-
tary coercive capacity of the state. "There was, however, a mechanism
which tended to restrain the *nai* (nobles) from making excessive demands on the services of their *phrai* (commoners). When the *phrai* could
no longer bear such excessive demands from their *nai,* they could simply
run away into the jungle."[49] Although this may exaggerate the ease with
which people left their village and land, a major preoccupation of the
Thai state in the early Bangkok period was holding the population it
administered and persuading runaways to return. The monarch tried to
restrain oppressive nobles who reduced the population of his kingdom;
tattooing was hit upon as a means to control subjects by indelibly iden-
tifying them; and Thai armies relocated whole conquered villages closer
to the center of the realm. As in most other traditional kingdoms,
however, the problem was persistent. The more burdensome the kingdom's taxes became, the more it lost population and encountered resistance until a temporary equilibrium was achieved. State revenue fluc-

ently missing from the published version, but were included in the manuscript version on
p. 68.

48. Guy Gran, "Vietnam and the Capitalist Route to Modernity: Village Cochinchina
1880–1940" (Ph.D. dissertation, University of Wisconsin, 1975), p. 342. See also Long,
*Before the Revolution,* pp. 33–34.

49. Akin Rabibhadana, *The Organization of Thai Society in the Early Bangkok Period,
1782–1873* (Ithaca, N.Y.: Cornell University Southeast Asia Program, No. 196).

tuated far more in response to peasant subsistence needs than either the king's ministers would have liked or the formal tax system implied.[50]

What evidence we have, then, suggests that invariable tax claims were both more onerous and more actively resented than tax claims which varied with the cultivator's resources. Our later examination of the rebellions of the 1930s will reveal how explosive such resentment could become. For if the traditional state could not prevent a certain amount of tax evasion by a beleaguered peasantry, the colonial state was much better equipped to make its claim to the peasant surplus stick.

I have tried to demonstrate in this chapter that there is a correspondence between the logic of the subsistence ethic and the concrete choices and values of much of the peasantry in Southeast Asia. At the level of village reciprocity, occupational preferences, and the evaluation of tenancy and taxation there appears to be a clear inclination to favor those institutions and relationships which minimize the risks to subsistence, though they may claim much of the surplus. These preferences grow out of the precarious human condition of subsistence farmers but they also take on a moral dimension as a claim on the society in which they live. The violation of this claim by the economic and social transformations of the colonial period is the subject of the next three chapters.

50. It should be added that excise taxes or monopoly profits on salt and other commodities were a sizable share of traditional revenue. To the extent that the commodities in question were subsistence necessities, such as salt, they constituted a fixed charge on peasant income. Even here, however, the illegal salt trade and traditional black markets which the state found difficult to control set a practical limit to the revenue-raising capacity of these devices.

# 3   The Distribution of Risk and Colonial Change

If we examine the experience of the Southeast Asian peasantry under colonialism in terms of the principle of subsistence security, our attention is drawn to events and processes that have rarely been center-stage in the analysis of colonialism. From this perspective the average per capita income of some statistically average peasant under colonialism is of less political interest than the relative instability of welfare levels of sharecroppers, smallholders, and laborers. It is in this area, I believe, that the social dynamite of the colonial transformation is to be sought.

In terms of subsistence security, colonialism created as many problems as it solved. It did, on the one hand, create the transportation networks and political capacity that could move grain from surplus to deficit areas, thereby easing the threat of local famine. On the other hand, that same transport and political capacity could be used to move grain out of an area in the form of rent and taxes. On the one hand, colonial policy and capital breached the agricultural frontier and, thanks to the labor of peasant pioneers, brought vast new tracts under the plow. On the other hand, much of this new land was controlled by a small class of landlords whose power over an exploding rural population tended to eliminate any improvement in living standards the peasantry might otherwise have realized.[1]

1. While the methodology of such comparisons is enormously complicated, the evidence suggests that the real per capita income of Southeast Asian peasants did not materially increase between 1910 and 1929 and may very well have declined from 1900 to 1940. For some fairly convincing evidence on Vietnam, see Sansom, *The Economics of Insurgency,* pp. 33–39; Jean Chesneaux, *Contribution à l'histoire de la nation vietnamienne* (Paris: Editions Sociales, 1955), chap. 9; Long, *Before the Revolution,* pp. 122–24; and especially Henri Lanoue, "L'Industrialization de l'Indochine," in *Sociéte d'études et d'informations économiques* (November 21, 1938). For Burma, see J. S. Furnivall, *Colonial Policy and Practice,* 2nd ed. (New York: New York University Press, 1956), pp. 103, 192–93; *Report of the Capitation and Thathameda Taxes Enquiry Committee, 1925–27* (Rangoon: Government of Burma, 1949), pp. 62–63; *The Couper Report,* p. 2 or "Summary," and pp. 49–50. Some of the most convincing evidence for Burma and other Southeast Asian states comes from the report on prewar agriculture in Burma by B. O. Binns, *Agricultural Economy in Burma* (Rangoon: Government of Burma, 1948). Binns's figures indicate a disparity between rice production and population that suggests declining consumption in Java, Indochina, and Siam as well. For the Philippines, see Generoso Rivera and Robert McMillan, *The Rural Philippines* (Manila: Office of Information, Mutual Security Agency, 1952), passim. I am not as familiar with the evidence for Indonesia, but the weight of opinion supports either a stable or a declining per capita income there (communication from Clifford Geertz). See, for example, A. M. P. A. Scheltema, *The Food Consumption of the Native Inhabitants of Java and Madura,* trans. A. H. Hamilton (New York: Institute of Pacific Relations, 1936), passim. Given the

The growth of the colonial state and the commercialization of agriculture complicated the subsistence security dilemma of the peasantry in at least five ways. First, it exposed an ever-widening sector of the peasantry to new market-based insecurities which increased the variability of their income above and beyond the traditional risk in yield fluctuation. Second, it operated to erode the protective, risk-sharing value of the village and kin-group for much of the peasantry. Third, it reduced or eliminated a variety of traditional subsistence "safety-valves," or subsidiary occupations which had previously helped peasant families scrape through a year of poor food crops. Fourth, it allowed landholders, who had once assumed responsibility for some of the hazards of agriculture, not only to extract more from the peasantry in rents but also to collect a fixed charge on tenant income, thereby exposing the peasantry more fully to crop and market risks. Finally, the state itself was increasingly able to stabilize its tax revenue at the expense of the cultivating class. Most of the agrarian unrest of the 1920s and 1930s in the region is tied to this new pattern of insecurity and exploitation. From the microperspective of a peasant family's budget, one could say that its income became more insecure, the charges on that income became ever more invariable and unrelated to its circumstances, and the locally available alternative sources of food and income tended to diminish.

What was critical in this transformation was not so much a decline in income per se as a decline of earlier social insurance patterns. The comparative agrarian history from 1900 to 1940 of, say, East and Central Java on the one hand and Lower Burma or Cochinchina on the other hand is suggestive here.[2] Peasant income in East and Central Java was almost certainly, on the average, well below the level for Lower Burma and Cochinchina but, by all accounts, it was far more stable. Owing to Dutch colonial policy and the redistributive elasticity of his village, the Javanese peasant retained much of his subsistence guarantee, though probably at declining levels of material welfare. In the boom and scramble atmosphere of the pioneer regions of Lower Burma and the Mekong Delta, however, higher average income levels were accompanied by the

statistical difficulties, all of this evidence remains circumstantial, but the case *against* assuming a rising level of material welfare among the peasantry is fairly convincing. For our purposes, of course, these statistics are far less important than the question of economic insurance.

2. This is not to say that Java was entirely peaceful, just that it was relatively calm by comparison. See Sartono Kartodirdjo's fine "Agrarian Radicalism in Java: Its Setting and Development," chap. 2 in Claire Holt, ed., *Culture and Politics in Indonesia* (Ithaca: Cornell University Press, 1971), and his later *Protest Movements in Rural Java: A Study of Agrarian Unrest in the Nineteenth and Early Twentieth Centuries* (Singapore: Oxford University Press, 1973).

absence of any of the traditional shock-absorbers that might provide some economic security. The comparatively tumultuous peasant politics in Cochinchina and Lower Burma would thus seem to stem less from absolute levels of poverty than from their complete exposure to the fluctuations of the world economy—an exposure which made stable social patterns and expectations impossible. Where abject poverty and insecurity were joined, of course, the situation became especially explosive.

The discussion of colonial change below can hardly do justice to the variety of experience in the region but is meant rather to sketch the main lines of what should be a more elaborate empirical inquiry. Of the five major changes cited earlier which made peasant subsistence security more problematic, we focus especially on the claims of landowners (in this chapter) and of the state (in Chapter 4) and only summarily treat the role of market forces, subsidiary occupations, and village leveling patterns. The reason for this emphasis is simply that landlords and the state were more politically salient. While the disappearance of traditional crafts, price-level changes, and weakening village charity narrowed the margin of peasant safety, they were all more or less impersonal processes without any readily identifiable human agency. The landlord and the official were, on the other hand, tangible indeed; they made direct claims on peasant produce which might be resisted.[3] Geographically, the major effort here is to present evidence for Vietnam and Lower Burma rather than for the rest of the region.

## MARKET-BASED INSTABILITIES

In a smallholding subsistence economy, despite its profound disadvantages, a peasant family knows that if the harvest is sufficient its food supply is more or less assured. When the crop is sold, however, or when portions of it are valued at current prices for rent or interest payments and taxes, there is no such assurance. The crop may be larger but a price fall will reduce its real value. To the extent that the market determines the value of the peasant's crop, to that extent is he exposed to the insecurities of the price mechanism.[4] Taxes, rents, and interest paid in

3. A more extended discussion of weakening village reciprocity and disappearing slack resources may be found in James C. Scott, "The Erosion of Patron-Client Bonds and Social Change in Rural Southeast Asia," *Journal of Asian Studies* 32:1 (November 1972), 25–30.

4. This may be the case whether the peasant physically sells his produce or not. So long as the landlord or moneylender figures his tenant/debtor's payment in rice according to its market value, the peasant is to that degree at the mercy of the price system. It is of course an advantage to have a cash crop like rice that is at the same time a staple food rather than, say, tobacco or rubber.

cash might cost twice as much *in rice* this year as they had last, even though the amount of cash required and the size of the crop remained constant.

The insecurities of the world market were, on balance, greater than those of the traditional local market. In a small restricted market, price and yield tended to offset one another; the smaller the local harvest, the greater the per unit price and vice versa, since supply and demand were largely determined by the harvest itself. Within a world market, however, this nexus between local harvest and price is broken and the world price varies more or less independently of local supply—a small harvest is as likely to fetch a small per unit price as a large harvest. The variability that price movements add to peasant real income over and above crop fluctuations can be determined by figuring the amplitude of price fluctuations and the extent of market valuation. Chayanov, for example, calculated that beyond the 20.6 percent variability in Russian peasant flax harvests per unit of land, the average variation in the price per unit of flax was 13 percent.[5] If the price rose as the yield declined, peasant income might remain the same, but price movements could just as easily compound as offset the effects of yields.

The commercialization of agriculture inevitably meant a marked increase in cash production costs for farming implements, the rental of plow cattle, and transplanting and harvest labor. Though the smallholder or tenant might try to minimize these expenses, they represented sunk costs (potential losses) which could be recovered or financed only through selling a part of the crop. The major impact of this development on income was noted in an inquiry into land revenue in Lower Burma in 1922:

> Owing to the increase of cost of cultivation, the income of the cultivators *varies within much wider limits* now than it did, say, twenty years ago. Now that the cost of cultivation absorbs one-half or two-thirds of the gross produce, a difference of one-fourth in the out-turn of the crop produces a great effect on income.[6]

We must also not ignore the fact that a growing concentration of landownership in lowland Southeast Asia itself served to expose peasants more fully to market forces. Everywhere, but most strikingly in the more commercialized lowlands such as the Mekong Delta and the Irrawaddy Delta, the proportion of rural wage laborers and tenants to

5. Chayanov, *On the Theory of Peasant Economy*, p. 137.
6. "Statement by S. N. Smyth," Indian Civil Service, Commissioner, Irrawaddy Division, in *Report of the Land and Agriculture Committee* (Rangoon: Government of Burma, 1938), vol. 2, p. 34.

smallholders increased dramatically. Wage laborers had both feet in the market economy; the price system fixed both the wage for their labor and the buying power of that wage. Tenants, though they might eat a portion of what they grew, increasingly faced rent, interest, and tax charges, the burden of which fluctuated with market prices. Small-holders were somewhat better insulated from market forces. But the fact that they had to pay taxes and mortgage and loan charges, and hire labor, left them far from invulnerable. Even in Thailand whose small-holding population was seen as the most stable in the region, much the same process was at work: "As they learned the advantages of credit and the dangers of foreclosure, owners became tenants and tenants became laborers. The most bounteous harvest was no avail against this kind of disaster."[7]

The impact of the market in wet rice areas was uneven. East and Central Java, Malaya's East Coast, the northern Central Plain in Thai-land, Tonkin and Annam, and Upper Burma retained more of a subsis-tence core than Lower Burma or Cochinchina. They were nonetheless variations on a central theme. The sources (for example, wages, prices of primary commodities) of the cash that the peasant *increasingly* needed tended to fluctuate, while the claims on his income (taxes, rents, a range of consumer necessities such as salt, cloth, kerosene, matches) tended to remain the same or steadily rise. Balancing the peasant budget became increasingly precarious.[8]

### The Weakening of Village Protection

Social change under colonialism did not destroy local redistributive norms. In fact, there is evidence that in the short run at least the new and intrusive economic demands of the colonial state served to enhance rather than erode the risk-sharing value of the village. This was certainly the case in those areas where the colonial state levied taxes collectively on villages as in Annam and Java.[9] Where these norms were weak to begin with, notably in the relatively atomized frontier regions of Cochinchina and Lower Burma, they never had provided much social insurance for the peasantry.

Over the long haul, even where village leveling traditions were strong, however, at least three structural changes served to attenuate their contribution to peasant subsistence. First, village redistributive pressures operated exclusively on locally held resources and thus the protective capacity of the village, as that of the kindred, was traditionally limited by

7. Hanks, *Rice and Man,* p. 141.

8. Boeke, *The Structure of the Netherlands' Indian Economy,* p. 58.

9. Cf. Geertz, *Agricultural Involution,* chap. 2.

its narrow scope.[10] If the village as a whole suffered a series of crop disasters, its internal capacity to share resources would be of little avail. The effect of colonial economic change was also to remove a steadily larger percentage of the real wealth of the village outside its jurisdiction. The disappearance of village lands was a particularly vital blow to the community's protective fabric. As Dumarest notes for Vietnam, "The commune, no longer owning communal land, no longer assures, as it had traditionally, assistance to inhabitants who find themselves in need."[11] In addition, with the rise of absentee owners who worked through hired agents, with the increase in laborers and tenants who worked in the village but resided elsewhere, and with debt structures that linked villagers more often to outsiders than to insiders, the leveling mechanisms of peasant villages reshuffled fewer resources.

Second, the objects of envy and pressure within the village, though hardly impervious, became less vulnerable to the demands of the local poor. The moderately well-to-do who did not actually leave the village were no longer so dependent on local validation and support for their position. Now the courts and the constabulary could, if need be, enforce their title to land and their claim to contractual debt. This new outside backing allowed them to incur local disapproval at less risk. The ethic remained but its capacity to protect was sharply reduced. The end result within the village was often a lower class communitarianism that could no longer guarantee a minimal subsistence to the poorest. Finally, even under the best of circumstances, it is doubtful if village redistributive pressures could have survived the new impact of fluctuating market prices and the long run growth of population.

## Loss of Secondary Subsistence Resources

Embedded within the traditional economy were a host of what might be called "fall-back" or subsidiary activities which in a time of dearth would provide a welcome margin. Trades such as basketry, pottery, and

10. In an interesting partial exception to this, Gourou mentions a traditional arrangement whereby sister villages, often in different regions, were pledged to assist one another. There is no indication whether this system was widespread or effective. Yves Henry mentions, at the other extreme, a village in Tonkin that in fact had *no* land of its own and whose inhabitants were all sharecroppers on land owned by a neighboring village. Gourou, *Peasants of the Tonkin Delta,* vol. 1, p. 306, and Henry, *Economie agricole de l'Indochine,* p. 113.

The atrophy of the kindred as it loses its protective power is supported by the common observation that the ideal of an extended family tends to be approximated only by relatively well-to-do families whose property increases their staying power as an institution. Steven Piker, in an excellent study in Central Plain Thailand, shows that membership in an effective kindred is strongly associated with landholding and nonmembership with landlessness. "The Post-Peasant Village in Central Plain Thai Society," unpublished ms, p. 7.

11. André Dumarest, *La Formation de classes sociales en pays annimites* (Lyon: P. Ferreal, 1935), p. 206.

weaving for local markets, which might occupy a family in the slack agricultural season, could be intensified, if yields were poor, to make good the shortfall. Subsidiary agriculture on land unsuitable for paddy-fields, gardening, the raising of chickens and ducks, fishing, and forest gathering were all sources of subsistence insurance that might carry a peasant family through a shortage of rice.

The existence of these options in a traditional peasant society gives it a certain elasticity—a capacity to absorb, for a short time at least, crop failures and the claims of outsiders. A critical fact about these options is that they are, even in normal times, an established part of local activity and their intensification does not greatly disturb the web of village life. Families remain on their holding and within the community. It is perhaps these traditionally available refuges which gave peasant society something of a retreatist character in periods of hardship and external pressure.

Economic change under colonialism steadily reduced the scope of these subsistence safety-valves. As these options narrowed, the peasant family economy became far more brittle; now, if the rice failed or the claims of rent and taxes threatened its subsistence, the alternatives to resistance or to leaving the village altogether were few. The disaster level became ever more sharply defined, thereby increasing the explosive potential of peasant politics.

Schematically we can identify the main features of this contraction of subsistence options, although the ecology of each region and village made its experience unique. There was in much of the area an enormous disruption of local craft and trade markets which had provided part-time employment for villagers. Local markets for cloth, household wares, and agricultural implements tended to recede before larger scale specialization or imports from the metropole.[12] Chesneaux describes, in this context, the many viable regional economies in Vietnam which collapsed as economic activity centered around the major port city or cities of the colony.[13] An analogous process must have occurred elsewhere. To be sure, the colonial economy created more jobs than it destroyed, but these new jobs tended to lie increasingly outside the village economy, in the provincial markets and major port cities which gained population at phenomenal rates.[14]

12. For a brief but illuminating discussion of the importance of this phenomenon in China, see Hsiao-tung Fei, *China's Gentry: Essays on Rural Urban Relations* (Chicago: Phoenix Books, 1953), pp. 116–18.

13. Jean Chesneaux, "L'Établissment géographique des interêts coloniales au Viet-Nam et leur rapports avec l'économie traditionelle," chap. 3 in Chesneaux, ed., *Tradition et revolution au Viet-Nam* (Paris: Éditions Anthropos, n.d.).

14. See, for example, G. T. McGee, *The Southeast Asian City: A Social Geography of the Primate Cities of Southeast Asia* (New York: Praeger, 1967).

More important in terms of the village economy was the gradual loss of local forests, village-held wasteland, and common pasturage. These resources had provided for an important share of peasant needs; they were essentially free gifts of nature and a bedrock of what independence the peasant family enjoyed. The Burmese peasants' experience was typical:

> In the old days of farming for subsistence, the cultivators would get free grass for thatching, free bamboos and free firewood from the public wastelands. They could get their fish in the neighboring pools or streams, and they could weave their own clothes in their own homes. As the public wastelands became converted to cultivation, as fisheries were declared the property of Government and as home weaving became unprofitable, the small proprietors like the tenants, were increasingly obliged to find money for needs which they could formerly supply themselves.[15]

The reasons for these changes were, as the report implies, both demographic change and conscious colonial policy. Demographically, the pressure of population on land meant the cultivation of hitherto marginal soil. The land around a man's paddy fields which might have served him for pasturage and fuel was gradually filled in. Similarly, the *cordon sanitaire* of public lands around each village narrowed or disappeared.[16] This process was far advanced in densely populated Tonkin even before colonialism and it could be observed in the pioneer areas of the Mekong and the Irrawaddy Deltas when the opening of new lands could no longer keep pace with population growth.[17]

The new hardships were not entirely, however, a matter of demography. Colonial legal forms allowed local officials and notables to lay successful claim to communal or public lands which had once been available to the poor. Fishing rights along streams that had once been the domain of all were auctioned to private bidders to raise revenue.[18] Colonial foresters and conservationists often attempted to restrict access to forest products in areas where they were still available to the peasantry.

Of all these changes, the restriction of forest use was one of the most

15. *Report of the Land and Agriculture Committee* (Rangoon: Superintendent of Government Printing, 1938), 2:51.

16. For a graphic representation of this difference in settlement patterns, see Gourou, *L'Utilisation du sol en Indochine,* p. 302.

17. The timing of this closing of the frontier varied greatly from district to district but it is fair to say that, with the exception of the trans-Bassac of southwestern Vietnam, the main rice districts of Lower Burma, Central Luzon, Java, and the Mekong Delta were fully occupied no later than the 1920s. See, for example, *The Couper Report,* pp. 28–29.

18. Ibid., pp. 55–56.

galling to peasants; resources that had always been as free as the air they breathed and that remained close at hand were suddenly being denied them. Forestry officials might be well-intentioned—though they seemed to be as much concerned with forest revenue as with conservation—but their actions deprived peasants of what seemed natural rights.[19] European peasants had reacted similarly to the game and fishing laws imposed on them: "The feeling that wild places and water, untouched by human hand, could not be appropriated by any individual (or the state) was deep rooted in man's primitive social conscience."[20] Such restrictions constituted, as we shall see, a leading grievance in more than one Southeast Asian peasant movement.

The narrowing of subsistence options had at least three major effects on the household economy. First, it forced the peasant family further out of production for its own use and further into the market. Bamboo and firewood could not be gathered but had to be purchased; more fish and meat had to be bought; buffalos, for whom there was not enough pasture, had now to be rented. For all such necessities cash was increasingly required and it could only be gotten by selling more rice or borrowing. As more of his production and consumption passed through the price system, the peasant might not be poorer but he was increasingly vulnerable to price fluctuations outside his control. Second, the loss of these free gifts of nature, together with the decline of labor intensive handicrafts, eliminated many of the possibilities for village poor to remain independent. A life on the margin was more difficult. Increasingly, the only route to survival *within* the village led to a permanent dependence on those who hired labor. For many peasants it represented a decisive break with the past as the means of their subsistence now passed entirely out of their hands.

A third consequence of the loss of "fall-back" resources was sharpened conflict in other areas. A tenant who, after he had paid the landlord's rent, found he could only scrape by if he hauled firewood or sowed a small plot on local wasteland, now found he could not so easily scrape by. The smallholder who had paid his head tax from the sale of handicrafts was also in trouble. Rents and taxes that had previously been tolerable only because this margin of subsidiary options remained open became more intolerable once they were closed. Before, if the state and landlords did not scale their demands to his circumstances or help him over a rough patch, well, he at least had what he could wring from the

19. Their reaction is probably not unlike that of the hill peoples of Thailand, the Philippines, and Burma who find their traditional slash-and-burn patterns being regulated by lowland governments.

20. Bloch, *French Rural History,* p. 182. Fragment in parentheses added.

public domain around him. Now, if the state and landlord did not show some flexibility, his line of retreat within the village economy was more restricted. Emigration, resistance, or dependence on wage labor were often the only options left.

## DETERIORATION OF AGRARIAN CLASS RELATIONS

The very statuses of landlord, tenant, and wage laborer are artifacts of the colonial integration of Southeast Asia into a capitalist legal order and a capitalist world market. Given this new class structure, the most striking fact about the relationship of landowners to their tenants or laborers was that it lost much of its protective, paternalistic content and became more impersonal and contractual. What had often been a diffuse and flexible relationship that provided subsistence insurance in poor years grew more explicit and rigid and was blind to good and bad years. Instead of beginning with the minimal needs of the tenant, it began, and often ended, with the fixed claim of the landholder.

This transformation was essentially a question of power. The tenant, as we have seen, would normally prefer the landlord to assume the risks of agriculture and to shield him against disaster; the landlord, in turn, would like to have tenants who hand over the rent come what may. Who stabilizes his income at whose expense, then, is a question of who can impose his will upon the other.[21] That the landlord could ordinarily shift the risk to the tenant's shoulders was an index of his growing relative strength. With the enormous growth in population in lowland areas (close to threefold from 1870 to 1940) and the occupation of most arable land, those who held land were much stronger than those who had only their labor.

The capacity of landowners to realize the full exploitative potential of their bargaining power, however, depended as much on political power as on owning the scarce factor of production. Their ability to break traditional terms of tenancy, to seize the land of defaulting debtors, to stop peasant mobilization, depended ultimately on the ability of the colonial state's militia and courts to enforce contracts that violated the moral economy of the peasantry.

In Table 4 are summarized the main structural changes we have discussed, together with their impact on the relationship between landowners and the landless.

21. There are, however, special circumstances when it is in the interest of the tenant to move to a system of shared risks and when the landowner would prefer giving the tenant a fixed reward. If technical advances in production make large increases in yields possible, if those yields involve little risk, or if the costs of the new technology are small, the tenant may have a greater interest in a share of the new yields than in a minimal but stable

Table 4.   The Commercialization of Agriculture and
Agrarian Class Relationships

| *Nature of change* | *Effect on class relationships* |
| --- | --- |
| 1. Growing inequality in landholding | Control of land becomes key basis of power; landholders' position strengthened in dealing with tenants seeking access to narrowly held land |
| 2. Population growth | Bargaining position of landowner vis-à-vis tenants and laborers strengthened |
| 3. Fluctuations of producer and consumer prices and market valuation | Landholders' position strengthened as tenants increasingly need credit for production and consumption |
| 4. Loss of "slack resources" (uncleared land, common pasture, free fuel, etc.) | Loss of alternatives weakens tenants' bargaining position vis-à-vis landowner |
| 5. Deterioration of village redistributive mechanisms | Loss of alternatives weakens tenants' bargaining position vis-à-vis landowner |
| 6. Colonial state protecting property rights of landowners | Landowner less in need of loyal local clientele, hence free to press his economic advantage |

There were two related changes in landowner-tenant relations, traced in some detail below. The first is what might be called the worsening of the "balance of exchange" between owners and tenants. That is, if we examine over time the goods and services the owner provides the tenant and the goods and services that the tenant provides the owner, we detect an unmistakable shift in the terms of trade against the tenant. Typically the landholder provided fewer services while exacting the same or more from the tenant or laborer. In this sense, the relationship becomes *objectively* more exploitative.[22]

return. By contrast, the owner may want to fix his labor costs so as to maximize his control of the new surplus. In such specific and relatively rare circumstances, the normal pattern of preferences is reversed. The explanation for this reversal is to be found in the lifting of the major restraints of risk that form the basis of the subsistence ethic.

22. For a much more elaborate discussion of the "balance of exchange" and exploitation as an objective phenomenon, see James Scott and Benedict Kerkvliet, "How Traditional Rural Patrons Lose Legitimacy," *Cultures et Développment* 5:3 (1973), 501–40; Barrington Moore, Jr., *Social Origins of Dictatorship and Democracy*, pp. 453–83; and Sydel F. Silverman, .

The critical change in terms of peasant perceptions, however, was not so much that the landlord might take more of the crop (which he generally did), but rather that the relationship as a whole lost whatever protective value it once had. As a relationship it moved from the realm of dependency within the context of a certain amount of security (that is, patron-client ties) to a more straightforward and more painful cash-nexus contract with little or no social insurance for the weaker party. The peasant reaction to this transformation in Southeast Asia bears many of the marks of the European peasants' reaction to the shift from feudal to capitalist labor relations in the West.

There were substantial variations on this theme within Southeast Asia. On the capitalist frontiers of Lower Burma and western Cochinchina, landlord paternalism was weak from the outset and it took little "deterioration" to make it entirely contractual. In the thickly settled traditional areas of Tonkin, East and Central Java, and Upper Burma the resistance of local social patterns to the full logic of the market preserved important remnants of feudal ties throughout the colonial period. Variation by size of landholding, by locality, by crop and planting techniques is also apparent. Nonetheless, the situation got generally worse for tenants and laborers. In one area landlords might refuse customary pre-harvest loans, in another they might insist on the full rent in a bad year, in another they were no longer lenient if the tenant fell ill, in another old tenants were replaced by more solvent competitors who required less assistance, in another sharecropping gave way to fixed rent. The signs varied enormously to suit the peculiarities of each region, but they all pointed in the same direction.

The growth of capitalist labor relations is nowhere more evident than in the two cases described below: Lower Burma and Cochinchina. Both are examples par excellence of the capitalist rice frontier in Southeast Asia. The classical centers of population for the Burmese and Vietnamese people had been in Upper Burma and the Red River Delta, respectively, although well before colonialism migrants had begun pushing south, displacing and/or assimilating other peoples (Mons and Karens in Burma, Khmers and Chams in the case of the Vietnamese). Under the impetus of colonial and local capital deployed in drainage and embankment construction, and the growing export market in rice, however, the movement of population to the south assumed massive proportions in the late nineteenth century. From the beginning, both areas were characterized by labor scarcity, widespread use of credit, land grabbing, and a cash economy. Socially, the frontier in each area pro-

"Exploitation in Rural Central Italy," *Comparative Studies in Society and History* 12 (1970), 327–39.

duced a fluid social structure with high rates of mobility, scattered rather than nucleated settlement patterns, low social cohesion, and not a little anarchy and disorder. These features of frontier capitalism were especially pronounced in the southern Delta in Lower Burma and in the trans-Bassac in Cochinchina (see maps, pp. 69, 77), and less so in areas somewhat to the north that had been settled earlier. Migrants moving onto the frontier at the outset could often acquire land and become smallholders but the regions as a whole came to be dominated by largeholdings and estates worked by masses of tenants and day laborers. As both areas represent rather extreme versions of the social and economic changes that affected much of lowland Southeast Asia, they offer striking examples of rapid growth combined with a painful shift in the balance of exchange in agrarian class relations.

*Lower Burma*

In Lower Burma the shift was unmistakable. It is fully in evidence in Couper's detailed 1924 "Report into the Condition of Agricultural Tenants and Laborers."[23] Here were all the constituent elements of a situation that was to grow far worse in the 1930s, and they had arisen in a period (1911–14 to 1920–23) of ostensible prosperity when the price of rice had climbed by one-third. The uniformly pessimistic tone of the report speaks for itself:

> [One] finds that the proportion of the area occupied for cultivation which is held by non-agriculturalists, and that the proportion of such area let at full rents, are both increasing, that the proportion of the area occupied for cultivation which is let at full rents (i.e., not privileged rentals to kinsmen, etc.) is no less than 38 percent and in some tracts amounts to 50, 60, and even 70 percent; that there has been a rise in the produce-rent paid by the tenant. . . . that the price of paddy has not risen in proportion to the cost of production, that the condition of the labourer has deteriorated . . . that, in short, a condition of things exists which urgently calls for remedial action.[24]

This more acute phase of agrarian conflict tended to coincide with the

23. Except where otherwise noted the factual material in these next paragraphs is drawn from Couper's excellent report.

24. *The Couper Report,* p. 2. The loss of land by smallholders proceeded apace in this period. "The amount of occupied area in Lower Burma controlled by non-agriculturalists rose from 18 percent in 1906–07 to 31 percent in 1929–30." Almost all of this newly alienated land was controlled by absentee landowners. Michael Adas, *The Burma Delta: Economic Development and Social Change on an Asian Rice Frontier* (Madison: University of Wisconsin Press, 1974), p. 142.

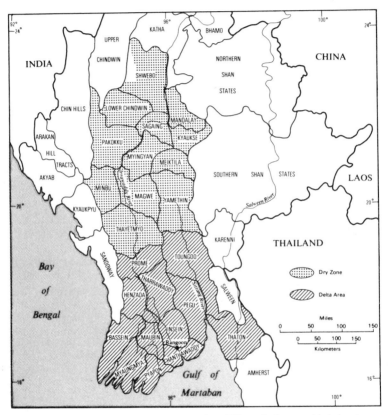

University of Wisconsin Cartographic Laboratory

Map 1  Political Divisions of the Province of Burma in the Twentieth Century.
Source: Michael Adas, *The Burma Delta* (Madison, Wis.: University of Wisconsin
Press, 1974). Used by permission.

closing of the frontier in district after district in the Delta. "The growing scarcity of land which can be worked at a profit and the growing population have placed the landlord in a stronger position than he occupied before the war."[25] The strength of the landlord found expression both in the rents and services he could exact and in the remorselessness with which he could exact them.

Fixed produce rents were nearly universal throughout the Delta. They were based on what the land would yield in a good year, although the general deterioration of yields from 1910 until 1940 made rents a growing proportion of the harvest for most tenants. While the landlord's return in rice was fixed, the amount left on the threshing floor for the tenant fluctuated dramatically. In Hanthawaddy, for example, produce rents in the late 1920s were set at what landlords decreed to be one-third of a good harvest. Even in a good year, however, the settlement officer estimated that rents took two-fifths of the harvest. In a bad year, of course, the rent could amount to two-thirds of the harvest.[26] Thus, the rent for a 25-acre holding would normally come to 350 baskets of rice out of an estimated yield of 1,000 baskets. The plot, however, would rarely yield more than 900 baskets.

Quite apart from the hardship that fixed produce rents worked on tenants in poor seasons, the level of rents, as the Couper Report notes, tended to edge up as landlords took full competitive advantage of the growing class of landless and the closing of the frontier. In the late nineteenth century, rents had been as low as 10 to 15 percent of the yield but as conditions permitted they rose to as much as 50 to 60 percent of the crop for larger fertile tenancies.[27] The official who examined tenancy in Bassein District, for example, found that between 1914 and 1935 average produce rents had risen in 20 of the district's 27 tracts and that "in many cases the rise has been considerable."[28] Increases in the Irrawaddy and Pegu divisions had been even more pronounced. Throughout the 1920s, at least, the cash value of the rents landlords took in was increasing merely by virtue of a buoyant market for paddy. The raising of produce rents thus represented a kind of surplus profit made possible by demographic pressure. Even in districts such as

25. *The Couper Report*, p. 8. See also Adas's excellent *The Burma Delta*, esp. chaps. 6 and 7. The closing of the frontier may be traced by its major symptom, the rise in land values.

26. *Third Revision Settlement of the Hanthawaddy District of Lower Burma, Seasons 1930–1933*, Settlement Officer U Tin Gyi, "Conference Minutes" (Rangoon: Government of Burma, 1934), pp. 3, 35, 36.

27. *Report on the Revision Settlement of Bassein District, Seasons 1935–1939*, Settlement Officer Maung Maung Gyi, p. 3.

28. *Report on the Revision Settlement of Maubin District, Seasons 1925–1928*, Settlement Officer U Tin Gyi, pp. 4–5.

Maubin, where population did not press so heavily on land as in the Upper Delta, tenants were worse off in 1925 than they had been in 1915.

Neither for tenants nor for smallholders did the increase in the price of rice make up the deficit produced by declining yields and higher rents. While the selling price of rice rose from 132 to 176 rupees in the decade from 1914 to 1924, the cost of implements and consumer necessities rose anywhere from 50 to 150 percent during the same period (for example, bullocks 57%, plows 100%, harrows 100%, salt 150%, chillies 80%, sessamum cooking oil 60%, shirts 83%, and *longyis*—the Burmese male's skirt—120%).[29] The disparity was inevitably reflected in the cultivator's standard of living.

In quite a few areas of longer settlement, local tradition resisted any increase in the traditional rents. Even here the landlord could maneuver the situation to his advantage. The most transparent and despised method of circumventing local traditions was to devise a "landlord's basket" that held more. The ingenuity of landowners and their agents in the design of such baskets was seemingly inexhaustible. Some baskets were constructed so as to balloon out as they received rice, others were shaped to prevent leveling and ensure a heaping basket, certain methods of pouring increased the basket's capacity, and if it were shaken vigorously several times as it was filled, it would hold more. Tenants tried to retaliate by putting chaff in the basket but, as the basket grew, they had either to pay the larger rent or lose the tenancy. The capacity of absentee landlords to adapt a special "rent-basket" that was always larger than the "village basket" came to be a galling symbol of their power to impose their will.

> The exact capacity of a landlord's basket is known to the landlord alone and the tenants may be prone to exaggeration. But the light in which the villagers regard these baskets may be seen from the names which they give to them; for example the basket of a Letpadan landlord is known as "the cart-breaker," this basket is said to equal 150 milk tins as compared with the village basket of 136.
>
> Tenants resent bitterly this right of enlarging the basket which the landlords have arrogated to themselves and many ascribe [to it] their present distress.[30]

The distress of the tenant in Lower Burma was less a matter of his average income (which was, in any case, considerably greater than that of his counterpart in Upper Burma) than of his insecurity. What hurt

---

29. *The Couper Report*, p. 7.
30. Ibid., pp. 16, 17.

him most, it seems clear, were the fluctuations in his income and the instability of his tenure—and the absence of any of the social restraints that provided at least some insurance to cultivators in Upper Burma.[31] Tenancy in Lower Burma had become, by contrast, far more rigid. The lease in Lower Burma was a standard formal document, a strict contract, while leases in Upper Burma were oral and circumscribed by tradition. Most tenants in Upper Burma were 50–50 sharecroppers living in the same village with the landlord and often related to him; most tenants in Lower Burma paid fixed rents to absentee landlords whom they might never have met.

The major insecurity for the Irrawaddy Delta cultivator was in his access to the land. A large proportion of Lower Burma's population was already in the pure wage labor category and was entirely at the mercy of the labor market and the price of necessities.[32] Those who were fortunate enough to be tenants could seldom count on keeping the same plot for long. Couper's sample findings in the early 1920s showed just how unstable tenancies had become; in Gyobingauk, Tharawaddy district, only 4 of 106 tenants had occupied their land for 12 years or more; in Letpadan, Tharawaddy, only 8 of 130 had such tenure; in Thongwa, Hanthawaddy, 7 of 99; and in Taikkyi, Insein, only a single tenant had been on the same land for 12 years.

At the turn of the century, this instability of tenancies was often a healthy sign that the tenant had managed to buy a plot and become a smallholder. By the 1920s, however, it was almost always a sign that the tenant had failed and had moved on to find another tenancy or, more likely, to join the ranks of agrarian labor. For tenants in the more heavily populated districts such as Tharrawaddy, upward mobility had become unlikely before 1920. "The transition from the status of a labourer to that of a landowner which was a comparatively simple matter some years ago is now almost impossible."[33]

One does not have to look far to discover why tenancies were unstable and why, therefore, tenants were likely to fall eventually into the class of wage laborers. The rents were simply so high that they could be paid only in good years without going more deeply into debt. The lucky four

31. Where fixed produce or money rents had been introduced, notably where cash crops such as groundnuts were grown, it was still the custom to lower rents in the event of a poor season. See *First Revision Settlement of the Pakokku District, Upper Burma, Seasons 1927–1931*, Settlement Officer R. Pearce (Rangoon: Government of Burma, 1932), especially pp. 3, 43.

32. Adas, *The Burma Delta*, pp. 151–53. Landless laborers came to be the "dominant element" in many Lower Burma villages.

33. *Third Settlement of Tharawaddy District, Seasons 1913–15*, Settlement Officer J. L. McCallum (Rangoon: Government of Burma, 1916), p. 24.

tenants in Gyobingauk who had held on for 12 years had comparatively smaller rents "but unless they had been granted reductions in bad years they could not have paid even this."[34]

For the vast majority of tenants the loss of access to land was linked directly to the fact that landlords now seldom gave remissions of rent in bad years.

> A rent which as originally fixed is fair, may become unfair when the outturn, through causes over which the tenant has no control, falls far below what the tenant and the landlord had in mind when the lease was made. *In such circumstances it has hitherto been the custom for the landlord to reduce the rent. But this custom is wearing thin*, now that money-lenders and other nonagriculturalists own so much land.[35]

Given the uneven demography of Lower Burma, the elimination of remissions was a complicated process. In relatively crowded districts such as Hanthawaddy where absentee landownership grew apace, remissions apparently had ceased as early as 1910.[36] Elsewhere, however, the agrarian system retained an important measure of flexibility until the 1920s. Even in Tharrawaddy, famous for its high rents, the settlement officer noted that in 1910 fixed rents were modified following harvest losses. "If the outturn falls below this amount [the amount on which the fixed rent was calculated], the rent actually paid is often less than the amount nominally agreed upon."[37] He went on to observe that "The Burman makes a good and lenient landlord and the second settlement year offered an example of his readiness to reduce rents in a poor season."[38] Even in this early period there were exceptions to the practice of liberal remissions, and when the landlord refused to grant them the tenant's reaction was predictable:

> This landlord [Martaban Hills, Moulmein District] is said to give no remission of rent in a bad season, and it may be that he pays back everything to which his tenants are strictly entitled when the arrears of rent from the past years are taken into consideration. I have only heard the tenants' statement of the case, but it is difficult to believe the detestation in which this landlord is held is altogether unjustified.[39]

34. *The Couper Report*, p. 31.

35. Ibid., p. 41, emphasis added.

36. *Report of the Third Settlement of the Hanthawaddy District, Seasons 1907–1910,* Settlement Officer R. E. V. Arbuthnot (Rangoon: Government of Burma, 1911), p. 20.

37. *Third Settlement of Tharawaddy District*, p. 4.

38. Ibid., p. 24.

39. *Moulmein Settlement Report, 1910,* Settlement Officer T. Couper, p. 19.

Beginning in the 1920s, however, remissions were increasingly the exception rather than the rule. As Adas notes, "in the decades of transition (1908–1930) many landlords would not allow them no matter how desperate their tenants' situation."[40] Despite poor crop yields in Bassein in the crop seasons 1936–37 and 1937–38, only a very few tenants secured rent reductions and those reductions were trivial compared with the extent of the crop failure.[41] What had been a system of fixed produce rents with a good deal of de facto flexibility became a pure fixed-rent system in earnest. As subsistence risks passed to the shoulders of cultivators, signs of discontent appeared. The settlement officer for Maubin District noted in 1928:

> In secure tracts the complaint is generally made that the full rent is almost invariably demanded by the landlord and no remission is granted on account of diminution of yield, and that even if an abatement of rent is granted, it bears no relation to the deficiency in outturn. But the landlord with so many tenants available to work his land at the stipulated rent does not see the need of a reduction. He looks upon the land merely as a source of income and makes no contribution to its cultivation.[42]

With the frontier closed and a growing reserve army of labor, it was now possible for the landlord to stabilize his income at the expense of the tenantry.

Typically, the landlord sought out solvent tenants who owned their own plow animals. This minimized the demands made on him for pre-harvest rice loans and allowed him to rent larger plots at premium rents. After a bad year, such a tenant would pay as much as he could possibly scrape together, even if it meant outside loans and the sale of a plow animal, for "a tenant fears above all that renewal will be refused to him."[43] When the tenant's resources were exhausted, he would be replaced with a more likely prospect. There was a ratcheting-down of the agrarian class structure generally. Just as bankrupt smallholders had fallen into the tenant class, so tenants who could no longer repay their debts and rents fell into the class of wage laborers. Cultivators who might have worked their way up this ladder in the 1890s were now working their way down.

The lack of remissions for tenants had its analogue in labor conditions for the landless. As early as 1910, Couper had observed that "with the increase in the population, the wages which a labourer can earn have

40. Adas, *The Burma Delta*, p. 149. See also the evidence referred to for this conclusion.
41. *Bassein Settlement Report, 1935–39*, p. 49.
42. *Maubin Settlement Report, 1925–1928*, p. 66.
43. *The Couper Report*, p. 31.

begun to fall."[44] Not only did the absolute money wage of plowmen decline by almost 20 percent from 1912 to 1922, but if we take into account the rise in the cost of rice as an index of consumer prices for this class, their real wage must have declined by as much as 35 percent.[45] Perhaps more important in terms of security, fewer laborers were now hired by the season rather than by the day or task and as a consequence "the same latitude is not now given in the event of illness as before; a man who falls sick is now more liable to be cut for every day he is absent."[46]

The bonds of protection and mutuality that still, to a large extent, characterized landlord-tenant relations in Upper Burma were completely broken in Lower Burma. Aside from the collection of a high and invariable rent and increasingly exacting loans, one would search in vain for any other links between landowner and cultivator in the Delta. All other services had been eliminated: the personal assistance and brokerage of the landholder, the contributions of landowners to village welfare, their technical assistance in cultivation, and above all the flexibility in the landlord's claim which had provided the tenant with some subsistence insurance. The elimination of these services meant a corresponding elimination of any claim the landholder might have had to legitimacy.

By the 1920s a growing hostility in landlord tenant relations was apparent. A relationship that had never been one of great personal loyalty was less often providing for the tenant's minimal needs. Tenants frequently violated the terms of their tenancy whenever they could. They harvested some of the crop early and sold it surreptitiously to small traders, claiming to the landlord that the grain was used to pay harvesters and threshers. Those tenants who received advances often fled with the advance and as much grain as they could carry off if a bad crop was in sight. The most characteristic resort of the peasant, however, seems to have been to withhold the rent on the basis of his right to subsistence in a poor year.

> In the years 1922 and 1923 landlords in the thirteen districts of this report instituted 918 and 797 suits against tenants for rent; and if I may draw an inference from such records as I looked through in the Insein and Bassein record-rooms, a large proportion of these suits had to be filed *because the tenant, considering that he was not receiving fair treatment in years of crop failure, refused to pay the rent in full.*[47]

44. *Moulmein Settlement Report, 1910*, p. 11.
45. Adas, *The Burma Delta*, p. 152.
46. *The Couper Report*, p. 49.
47. Ibid., p. 41.

Hauled into court, the tenant was virtually always made responsible for the full amount stipulated in his tenancy contract. The form of his resistance was nonetheless an accurate expression of his moral economy; he evidently felt that the landlord's claim could not justifiably extend to his subsistence resources. In a good year, both the tenant's claim to subsistence and the landlord's claim to the surplus can be satisfied; in a bad year, the landlord can collect his rent only by violating what the tenant sees as his prior moral claim to the harvest.

The increasing resort to force by landlords in the Delta reflected the growing resistance to their claims. Each violation of local norms implied a greater reliance on coercion. Couper, for example, writes of a landlord who had violated the norm of employing villagers before outsiders and who, because he "imports tenants from a distance . . . is afraid to visit his fields toward nightfall in case he gets his head broken."[48] Gradually, even the courts were inadequate to enforce the rental claims of land-lords. They had to have more watchmen as the harvest neared and more toughs to protect them against the tenants they had dismissed. As rural security became more problematic, more landlords moved to the pro-vincial towns where they could find safety as well as credit. "The fear of dacoities and robberies has also driven many of those who possess a little money to the large towns and villages. Many of them would no doubt like to live in their native places but the insecurity of life and property in recent years has forced them to seek the protection of more thickly populated areas."[49] The growth of private landlord armies was paral-leled by the growth of tumultuous tenant organizations seeking rent remissions and security of tenure. This growing structural antagonism would deepen and take a more communal form as a result of the Great Depression and culminate in the Saya San rebellion which swept Lower Burma from 1930 to 1932. But its constituent elements were in place a decade earlier.

## Cochinchina, Vietnam

The course of landlord-tenant relations in the Mekong Delta of Cochinchina follows the pattern of Lower Burma. Here too was a fron-tier area where market forces did not have to contend with an estab-lished precapitalist social order. Here too, as population grew and the frontier was exhausted, the terms of tenancy stiffened.[50] Landlords used

48. Ibid., p. 33. A landlord may prefer to hire outsiders who have little moral claim on him as opposed to fellow villagers who will expect him to observe local norms and will be indignant if he refuses.

49. *Maubin Settlement Report, 1925–1928*, p. 64. See also the statistics on "the growing" crime rate from 1905 to 1922 in *The Couper Report,* p. 10.

50. "Grand propriétaires et fermiers dans l'ouest de la Cochinchine pendant le periode coloniale," *Revue historique* 249:499 (1971), 71.

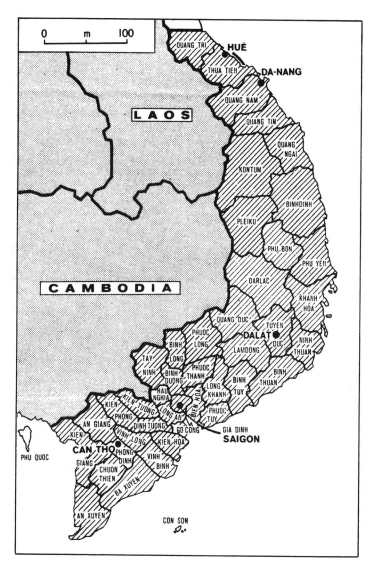

QUANG TRI
HUÉ
THUA TIEN
DA-NANG
QUANG NAM
QUANG TIN
LAOS
QUANG NGAI
KONTUM
BINHDINH
PLEIKU
PHU BON
PHU YEN
DARLAC
KHANH HOA
CAMBODIA
QUANG DUC
TUYEN
DALAT
PHUOC LONG
NINH THUAN
BINH LONG
LAMDONG
DUC
TAY NINH
PHUOC THANH
BINH DUONG
BINH TUY
BINH THUAN
HAU NGHIA
LONG KHANH
KIEN TUONG
BIEN HOA
LONG AN
KIEN PHONG
PHUOC TUY
DINH TUONG
GO CONG
GIA DINH
AN GIANG
KIEN
VINH LONG
KIEN HOA
SAIGON
PHU QUOC
CAN THO
PHONG DINH
GIANG
VINH BINH
CHUON THIEN
BA XUYEN
AN XUYEN
CON SON

0    m    100

Map 2   South Vietnam.

their growing bargaining power to increase rents, eliminate previous services and, above all, guarantee themselves a steady take by shifting risks to the tenant.

Here too the problem was not so much poverty per se as economic insecurity and the absence of a protective social fabric. Just as the Lower Burma cultivator ate better, on the average, and worked less intensively on the average than his counterpart in Upper Burma, so did the Cochinchinese tenant eat better and work less intensively than his counterpart in the more densely populated traditional areas of Annam and Tonkin to the north. The difference was thus not one of the tenant's average income; it was rather a difference in the extent to which the agrarian system made him shoulder the risks of weather and the marketplace. In this sense, the higher income of the Vietnamese tenant in the south did not prevent the growth of explosive rural class relations.

Even before the arrival of the French, Cochinchina had been the domain of the large landowner and the landless peasant. An 1840 report from the Financial Commissioner of Vinh Long Province in the Mekong Delta to Emperor Minh Mang noted that a few families held most of the land and 70 to 80 percent of the population had none.[51] These frontier tendencies were given further impetus by the French policy which included liberal land concessions to French citizens and Vietnamese collaborators and cast a blind eye toward an enormous amount of land grabbing and corruption in the issuance of titles. Together with the steady loss of land through smallholder indebtedness, this policy created a situation of extreme inequality by the 1930s, as shown in Table 5.

Table 5.   Inequality in Landownership in Cochinchina, 1930[52]

|  | Percent of all households | Percent of landowners | Percent of cultivated land |
|---|---|---|---|
| Landless | 67 | | |
| 0–5 hectares | 24 | 72 | 12.5 |
| 5–10 hectares | 5 | 15 | 42.5 |
| 10–50 hectares | 4 | 11 | |
| Over 50 hectares | 0.8 | 2.5 | 45.0 |

From province to province the figures varied greatly; in the more recently settled areas such as Bac Lieu at the tip of Cochinchina ownership was even more skewed, while in older areas such as My Tho in central Cochinchina there were proportionally more smallholders. Despite the

51. Alexander Woodside, *Community and Revolution in Modern Vietnam*, (New York: Houghton Mifflin, 1976), p. 76.

52. Gourou, *L'Utilisation du sol*, pp. 272–74.

variation, nothing could mask the fact that the social fabric of Cochinchina was polarized by a mass of landless facing a powerful group of largeholders some 8,000 strong. There were not more than 500 such magnates in Tonkin, and in Annam there were fewer than 100.[53]

Paternalism was never the hallmark of Delta landlords but, when labor was still scarce and the frontier still open, elements of paternalism were not precluded. Descriptions of class relationships in this period refer to the "quasi-feudal authority" exercised by the large landowners who then often resided on their holdings and of the "protection" which they extended to their dependents.[54] "They group on their estates numerous families of tenants who cultivate the land in lots from 5–20 hectares. These tenants as well as any small owners for whom they are moneylenders, constitute a veritable clientele of theirs."[55] We find older landlords recalling nostalgically the days when, in return for deference, tenants were assisted at births and funerals, and given loans when they were in need.[56] It would hardly do to exaggerate the liberality of landlords, who from the beginning were speculators. But it is probably accurate to conclude, as Brocheux does, that "The doctor-landlord who gives assistance and distributes medicines free, the *dien chu* who lowers rents on account of a bad harvest, one who adopts the children of tenants, *were not rare.*"[57] Of course, to say that humane landlords "were not rare" is to imply that they were not typical either.

One key test of an agrarian system for the tenant, as we have seen, is what happens when the harvest fails. While the tenancy contract itself did not entitle the *ta-dien* (tenant) to any reduction in rent in such circumstances, there is some evidence that until at least the 1920s the landlord found it in his interest to meet the minimum needs of his cultivators. "It is common practice (*courant et effectif*) for the landlord to take from his tenants whatever is left over above that which is necessary for their family subsistence."[58] The exploitativeness of a system that transfers the entire surplus above subsistence to the landowner is perfectly evident. Nonetheless, the tenants' basic needs did at least consti-

53. Paul Bernard, *Le Probleme économique indochinois* (Paris: Nouvelles Editions latines, 1934), chap. 1. Bernard's figures come, as do many of Gourou's, from Yves Henry, *Economie agricole de l'Indochine.*

54. Gourou, *L'Utilisation du sol,* p. 284.

55. Henry, *Economie agricole,* p. 57. See also Brocheux, "Grands proprietaires," p. 66, who notes: "The large owners grouped around them more or less numerous clienteles which reinforced their already extended patron-client networks."

56. Sansom, *The Economics of Insurgency,* p. 29.

57. Pierre Brocheux, "Les Grands *dien chu* de la Cochinchine occidentale pendant la periode coloniale," in Jean Chesneaux, ed., *Tradition et revolution au Vietnam,* p. 151.

58. Brocheux, "Grands proprietaires," p. 64.

tute the first claim on the harvest. This practice owed most, in all probability, to the scarcity of labor on the frontier, although it is not inconceivable that Confucian traditions of obligation may have also played a contributory role.

In the second two decades of this century a tightening of the smallholders', tenants', and laborers' situation was evident. The smallholders' need for cash for production costs, taxes, and consumption led to indebtedness and often to the loss of land. Local largeholders became the creditors of a smallholding clientele who mortgaged their land by what was called *vente à réméré* (conditional sale). When the smallholder failed to make the required payments, his land passed into the hands of his creditor and he became a tenant. As Yves Henry observed, "this concentration [of landownership] is particularly intense following each bad harvest."[59]

Tenants, a majority of the Delta population by 1920, saw rents edge up from the equivalent of 40 percent to as much as 60 or 70 percent of the harvest depending upon the size and fertility of the plot and upon the degree of competition among would-be tenants for the land.[60] The surplus value appropriated by the owner was as much a function of moneylending as of the stipulated rent. Since most tenants lacked working capital as well as a consumption fund, they were obliged to take loans in cash at the beginning of the season when rice prices were high and pay back an *equivalent amount in rice* at harvest time when the rice price was much lower. The result was an effective interest rate approaching 200 percent.

As the balance of power changed, most tenancies became written contracts with a fixed rent in kind established on the basis of what the land would produce in a good year.[61] The notion of the "good year" was, of course, as in Burma, an increasingly utopian figure designed to maximize rents. Nearer Saigon a large rentier landowning class more often insisted on cash rents to avoid the expense of marketing rice and to insulate themselves from fluctuations in the paddy market.[62]

As the large moneylending landowners gravitated toward the provincial cities or Saigon and began acting through agents, the practice of "tolerance,"—the reduction of rents after a poor harvest—became increasingly rare. In fact, a great many landowners insisted on renting only to solvent tenants with working capital and plow animals in order to

59. Henry, *Economie agricole,* p. 192.
60. Sansom, *Economics of Insurgency,* pp. 30–33.
61. Henry, *Economie agricole,* p. 192.
62. Ibid., p. 193.

reduce the need for "tolerance" and avoid the anger which a refusal would provoke.[63]

Finally, the security of tenure itself declined as ruined tenants were dismissed in favor of those more capable of meeting the rent. Dismissed tenants, unless they moved to the city, had little chance of establishing themselves as smallholders by the 1920s, since the frontier land which could still be brought under the plow was fast disappearing. Instead, they either competed with others for the available tenancies or else fell into the agrarian wage labor class. A comparable loss of security hit the ranks of wage labor. More and more laborers were hired by the day or week rather than the season or year, and wages were more often in cash than in kind.

Some of the same economic forces that were eroding the peasant's bargaining position in Cochinchina were at work in Tonkin and Annam as well. Henry's study of Tonkin prior to 1930 noted that "Tenancy [fixed rent] is the form of tenure preferred by owners in regions vulnerable to big crop losses: drought, floods. . . . This mode of tenure was very rare before. It grows little by little, along with the increase of town dwellers, some of whom wish to own rural property."[64] The direction of change may have been the same but the traditional local social structures in Tonkin and Annam were far more resistant. Tonkin and Annam remained the strongholds of the smallholding peasant. Most of those without land were sharecroppers with security of tenure who cultivated land owned by village-based landowners rather than outsiders. Above all, the norms of sharecropping recognized the priority of the cultivator's subsistence claim, for "the owner leaves the entire harvest to the sharecropper in the event of a poor harvest."[65]

A certain consolidation of landholding and rural power did occur in Annam and Tonkin, but it neither went so far nor produced such economic insecurities as it had in Cochinchina. In Hungyen province (Tonkin), for example, a large number of peasants lost their plots to moneylenders in the wake of six consecutive crop failures in the 1920s. "These who thus acquired these large holdings," however, "keep, in general, the old owners as sharecroppers and sometimes even shelter them from crop risks as tenants."[66] Rural laborers, for their part, were both less numerous and somewhat better protected than their Cochinchina counterparts. Many more of them were hired on an annual basis and, "when the yearly worker [Tonkin] suffers an accident or illness due

63. Sansom, *Economics of Insurgency,* p. 32.

64. Henry, *Economie agricole,* p. 113.

65. Ibid., p. 35.

66. Ibid., p. 122. See also p. 46 on Annam.

to his work, the employer must provide for his food, his needs and the payment of wages."[67] The practical importance of these mechanisms of social insurance is evident from the relative lack of immigration from Tonkin and Annam to Cochinchina. Despite the much higher average income in the south, relatively few peasants in the 1920s elected to abandon their comparatively secure poverty for the risks of the southern frontier.[68] And of those who did go, a large portion were press-ganged by plantation agents with the help of local authorities.

The relation of most landowners to their tenants in Cochinchina was unambiguous; they were becoming mere rent-collectors and usurers who, far from protecting their tenants, exposed them to the full penalties of crop failures. The relation of landowners in Annam and Tonkin to their sharecroppers was, by contrast, ambiguous; it still involved elements of patronage as well as of exploitation. Henry's description of middle owners and large owners in Tonkin catches this duality.

> These middle owners are generally at the same time notables or holders of some public post, which they often abuse. They know how to put themselves in the good graces of the population by being generous on holidays or by giving gifts to the village or to religious groups.
>
> Many of them (large owners) are very clever and know, by a calculated and self-interested generosity, and by forceful repression (for its demonstration effect) against certain recalcitrant debtors, to make themselves known as just men.[69]

Tonkin landowners were not a public-spirited lot, but they operated in a context which restrained them. Local authority and popular norms were stronger; landlords themselves did not have the vast domains their counterparts ruled in the south, and the day-to-day presence of colonial power was less pervasive than in the south. Landlords were not above employing *lumpen* toughs (*nacno*) to whom they supplied opium and alcohol, but the evidence suggests that they also felt it advisable to maintain at least a modest degree of local respect.

If the texture of agrarian class relations was hardly cordial in Annam and Tonkin, the absence of any social guarantees in the terms of tenancy in Cochinchina made for incipient warfare. "The absconding of tenants and the disputes over the division of the harvests are the indications that

67. Ibid., p. 30.

68. Charles Robequain, *The Economic Development of French Indochina* (New York: Oxford University Press, 1944), chap. 3.

69. Henry, *Economie agricole,* p. 37.

[agrarian] contracts are imposed and endured [*subis*] rather than accepted."[70]

A particular fact, like that reported by *L'Opinion* [11/5/28] tells us more than psychological explanations about the motives of the fugitives: four tenants assault Mr. Duong Hoa Loi, landowner in Camau, they take from him 60 debt notes having a value of 20,000 piastres and 2,000 piasters in cash. The day before they carried off 1,600 gia [gia = 20 kg.] of paddy.[71]

As resistance was encountered among tenants, a parallel mobilization occurred among landlords. More overseers were hired to guard the ripening paddy and, as in Burma, false weights were increasingly used to enlarge the landlord's share of the harvest.[72] By 1922 it was remarked that landowners in Cochinchina were installing grilles in their windows as protection against thefts and banditry.[73] Investment in more straightforward measures of control grew too; the police budget went from 7.7 million francs in 1919 to over 20.7 million francs in 1929.[74] These are gross measures, to be sure, but they strongly suggest a qualitative shift in rural class relations.

Although it was especially in Cochinchina and Lower Burma where the failure of the tenancy system to protect the cultivator from the worst outcomes was most pronounced, elsewhere in lowland Southeast Asia the same tendencies could be detected.[75] How far they went, however, depended on the resistance of local social structures and the intrusiveness of the colonial regime in that area. In the traditional core regions of older kingdoms such as Upper Burma, Tonkin, Annam, and Java, capitalist patterns of land tenure distorted but did not entirely smash the older forms of social protection and patronage. The frontier, however, allowed full play to market forces and allowed landowners to take full

70. Brocheux, "Grands proprietaires," p. 67.

71. Ibid. The pattern of such incidents may be followed in detail in the newspapers of that period such as *La Lutte, Le Paysan de Cochinchine,* and *La Tribune Indochinoise.*

72. Ibid.

73. Guy Gran, "Vietnam and the Capitalist Route to Modernity" (Ph.D. dissertation, University of Wisconsin, 1975), p. 218.

74. Ibid., p. 226.

75. For other regions see, for example, Benedict J. Kerkvliet, "Peasant Unrest Prior to the Huk Revolution in the Philippines," *Asian Studies* 9 (August 1971); Anderson, "Some Aspects of Land and Society in a Pangasinan Community"; M. G. Swift, "Economic Concentration and Malay Peasant Society," in Maurice Freedman, ed., *Social Organization: Essays Presented to Raymond Firth* (London: Cass, 1967); Margo Lyon, *Bases of Conflict in Rural Java* (Berkeley: University of California Center for South and Southeast Asian Studies, Monograph No. 3, December 1970); and Piker, "The Post-Peasant Village in Central Plain Thai Society."

competitive advantage of the power that the competition for land and the colonial legal order placed in their hands.

## AGRARIAN CHANGE AND THE WORLD ECONOMY

The history of the shift from more flexible, diffuse landlord-tenant bonds to a more straightforward cash nexus is, at the same time, the history of the incorporation of Southeast Asia into the world capitalist economy. Where that incorporation was most thoroughgoing, as in Lower Burma and Cochinchina, the extirpation of what few customary ties still existed was also most thorough.

If the tenant felt cheated of the relative security that customary tenancy had once provided, we must recognize in turn that the landowner was enmeshed in a wider financial network that made its own demands upon him. The social insurance he might once have given tenants had become a vastly more expensive luxury. Prices for land had shot up fantastically between 1870 and 1925 and the same profit per hectare would now represent a much smaller return on invested capital.[76] If land could not be made to yield more, it could be sold at a profit and the proceeds invested elsewhere.[77] To make the land yield more was, in effect, to make the tenant yield more. As the price of grain increased, interest-free loans of seed paddy to tenants cost the landlord more in money terms—money that also might be deployed to better advantage elsewhere. It is, incidentally, for this reason that the high interest moneylending operations of landlords in Cochinchina and Lower Burma were the most profitable feature of landownership. "It is the tenant who is exploited, the paddy land is only exploited on the rebound (*que par le ricochet*)."[78] Once labor is abundant it makes no economic sense for the landowner to hire laborers for an entire season when he can hire them for the day or at piecework rates and assume no further responsibility for their welfare. In short, the opportunity costs of customary tenancy and employment arrangements increased greatly, and the landowner correspondingly moved to eliminate them or to charge what they now cost him in market terms. How far he could move in this direction depended not only on his bargaining strength with land-

76. The rise in the price of rice would, of course, work in a compensating way to raise the landlord's return. Rampant speculation in the 1920s, however, caused the increase in land values to stay far ahead of the market price for rice.

77. A lower return might be acceptable for land in view of its long-run security but it was not immune to the market logic of comparative rates of return.

78. Pierre Melin, *L'Endettement agraire et la liquidation des dettes agricole en Cochinchina* (Thèse, Université de Paris, Faculté de Droit, Librarie Sociale et Économique, 1939), p. 25. Melin is quoting a colonial official.

hungry peasants but also on the coercive capacity of the state to contain the anger that his violation of traditional norms would provoke.

The account thus far may have left the impression that the loss of subsistence security was, for the tenant and laborer, a seamless web of gradual change. The opposite would be more nearly correct. The change was transmitted in a series of rude shocks linked, for the most part, to the world market.

It is in the nature of the fail-safe arrangements that a peasant strives to create that their reliability and value are only fully tested in a crisis. Throughout much of the early twentieth century the Burman or Vietnamese cultivator must have known that his social insurance in patronage was increasingly tenuous, but exactly how tenuous he could not know until he needed to press a claim. As long as the frontier was open and labor scarce, the wealth of alternatives meant that the potential default of a landowner's patronage was less catastrophic in a bad year. Even when demographic change had put landowners in the driver's seat, the full social implications of the failure of patronage could be masked and contained by a buoyant economy. This was to a great extent the situation in the 1920s. Subsistence guarantees *were* eroding but the high price of rice, the resulting availability of agricultural employment, and an expanding nonagricultural sector of trade and industry helped compensate for the default of patronage. It was only with the Great Depression, when all these opportunities were stripped away, that the exploitative role of landowners was cast in stark relief.

There was what we might call a small-scale dress rehearsal in 1907. In that year a credit crisis originating in the United States swept under many small proprietors in Lower Burma and Cochinchina who had gone deeply into debt on the basis of the preceding land boom. As the Chettiars (a moneylending caste from southern India) foreclosed on their loans, many smallholders lost their land and became tenants. The dress rehearsal extended as well to forms of resistance. "It has been pointed out to me that the beginning of the market rise in dacoity and robbery [Lower Burma] is to be traced to the years 1905–10 when the collapse of the land boom parted many people from their lands."[79] Of the land lost in Lower Burma between 1900 and 1920, most was lost in this brief period. The massive peasant tax protests of 1908 in Vietnam may also have been triggered by the shortage of cash occasioned by the credit crisis.

The shock of 1907, traumatic as it was for some, was little preparation for the shock of 1930. Rice which had sold for 1.40 piastres per gia (20

79. *The Couper Report,* p. 10.

kg.) in 1929 fetched only .72 piastres in 1931 and .30 piastres in 1934. These paddy price movements triggered much larger losses of net income from landowning; the higher the cash costs of agriculture and the weight of debt, the greater the loss. In the older provinces of central Cochinchina, net income slipped from 34.30 piastres per hectare in 1929 to 4.60 piastres per hectare in 1934. In the credit-soaked boom area of the trans-Bassac, however, net income fell from 33.70 per hectare in 1929 all the way to 1.80 per hectare in 1934.[80]

The shock of the crises passed down the social structure with each victim passing on as much of the loss as possible to weaker parties. Largeholders with debts predicated on a continuation of the boom of the 1920s lost fortunes virtually overnight and suicides among this class were not uncommon.[81] The indebted smallholders of Cochinchina and Lower Burma were naturally among the great losers.[82] With the price of rice as low as it was they could not meet the demands of their creditors who, for their part, were operating on a margin and unable to meet the demands on them from higher up the pyramid of credit. Chettiar moneylenders, almost as important in Cochinchina as they were in Lower Burma, foreclosed and became owners of land they would have preferred not to hold. In 1930 they had controlled 6 percent of the land in the Irrawaddy Delta, while nonagriculturalists in general held 19 percent; in 1937 they had 25 percent of the Delta and nonagriculturalists as a whole now controlled fully 50 percent.[83] Land was lost on a nearly comparable scale in Cochinchina. For a large proportion of small propertied peasants it meant being swept from a comparatively secure subsistence into the class of tenants or wage laborers. A number of large owners were rescued by emergency credit and negotiated settlements encouraged by the colonial governments, but little of this credit ever reached smallholders.[84]

Tenants suffered as well. Most of them had crop loans payable in cash equivalent which they could not pay when the price of rice plummeted. Although they had no land to lose, they were likely to lose all of their crop together with their savings and plow animals as their landlord/

80. Melin, *L'Endettement agraire*, pp. 34–40.

81. Communication from Alexander Woodside. See also, Adas, *The Burma Delta*, pp. 188–89.

82. The same process in varying degrees can be observed elsewhere as well. In the case of Indonesia, Justus van der Kroef noted that in the financial crisis of the 1930s "thousands and again thousands of peasants in Java were forced to pawn away their land for practically nothing." "Peasants and Land Reform in Indonesian Communism," *Journal of Southeast Asian History* 4:1 (March 1963), 42.

83. Adas, *The Burma Delta*, p. 188.

84. On the French efforts, see Melin, *L'Endettement agraire*, pp. 76–82; on the British efforts, see Binns, *Agricultural Economy in Burma*, Appendix B, p. 8.

creditor squeezed what he could from them. "In 1930–31 an unusually high number of tenants were turned off the holding which they had rented" and swelled the ranks of the landless laborers who wandered around the Irrawaddy Delta in search of work.[85] Even those who stayed on the same plot could not look forward to any credit or subsistence loans for the succeeding season. Tenants were on their own; far from assisting them, their landlords and creditors were pushing them further under in a desperate effort to stay afloat themselves.

Laborers were the worst hit. As the economy contracted their numbers grew and they competed for fewer and fewer jobs. Where they had been working on marginal land that had been cultivated on the strength of a buoyant rice market, their jobs disappeared, and work outside the agrarian sector evaporated. A report on conditions in Hanthawaddy in the early 1930s noted that "this class of people has suffered most and are at present living from hand to mouth."[86] In Cochinchina, according to the calculations of Robert Sansom, the average rice consumption of a family of five supported by a wage laborer fell from 800 kg. in 1929 to 267 kg. by 1938. Such tragic figures speak for themselves.[87]

Perhaps the starkest testimony to the power of landowners and creditors to pass on a crushing share of the burden to tenants and laborers were the export figures. In both Lower Burma and Cochinchina the volume of rice exports actually grew during the depression. Despite a contraction of acreage planted in each area, the landowners, assisted by the state, were able to extract more grain from the countryside in the attempt to make good their losses. The result was a sharply reduced consumption of rice per capita. In Burma, Binns concluded that "during the 1930s the population consumed less rice per head than in the 1920s without any social or occupational change occurring which would make such a change a natural and voluntary phenomenon."[88] His all-Burma figures indicate a drop of something more than 10 percent in average

85. Adas, *The Burma Delta*, p. 189. The pattern we are describing is hardly unique to Southeast Asia. In the United States much of the impetus for the growth of the Sharecroppers' Union in 1931 was the refusal of landowners to give the customary working capital and credit to their tenants. The parallel, it would appear, extends even to the moral economy of its participants. See the moving account of one courageous union member in Theodore Rosengarten, *All God's Dangers: The Life of Nate Shaw* (New York: Alfred A. Knopf, 1974), pp. 287–310.

86. Binns, *Agricultural Economy in Burma*, p. 73.

87. Sansom, *The Economics of Insurgency*, p. 41. As Sansom points out, these figures give a rough estimate of the decline in welfare levels among tenants too, since the ability of laborers to bid against established tenants would drive rents up correspondingly.

88. Binns, *Agricultural Economy in Burma*, p. 59. Binns puts the change down to demographic factors and, indeed, there is evidence of a deterioration in per capita rice consumption well before the depression.

rice consumption, but the drop was far more severe in Lower Burma. In Vietnam as well, most figures show a deterioration in rice consumption that is sharpest in Cochinchina.[89]

Actual starvation, at least in Cochinchina and Lower Burma, was rare. By reducing expenses to the bone, switching from rice to less desirable foods, and by refusing to pay rents and taking as much of the harvest as possible, most survived. In fact, in terms of brute calorie intake, the cultivators of Lower Burma and Cochinchina were probably *still* better off than their compatriots in Upper Burma, Annam, and Tonkin. What had happened, however, was that the balance of exchange between tenants and landlords in the Mekong and Irrawaddy Deltas had moved dramatically in the landlords' favor and, above all, the provision for the tenants' primary needs, whether by remissions of rent or liberal credit, that had already been crippled by two decades of structural change was now dealt the coup de grâce. The peasants of Annam, by contrast, had subsistence problems that threatened their very lives, but the issue there was largely one of taxes and not a massive deterioration in rural class relations.

Peasants resisted as best they could this assault on their subsistence security. In Cochinchina they refused to pay any claim on their shrunken resources. "A true spirit of non-payment swept through the countryside of Cochinchina. One no longer payed debts nor taxes, because it was a crisis."[90] Tenants took to paying what they wished or not at all. In some cases they based their refusal both on the crisis and on the fact that the land had been more or less stolen from them by legal tricks, colonial grants, or defaulted loans. Others who paid something often gave the owner half of the remaining crop *after* they had taken what they needed to feed their family and their animals and pay the expenses of the next crop season.[91] Nothing expresses more clearly the popular belief in the priority of subsistence needs over any other claim on the harvest.

What we witness in the early 1930s is the stripping away of the few remaining economic guarantees provided by the earlier agrarian order. The older system was anything but utopian but, of necessity, it had offered more security. "As long as the old owners lived, they kept the tradition of their fathers, but many of them are dead; their sons and grandsons no longer follow their old patriarchal customs; they exercise their rights and neglect their duties."[92] In the Hobbesian financial world

89. See Sansom, *Economics of Insurgency*, p. 41, and note 1, p. 56.
90. Melin, *L'Endettement agraire*, p. 3.
91. Brocheux, "Grands proprietaires," p. 69.
92. Ibid., p. 73.

of the depression, the landowners missed no opportunity to recover their losses from the tenantry. "They put the maximum pressure on their tenants." "Their behavior was the negation of their proclaimed solidarity [with tenants] or of a practical complementarity of interests."[93] What is important here is that the agrarian order had lost its economic elasticity for the tenant and therefore its moral underpinning as well. The tenuous claim of the landowner to compliance had depended on his meeting the minimal demand for social justice—subsistence protection. Once that protection disappeared so did the last vestige of voluntary compliance. Collecting rents and taxes or dismissing recalcitrant tenants required a growing increment of coercion; old tenants fought the new tenants brought in to replace them. Tenants and laborers moved beyond formal complaints and protest meetings to land invasions and refusals to clear out when the landlord revoked a tenancy. Within a year, as we shall see in Chapter 5, this resistance assumed the proportions of a regional insurrection.

The response of the Burman peasantry in the Irrawaddy Delta was, if anything, even more violent. Landlords hired more of the rural lumpenproletariat to collect their rent while tenants pressed for rent reductions and other concessions. The fact that much land had passed from the hands of bankrupt Burman landlords into the hands of their Chettiar creditors and that the competition between Burman and Indian laborers for a diminishing supply of jobs was so ferocious, lent a strong communal tone to the violence there.[94] Burman landlords would gain if they could cancel their debts to the Chettiar; Burman paddy brokers would gain if they could replace Indian brokers; Burman tenants and laborers would gain if they did not have to compete with Indians for tenancies or for jobs in the rice mills or on the docks. Violence erupted in those provinces where the economic dislocation was most severe and the competition with Indians most intense—that is, in the East and Central Delta.

Resistance ranged all the way from banditry and looting to a more premeditated effort at revolution (see Chapter 5). The issues were virtually the same as in Cochinchina—security of tenure, remissions of rent, debts, and taxes in the crisis, and subsistence loans—except that in

93. Ibid., p. 71. See also Pierre Gourou: "In the crisis precipitated by the fall in the price of rice around 1930, the Annamite owners were most intractable; they did not understand that one could induce them by grants and guaranteed loans not to grab the lands they desired, the acquisition of which was always the logical goal of their loans." *L'Utilisation du sol,* p. 277.

94. See Adas, *The Burma Delta,* chap. 10, for an excellent analysis of the communal impact of the economic crisis.

Burma the fact that the competition and creditor was often an Indian seemed to offer a minimal basis of collaboration between different classes of Burmans.

If it is possible to speak of peasants in both Cochinchina and Lower Burma in virtually the same breath, this is precisely because the integration of these two areas into the world market had, even before the 1930s, produced a convergence in their social histories. They had become capillaries of a network of financial arteries leading to the banks of London and Paris. As capillaries, their growth was promoted by the heavy flow of capital from the metropole and they were, in turn, fully vulnerable to a failure of the financial center that nourished them. The agrarian histories of the Mekong and Irrawaddy Deltas became, at this point, a provincial variant of world economic history.[95] They remained distinctive, to be sure, but the major economic events that transformed their inhabitants' lives originated elsewhere. In contrast, the traditional heartlands of Upper Burma, Annam, and Tonkin, though hardly untouched, retained a certain autonomy and inner dynamic of their own due to their relative insulation from the world economy.

The impact of market integration on the subsistence guarantees of the peasantry is simply that it unifies and homogenizes economic life for those it embraces and, for the first time, makes possible a failure of social guarantees on a far larger scale than previously. In contrast, relations between a patron and his client in nineteenth-century Southeast Asia varied from region to region, depending on mainly local factors. A deterioration in a peasant's welfare and bargaining position could thus normally be attributed to such local conditions as labor supply, crop losses, and warfare. The penetration of the world economy, however, steadily eliminated the local idiosyncrasies of fragmented subsistence economies. Tenancy became increasingly more uniform from one landlord to the next and created a new set of shared experiences.

Viewed from the bottom, the depression was not the same as a crop failure; crops grew more or less as before, but the remaining securities of tenancy or rural labor were eliminated and claims on the crop were pressed remorselessly. Elites failed to observe the minimal obligations that the moral economy of the peasantry required of them. Such a large-scale rupture of interclass bonds is scarcely conceivable except in a market economy.

95. An attempt to analyze the early development of capitalism in Europe in terms of this center-periphery dimension may be found in Immanuel Wallerstein, *The Modern World System* (New York: Academic Press, 1974).

# 4 The State as Claimant

Nothing about the colonial order seemed to infuriate the peasantry more than its taxes. One would be hard pressed to find many demonstrations, petitions, or rebellions involving the peasantry in which the burdens of taxation were not a prominent grievance. Large-scale tax and corvée protests convulsed parts of Indochina in 1848, following floods and crop failures in the Red River Delta, and again in 1908, following a world credit crisis.[1] Most of the protests which preceded both the 1930–31 riots and the rural insurrection known as the Nghe-An, Ha-Tinh Soviets of 1931 were, in large part, directed against the tax claim of the state.

In the Philippines under the Spanish and Americans, a long lineage of peasant leaders from the late nineteenth-century Colorum sects all the way to Sakdal leader Benigno Ramos in the 1930s traded on a persistent peasant vision of a reconstituted village world without the state—that is to say, without taxes.[2] Many of the peasants and rural laborers captured in the ill-fated Sakdal revolt had been too poor to pay their *cedula* or poll tax. The husband of a heroine of that revolt had been thrown in jail for his failure to pay. Although the leaders sought independence, the primary meaning of independence for the rank-and-file was an end to taxes. As one rebel put it, "Under independence I would pay no taxes. No cedula." Another echoed, "They told me independence would be a good thing with no cedula to pay, or a cedula for a peseta."[3] It was a vision they shared with peasants elsewhere in colonial Southeast Asia.

Fifty years earlier in the Madiun Residency of Java, peasants rose for essentially the same reasons in what was known as the Pulung Affair. "A little man (*wong cilik*) cannot even wear trousers because his money is used for paying taxes," explained one rebel. "We want to kill the Dutch because they impose taxes on us," said another.[4] This was hardly the

1. For brief accounts of each of these episodes, see David Marr, *Viet-Nam's Anti-Colonial Movements: The Early Years, 1885–1925* (Berkeley and Los Angeles: University of California Press, 1971), chaps. 1 and 8.

2. See David R. Sturtevant's superb book, *The Last Shall Be First: Millennial Movements in the Philippines: 1840–1940* (Ithaca, N.Y.: Cornell University Press, 1976).

3. See Appendix I, pp. 4, 6, of "Sakdal Uprising Report," by J. R. Hayden, Acting Governor General, May 27, 1935 (Hayden Collection, University of Michigan Library). For more on the rebellion and on Primitivo Algabre, the rebel from whose interrogation this quote comes, and his sister Salud, see Sturtevant, *The Last Shall Be First.*

4. Onghokham, "The Residency of Madiun: Prijaji and Peasant in the Nineteenth Century" (Ph.D. dissertation, Yale University, 1975). See also Kartodirdjo, *Peasant Movements,* chap. 2.

only occasion on which the Dutch were obliged to deal with anti-tax uprisings. The abolition of taxes was a central goal in such diverse peasant settings as the folk anarchism of the Saminists, the religious utopia promised by the leaders of the Banten Islamic brotherhoods, and the more secular paradise envisioned by the peasant followers of the left-wing Sarekat Rakjat in the 1920s.[5]

Taxes and rents, together or individually, form the twin issues around which peasant anger in Southeast Asia has classically coalesced. They were, and often still are, the major institutional threats to peasant welfare. Where a frontier and a growing export market conspired to transform rural class relations (as in Central Luzon, Lower Burma, and Cochinchina), agrarian movements often fastened on such landlord-tenant issues as rents, "remissions," and credit, with taxes increasingly a secondary issue. Where customary reciprocity weathered the assault of market forces more successfully (as in Tonkin, Annam, and Java), taxes often remained the major cause of peasant unrest. The more rigid, inflexible, and regressive the tax regime, the more social dynamite it engendered.

That taxes should periodically enrage the peasantry should hardly occasion surprise. Before the development of absentee landownership, taxes were the main route by which wealth in labor or kind was taken from the village. The threat of tax insurrections led by rivals or of mass emigrations of subjects voting with their feet was a constant preoccupation of precolonial Southeast Asian monarchs.

By almost any criterion, however, taxation as a popular agrarian issue achieved its apotheosis under the colonial regime. The reasons for this demonstrate how the fiscal policy of the colonial state increasingly violated the moral economy of the subsistence ethic.

There is little doubt that the *average* burden of the colonial government on a peasant's income was greater than that of the indigenous governments that had preceded it. The growing average fiscal levy of the colonial state, though symptomatic, misses the most oppressive features of taxation in terms of peasant subsistence needs. The distinctiveness of colonial taxes lay not so much in the fact that they were higher but in the nature of those taxes and the blind rigor with which they were imposed.

    5. For the Saminists, see Harry J. Benda and Lance Castles, "The Samin Movement," *Bijdragen tot de Taal-Land-, en Volkenkunde* 125:2 (1969), passim; for the Banten revolt, see Sartono Kartodirdjo, *The Peasants' Revolt of Banten in 1888* (The Hague: Martinus Nijhoff, 1966), pp. 63; 104, 280; and for the rebellion of 1926–27, see Harry Benda and Ruth McVey, *The Communist Uprisings in 1926–27 in Indonesia* (Ithaca: Modern Indonesia Project, Cornell Southeast Asian Program, 1960), pp. 38, 42, 47.

First, and most important, the taxes that bore most heavily on the peasant were fixed charges that had no relation to his ability to pay or to his subsistence needs. The head tax (*impôt personnel*), as it was called in Vietnam, or capitation tax, as it was called in Burma, was the ultimate in regressive fiscal measures. It fell indifferently on rich heads and poor heads in good times and in bad, with the result that its actual burden on the tax-paying family fluctuated wildly from season to season. The state, for its part, could count on a steady yield that grew with population. Land taxes were almost as regressive, based as they were on per hectare assessments according to what was thought the average yield. Thus, the substantial landowner of 100 hectares, though he paid more absolutely, paid the same average proportion of his crop as the smallholder with a single hectare. The rate was a fixed tax that was exacted without respect to what the land had actually produced that season. If half a crop was lost, the land tax was in effect twice the burden it would have been in a good season. Colonial regimes also instituted or "improved upon" a wide variety of excise taxes on such items as salt, alcohol, wood products, boats, marketing, and in the sale of water buffalos. To the extent that these products or activities were a normal part of subsistence routines, such taxes also represented a fixed charge on a variable peasant income.

The way in which taxes were administered in the colony was at least as important as the form they took. Many precolonial taxes were, in principle, fixed as well; the chief difference was that the traditional state did not have the means to impose its will and there was a corresponding slippage between what the king decreed and what his ministers could deliver. Subjects fled, black markets circumvented state monopolies, villages faked records and pleaded poverty; the more effective a kingdom was in imposing its taxes, the more its tax base leaked away.[6]

6. It is hard to assess the restraining effect of the moral injunctions and the metaphysical beliefs of traditional Southeast Asian monarchs on their fiscal policies. It is entirely possible that the Hindu and Buddhist doctrines of the responsibility of the king for the welfare of his subjects made for monarchs who went easy in times of dearth and devoted much public revenue to irrigation works and public relief. This is certainly a recurrent theme in traditional literature. The ideal king is "generous in giving alms, gives clothes to those who have none . . . food to those in hunger." Onghokham, *The Residency of Madiun*, p. 16, quoting Tjan Tjoe Siem, "Hoe Koeroepati Zijn Vruaw Verwief" (Ph.D. dissertation, Leiden, 1930). See also, Somersaid Moertono, *State and Statecraft in Old Java* (Ithaca: Modern Indonesia Project, Cornell Southeast Asian Program, 1968). One thing, however, is clear. A rapacious Southeast Asian monarch paid immediate and palpable costs if he pressed too hard on his subjects. Witness the admonition of Queen Saw to King Narathihapate: "Consider the state of the realm. Thou hast no folk or people, no host of countrymen and countrywomen around thee. . . . Thy countrymen and countrywomen tarry and will not enter thy kingdom. They fear thy domination; for thou, O King Alaung, art a hard master. Therefore, I, thy servant, spake to thee of old; but thou wouldst not

With the colonial regime the degree of slippage was less and less. With its monopoly of modern weapons and its more disciplined standing army, the colonial regime expanded the radius of its power and eventually made its presence felt at the periphery. Unlike most traditional rulers, it was not often obliged to come to terms with regional chiefs who could have defied its predecessors.

The decisive advantage of the colonial apparatus, however, lay as much in paperwork as in rifles. To follow the development of the colonial regime is to follow the inexorable progress of cadastral surveys, settlement reports for land revenue, censuses, the issuance of land titles and licenses, identity cards, tax rolls and receipts, and a growing body of regulations and procedures. The collection of revenue was the end of much of this activity. Nets of finer and finer official weave caught and recorded the status of each inhabitant, each piece of land, each transaction, each activity that was assessable. Although it may be possible to exaggerate the official reach of established colonial regimes, there is little doubt that, compared to the kingdoms they replaced, they left few places to hide.

*The power of the colonial order in the countryside finds expression precisely in its capacity to stabilize its income at the expense of its rural subjects.* Both the colonial bureaucracy and the tax receipts which support it show a more or less steady upward trend, at least until 1930. The variability of crop yields and peasant income is almost always far greater than the variability of the state's claim on them. Remissions of personal taxes and land rates are comparatively rare, and, when extended, are seldom more than a small percentage of the loss in crops or income.[7] Even in 1930 when the colonial bureaucracies were finally obliged to retrench and tighten their belts, the contraction of the state was nothing compared to the contraction of the income of the tax-paying public.[8] At those times and in those regions when peasants found themselves closest to the margin, any tax, let alone a substantial one, was seen as totally unjust; the fact that it could nevertheless be collected was testimony to the extractive capacity of the colonial state.

Finally, the colonial leviathan seemed often to inspire a certain hysteria by the very scope of its taxes. Villagers found their immemorial rights to the forest and its products were suddenly and unaccountably circumscribed. Their rights to the fish in local streams and the game in the forest were taxed and licensed. In some cases, notably Vietnam, their

hearken. I said, bore not thy country's belly . . . cut not thy country's feet and hands!" *The Glass Palace Chronicle of the Kings of Burma*, trans. Pe Maung Tin and G. H. Luce (London: Oxford University Press, 1923), p. 177.

7. *Land Revenue System Committee Report*, vol. 2, pp. 4, 233, et seq.

8. Paul Bernard, *Le Problème économique indochinois*, pp. 50–55.

right to distill a portion of their own rice into alcohol for their own use was withdrawn and a state monopoly created. The imposition of registration fees, stamp duties, heavier salt taxes, marketing fees, and boat taxes moved the state further into the individual peasant's life than the traditional state had ever gone. In the case of forests and streams, the state seemed to be taxing the free gifts of nature. Where would it stop? If the state could tax firewood and fish, why not the banana tree by the house, or the peasant's clothes, or the very air he breathed. The prevailing atmosphere is captured by the "Asia Ballad," popular in Vietnamese nationalist circles at the Tonkin Free School in 1907. It complained of

> oxen taxes, taxes on "chattering pigs," salt taxes, rice field taxes, ferry boat taxes, bicycle or conveyance taxes, taxes on betel or areca nuts, tea and drug taxes, commercial license taxes, water taxes, lamp taxes, housing taxes, temple taxes, bamboo and timber taxes, taxes on peddler's boats, tallow taxes, lacquer taxes, rice and vegetable taxes, taxes on cotton and silk, iron taxes, fishing taxes, bird taxes, and copper taxes.[9]

Nothing seemed immune from taxation and the hysteria about what was in store played an important role in local rebellions. Among the Saminists of Java, smarting under new forest regulations, "stories spread that there would be new taxes on the burial of the dead, on bathing buffalos in streams, on travelling the road, and so on."[10] A document of prophesy seized in connection with the Saya San rebellion in Burma, struck the same note: "Taxes in different forms were levied on all pieces of land and it went nearly so far as to levy a tax on flower pots in houses till Burma is helpless. No piece of land would be left untaxed *not even forest*."[11] Yet another document from the rebellion declared that "although the 12 kinds of timber together with precious minerals came into existence for the use of Burmans, they are prohibited from picking up the smallest splinter even the size of a toothpick or earstud, that royalty is imposed on bamboo and firewood and that the heathens have done very unfairly regarding these things."[12] Allowing for the polemical intent of these declarations, it is clear that they touched a responsive note among the peasantry. Facing what already must have seemed a mind-boggling array of taxes, the peasant easily succumbed to panic.[13]

9. Woodside, *Community and Revolution*, p. 153.

10. Benda and Castles, "The Samin Movement," p. 222.

11. *The Origin and Causes of the Burma Rebellion, 1930–1932* (Rangoon: Government of Burma, 1934), p. 26, emphasis added.

12. Ibid., p. 33.

13. The caprice of taxation must also have stirred indignation. Local authorities abused their power to reward themselves and their friends and abuse their enemies. However

The experience of the Southeast Asian peasantry with the fiscal practices of the colonial state is analogous in many respects to the experience
of the European peasantry with the centralizing states of the seventeenth
and eighteenth centuries. As Charles Tilly has noted, "Taxation was the
most prominent single issue in the large-scale rebellions during the
European state-making of the sixteenth to nineteenth centuries."[14] In
each case, a growing central authority that increasingly intruded in the
daily life of its subjects with administrative and fiscal demands produced
comparable results.

The most obvious, if not most important, of these was the rate of
expansion of the state's fiscal claim, exceeding rates of economic or
population growth. Burgeoning public payrolls required ever larger
and *stable* sources of revenue which, in an agrarian economy, meant
extracting what was needed from the rural sector. This steadily growing
claim had an internal dynamic of its own that was independent and more
or less heedless of cycles of prosperity and dearth in the countryside. If
widespread crop failure reduced the taxpaying capacity of an already
hard-pressed peasantry by 80 percent, it would certainly never do to
reduce the personnel and budget of the central state by a similar figure.
Rational administration would be inconceivable under such conditions.
Instead, the state sought to stabilize if not expand its claim on society
even though the weight of its demands and its consequences for rural
life might fluctuate dramatically according to the health of the rural
economy. The magic in this recipe, of course, was that the very size of
the state apparatus was precisely what allowed it, not without difficulty to
be sure, to meet its annual budget at the expense of its subjects.

The new state, moreover, was a *bureaucratic* state. That is, it worked
increasingly through formulas, regulations, and laws that could be
applied across the board by its agents. Creating a central administration
meant the unification of what had been fragmented local customs and
procedures into a more homogeneous whole. Roland Mousnier, in in-
terpreting the rural rebellions of seventeenth-century France, sees such
infringements of local traditions of substantive justice as a major pre-
cipitating factor. "Royal taxation was the way in which people were most
directly made aware of the modern state, centralizing and reducing all to
equality and uniformity."[15] The logic of uniform administration, in
seventeenth-century France as in colonial Southeast Asia, meant that the

---

infuriating this aspect of the state's fiscal squeeze may have been, it seems less distinctive of
the colonial regime inasmuch as traditional taxation must have been equally or more
Caligulan.

14. Charles Tilly, "Do Communities Act?," *Sociological Inquiry* 43:3,4 (1973), 221.

15. Mousnier, *Peasant Uprisings*, p. 329.

tax collector as often as not ignored local crop failures in imposing the land revenue system. It meant that a host of customary rights regarding land and forest use were swept away in the pursuit of a national pattern of land administration. It meant that small but important differences in soil fertility and cropping patterns were ignored in order to create a uniform classification of land that was simpler for assessment purposes.

The new state was not only larger and more bureaucratic, it was also centrally administered. In a more feudal system, local chiefs, though they might have been far more capricious, had an interest in keeping their ears to the ground and adjusting their claims to the ability of their subjects to pay. So long as their local power rested on their ability to summon the necessary manpower in a conflict, they found it prudent to avoid excesses that would provide potential rivals a base of recruitment. The new agents of the center, however, had far less interest in maintaining a local following. They rose or fell according to how well they pleased their bureaucratic superiors, not according to how well they protected the local population. In revenue matters, especially, the satisfaction of the center with its agents tended to vary directly with the receipts they forwarded; short of provoking a rebellion, pleasing the center implied squeezing the local population.

In seventeenth-century France as in Southeast Asia, the new fiscal claims and administrative ways of the central state produced a bountiful harvest of peasant resistance and rebellion. Resistance was most tenacious in regions where crop yields were especially vulnerable to the vagaries of weather. It was in precisely such regions where a rigid fiscal claim of the state was most often pressed on a peasantry with its back to the wall. The peasant movements that emerged were "reactions against the state."[16] In the Jean Nu-pieds revolt in Normandy the rebels called for an end to *la gabelle* (the salt tax) and other new taxes and a return to the lighter fiscal regime of Henri IV.[17] Their immediate targets were the minions of the new order—the tax monopolists, state officials, and their local collaborators—and they seldom failed to burn the tax rolls and records which they understood, correctly, to be an integral part of the new order.

The new state both in Europe and in Southeast Asia moved as quickly as possible from taxes in kind and in corvée labor to cash. Within a still largely subsistence economy, the demand for cash imposed new hardships; it drove peasants into cash crops or into the labor market. Much of

16. Ibid., p. 348.
17. Cf. Boris Porchnev, "Popular Uprisings as Class War/The Revolt of the Nu-pieds," pp. 42–51, in Isser Woloch, ed., *The Peasantry in the Old Regime: Conditions and Protests* (New York: Holt, Rinehart, 1970).

what economists and anthropologists have called "cash hunger" in the
Third World owes its origin to colonial fiscal policy. Ardant claims that
tax rebellions in Europe arose most commonly in communities that were
unable to market enough to meet their tax obligations.[18] A number of
anti-tax movements in Indonesia developed because "Peasants were
paralyzed by their inability to find money to pay their taxes and rents."[19]
In the Tangerang tax protests near Jakarta in 1924, for example, "the
general complaint was that it was hard to earn money and that money
was scarce."[20] It was, of course, far more rational for the colonial regime
to collect cash rather than tribute in kind or corvée, but in areas of
subsistence production or following a market slump or crop failure, the
shortage of cash could vastly magnify the tax burden.

Viewed from the top, such peasant tax revolts have a vaguely archaic
air. Their principal target, after all, was the fiscal edifice of the modern
state. Their vision was, for the most part, one of local autonomy and a
world without taxes. Viewed from the bottom, however, they expressed
a natural resistance to new demands that took little or no heed of the
local situation or of the fluctuating real burden they might represent
from one year to the next. They represented, in short, the defense of the
peasant and little community's claim to a stable subsistencè against the
new state's effort to extract a reliable and growing income from its
subjects.

If anything, the confrontation between the peasant and the modern
state was more traumatic in Southeast Asia than in Western Europe. The
imposition of the state was a lengthy process in Europe, while in Southeast Asia most of the populated lowlands were brought under colonial
administration within a few decades. Colonial officials, sealed off from
the indigenous population by barriers of language, culture, and religion,
were even less responsive to local customs and conditions than were the
*intendants* of France. The taxes they imposed and the administrative
forms they followed, borrowed as they were from the metropole (or in
the British case, from India) were even less accessible to the populations
they governed.

The impact of the colonial tax system on the peasant economy is
apparent from the cases of Burma and Vietnam which are discussed
below. As the system's explosive potential was realized only during the
world depression of the 1930s, a brief section is devoted to that period.

18. Gabriel Ardant, *Théorie sociologique de l'impôt,* Livre IV (Paris: S.E.V.P.N., 1965),
pp. 751–837.

19. Kartodirdjo, *Protest Movements in Rural Java*, p. 43.

20. Ibid., p. 47.

## BURMA

### Head Taxes

The head tax was hardly a fiscal invention of the colonial state. Such a tax, in one form or another, was a traditional device of precolonial kingdoms as well. What was new were the manner and thoroughness of its application. In the portions of Upper Burma where a land revenue system had not yet been applied, a *thathameda* tax was levied on each village. An estimate was made of the nonagricultural income of a village tract and that figure was then divided by the number of households in the tract to arrive at a standard tax. The tax per household thus varied from village to village (from two to twelve rupees) though the average figure was eight or nine rupees. It is likely, but not entirely certain, that this amount represented a greater burden for the cultivator than pre-colonial taxes.[21] Raising the necessary cash was particularly difficult given the closed subsistence character of Upper Burma's economy in the early colonial period. Theoretically, provisions that allowed a village to collect the sum due after its own fashion and to exclude households on grounds of poverty left some flexibility in the system. In practice, how-ever, the government committee that examined its operation found that the tax was both systematically collected and regressive.[22]

The capitation tax in Lower Burma was more straightforward. It was a fixed *individual* tax in rupees. Since it varied neither by individual nor by village it was especially regressive. In the best of times it bore particularly hard on tenants and laborers whose cash resources were slender and uncertain. After crop failure, or after a fall in wages or employment, it might represent a direct threat to consumption needs.

Heavy though it may have been, the *average* burden of the head tax—the percentage of average net income it represented—cannot ex-plain why it should have stirred so much resentment and violence. The hatred it engendered was disproportionate to its relative importance for colonial revenue. As a fiscal device it produced less than one-third the amount derived from land revenue, for example, and its total proceeds amounted to only 5 percent of the colony's receipts in 1925–26.[23] Yet, the campaign against head taxes was the central issue of popular nationalist agitation from 1915 until World War II. The abolition of these taxes was the first and seemingly most popular demand of Saya

21. *Report of the Capitation and Thathameda Taxes Enquiry Committee 1926–27* (Rangoon: Government of Burma, 1949), pp. 1–20. Hereafter referred to as the *Capitation Taxes Enquiry Committee*.

22. Ibid., p. 21.

23. Ibid., p. 3.

San's Galon Party in the rebellion of 1930. "There is plenty of oral evidence to show that Saya San and his lieutenants, in their efforts to raise the countryside in open rebellion, had taken pains to exploit the dislike of taxes in general and of capitation and *thathameda* taxes in particular."[24] Saya San had hardly created this issue; he presumably discovered in the course of his travels for the General Council of Buddhist Associations just how bitterly the head tax was resented by cultivators.

The reason behind the furor generated by the head tax is, I believe, to be sought both in the rigor with which it was collected and in the fact that it bore "more heavily on the poor than on the well-to-do."[25] It was also implemented with such a disregard for the agricultural cycle that its net burden was much larger than intended. Collection took place between April and October, before the main harvest, and often at precisely the period when the agriculturalist was short of cash and rice. Fully two-thirds of those who paid were obliged to borrow the cash privately and repay the loan in rice of equivalent value at a time, after the harvest, when rice prices were comparatively low. In practice, the rice cost of the loan was roughly five baskets (circa 1923). Since a single basket (9–10 gallons) was sufficient to feed a peasant family of four for 21 days, the actual cost of the loan to the cultivator's family was the equivalent of over three months' supply of its main staple.[26] The timing of this fixed claim on peasant income, when its threat to subsistence routines was greatest, had much to do with the anger it provoked.

It is possible to grasp something of the impact of these taxes on peasant subsistence by comparing the receipts they produced over time with the much larger fluctuations in crop yields. On the basis of incomplete figures, it seems that until 1930 the receipts from head taxes expanded steadily with the growth of population and seldom fell back more than 2 to 3 percent after a bad harvest.[27] Yields on the other hand were far more variable, the differences ranging from at least 10 to 20 percent in Lower Burma to much higher figures in the Dry Zone of Upper Burma. Such averages, moreover, tend to understate the burden of the head tax after a bad year in at least two ways. First, an *average* fluctuation in crop yield of 20 percent masks fluctuations of much greater magnitude in the income of individual farmers or of certain districts. The head tax, in its administrative simplicity, was no respecter of these differences in ability to pay. Second, it is critical to recall that,

24. *The Origin and Causes of the Burma Rebellion, 1930–32,* p. 43.
25. *Capitation Taxes Enquiry Committee,* Appendix, p. 42.
26. *The Couper Report,* pp. 50–54.
27. *Capitation Taxes Enquiry Committee,* p. 33.

for cultivators who are close to the margin, a 20 percent loss of yield may well threaten their tenancy and their subsistence. The tax in this case is not, say, 20 percent more burdensome but may well threaten the central ligaments of a family's livelihood.

What is involved here is essentially the difference between quantity and quality or, put another way, the problem of thresholds. As Lukács has noted in another context, "The qualitative differences in exploitation which appear to the capitalist [or the state] in the form of quantitative determinants of the objects of his calculation, must appear to the worker [peasant] as the decisive, qualitative categories of his whole physical, mental, and moral existence."[28] Viewed from the budget office in the colonial capital, an increase in taxes from five rupees to six rupees amounts to a 20 percent increase in the taxpayer's obligation. Viewed from the taxpayer's perspective, however, the surrender of five rupees one year may still permit a family to maintain the basic features of its life style. But take one additional rupee or, what amounts to the same thing, five rupees after the family has had a bad year, and you may thrust it over a social precipice from which there is no return.

Another measure of the oppressiveness of head taxes would be to compare them with the actual cash resources of tenants and laborers. No direct figures are available but the fact that average per capita consumption of staple consumer goods such as *ngapi* (fish paste), salted fish, milk, and sugar actually declined between 1911–14 and 1923–26 suggests that the disposable cash resources of the peasantry were diminishing.[29] If this was so, and it is in line with statements by Furnivall and others about the increasing penury of the cultivator, it indicates that the real burden of the head tax was increasing well before 1930.

For the colonial state, the capitation tax had a captivating simplicity. Assessment was automatic and required no administration. This meant, not incidentally, that a certain amount of corruption was avoided that would have inevitably followed any attempt to give local officials the discretion to implement a progressive income tax. It had the further advantage that receipts were stable and grew in direct proportion with population. Its effect, and its intention, was to insulate the bureaucratic center from the fluctuations of the rural economy. In terms of subsistence security, however, it was the most onerous form of taxation imaginable. The nature of the peasant reaction can be gauged from the growing level of coercion needed to collect the head tax after crop

28. Georg Lukács, *History and Class Consciousness: Studies in Marxist Dialectics,* trans. Rodney Livingstone (Cambridge, Mass.: M.I.T. Press, 1971), p. 166.

29. *Capitation Taxes Enquiry Committee,* pp. 62–63.

failures and slumps in prices or employment, and by the uniquely privileged place it enjoyed among peasant grievances.

## Land Revenue

The land revenue system of Burma provided for the government the same advantages of a secure fiscal intake as did the capitation tax. Again, it was the cultivator whose economic insecurity was magnified as he was asked to underwrite the fiscal insurance of the state.

As settlement officers made their way slowly through Burma, they established fixed annual land rates according to the quality of the land, an estimate of the average yield, and the average crop prices for the period immediately preceding the assessment. Reassessments were made at 15 to 20 year intervals. The result was a fixed per acre tax on every cultivated acre in Burma—*a tax whose revenue yield was far more dependable than crop yields.*

The most evident victims of fixed assessments were naturally the smallholders in the northern portions of the Irrawaddy Delta and in Upper Burma. A default of two or three years following bad harvests or a fall in prices would lead to the seizure and auction of their land by district revenue officials. Inasmuch as larger landowners could increasingly pass on most of the added cost of tax charges to their tenants and laborers, the impact of the tax was not limited to smallholders. It seems, in fact, to have been normal for a round of compensating rent increases to follow each upward revision in land rates. But nonowning tenants and laborers, though they might in effect pay the land rate, paid it through the landlord who became the natural and most immediate target of their anger. This may explain why the land revenue issue never elicited quite the same level of anger as did head taxes which, while constituting a smaller share of colonial income, struck all poor cultivators more or less equally.

The land tax represented a substantial charge on the cultivator. Settlement officers generally figured that land rates took roughly 10 percent of his gross return and as much as 25 to 40 percent of his net return (gross return minus production costs, including an estimate of the value of home labor). Such average figures are, as usual, somewhat misleading inasmuch as the actual take varied greatly from settlement area to settlement area and even from tract to tract. Inequalities such as these were a logical result of the administrative need to establish a limited number of land categories, each of which included substantial differences in productivity. There were also important variations over time. As land rates were in part based on rice prices up to the time of settlement, their real burden varied according to price movements after the assessment date.

In theory, land rates were less regressive than the head tax. Because it was a tax on units of land rather than heads, the man with ten acres paid ten times the tax paid by the owner of a single acre. To the extent, however, that the large owner sublet the land to small tenants from whom he could recoup his tax costs, the progressive aspect of the tax was fictitious.

The land rate menaced the marginal smallholder in three ways. First, assuming that yields are steady, such a proportional tax of 20 percent threatens his livelihood far more than that of the larger owner. For peasants with small plots and/or large families, the tax might mean the difference between remaining an independent cultivator and falling into the tenant or laborer class. Far more important, however, was the fact that the tax was fixed, albeit by acre. With few exceptions, it was administratively blind to the large variations in annual yield throughout the country. Such variations might not be a disaster for the large owner, but a smallholder who lost most of his crop might not have *any* profits with which to pay the land revenue rates. In practice, then, the tax tended to be regressive on an annual basis, for "*as the agriculturalist's income diminishes, the proportion of his income taken away from him to meet land revenue charges increases.*"[30] Though the burden of the land tax may have been fixed from the government's point of view, its effect on the peasant was hardly uniform.

There was, in theory, a remedy for these inequities in the remission of a proportion of the tax following widespread crop failures. In practice, remissions failed to bring much relief to those who most needed it. The procedures of application were unknown to small scale cultivators, they were cumbersome, and remissions were only rarely granted.[31] An Englishman who was presumably not handicapped as were the peasants by the social distance between himself and the revenue officials complained that the time and money consumed by the application cost him more than he gained when it was finally granted.[32] There is evidence, in fact, that revenue surveyors in Lower Burma *consistently* failed to apply the provisions for across-the-board remissions of land rates in those seasons in which the whole crop of an assessment tract was lost.[33] Above and beyond the imposing administrative obstacles, remissions if granted tended to be inferior to the actual proportion of the crop lost. In the

---

30. Binns, *Agricultural Economy in Burma*, p. 16.

31. *Land Revenue System Committee Report*, vol. 2, pp. 3–4.

32. Ibid., p. 54.

33. *Maubin Settlement Report*, p. 60. "It appears that from 1924–25 only, have revenue surveyors omitted to assess completely failed areas under the provisions of Direction 122 of the Land Revenue Manual."

disastrous year of 1937–38 when, due to a failure of late rains, the crop losses in Lower Burma approached 40 percent, the remissions of land revenue amounted to only 11 percent.[34] A tax system which was attentive to subsistence needs would have reversed the procedure; it would have accorded a remission well above the proportion of crop loss to compensate for the drastically reduced capacity of the cultivator to pay.

Finally, the real burden of the revenue rates on the smallholder varied as much with the price of rice and with the availability and cost of credit as it did with the actual crop yield. The lower the price of rice fell, the greater the share of the harvest that had to be sold to meet the annual tax. As one ex-settlement officer laconically explained as early as 1922, "fluctuations in the general level of prices have in recent years been a further factor upsetting suddenly the data on which settlements had been based."[35] The remedy proposed by many officials closest to the problems of the cultivator was to move to an annual income tax that would assess the cultivator only in proportion to the real value of his actual harvest.

> The need to do so [switch to an income tax] arose about thirty-three years ago [circa 1911] but the steady rise in prices obscured the threat of difficulty. The system worked well enough when the rates were as low as Rs 2 per acre; but these are now Rs 7 or 8 in many districts. Land revenue brought in a steadily increasing revenue, *which did not fall off heavily in bad times and for this reason was no doubt highly valued.* But times have greatly changed. Prices are now subject to violent fluctuations even in the course of a single season.[36]

The reason a shift to an income tax was resisted throughout the colonial period is clearly implied in this evaluation. To shift would have required the colonial government to assume the burden of economic fluctuations and to insure that its claim did not disrupt peasant subsistence. But the government wanted things just the other way around and could have its way.

The consequences of this policy contributed more than a little to the liquidation of the Burman smallholder class. In 1908, following the world credit crisis, many smallholders defaulted on their taxes as well as their debts and lost their land. In the early 1930s the tragedy was repeated on a much larger scale, when even large financiers were unable

---

34. Binns, *Agricultural Economy of Burma*, p. 75.

35. *Land Revenue System Committee Report*, vol. 2, p. 94.

36. Binns, *Agricultural Economy in Burma*, Appendix B, extracts from Memorandum by L. Dawson, p. 17, emphasis added.

to pay the tax claim on the land that fell into their hands. The tragic ruin of thousands of cultivators at such times of world economic crisis demonstrated how colonial fiscal policy had systematically undermined the already tenuous position of marginal smallholders. On the expense side of the smallholder's family budget, it had added the fixed charges of the head tax and land rate to the production costs and consumption needs of the household.[37] A farmer needed to grow more, simply to stay even. An off year that he might have otherwise managed, with difficulty, to get through would now more likely cost him his land. To the already considerable risks of drought, flood, pests, and plant disease the colonial economy added price fluctuations and credit crises. Returning to the felicitous metaphor of Tawney, it is as if the colonial government had found a peasant smallholder up to his neck in water and had first proceeded, by its tax policy, to raise the water level to just beneath his nose and then, by integrating him into a cash economy, to increase the wave action enough to drown him.

The head tax and fixed land assessments, despite a widespread recognition of the inequities they worked, continued to be applied. They were as advantageous for the colonial budget as they were ruinous for the peasantry, even though increased policing and coercion were needed to implement them. After crop failures, particularly in Upper Burma, even nominal land rates were difficult to collect. Petty crimes and protests became increasingly common before the capitation tax was due and defaults multiplied. So long as the price of rice remained buoyant and jobs plentiful, these difficulties posed no serious threat to the colonial order. Beginning in 1930, however, as we shall see, the conflict between the colonial budget and household budget became irreconcilable.

## Vietnam

In a country that already boasted a long tradition of tax rebellions and protests,[38] the imposition of the French fiscal system created burdens of an entirely new order and reactions to match. The basic pattern was remarkably similar to that in Burma. A colonial regime, with an administrative capacity and bureaucratic reach far more developed than the traditional regime it replaced, extracted the revenue needs of a growing bureaucracy from the agrarian economy. If anything, the consequences

37. I have not discussed other fiscal measures that might be included under this heading such as the salt tax which, due to the importance of salt in making *ngapi* (fish paste condiment), represented a regressive tax that amounted to as much as 25 percent of the onerous capitation tax. Cf. *The Couper Report*, p. 50.

38. See Marr, *Viet-Nam's Anti-Colonial Movements*, chaps. 1–2.

for the Vietnamese peasant were even worse than for the Burman peasant. While the French may not have taken a larger proportion of the peasant's income than the British, they took it, especially in Annam and Tonkin, from a mass of peasantry who lived even closer to the famine line than the cultivators of Upper Burma. The administration of taxes in Vietnam seemed, in addition, to be even more corrupt and capricious than in Burma.[39] Remissions of land or head taxes were even rarer. Finally, there were a host of excise charges and monopolies, perhaps due to the stronger statist fiscal tradition of France vis-à-vis liberal England, which imposed an added burden on the peasant as consumer. The net result was to make colonial taxes an issue of even more transcendent importance for the Vietnamese cultivator than for his Burmese counterpart.

There is no doubt that the fiscal claim of the colonial regime was far above that of the traditional Vietnamese court. Ngo Vinh Long's careful comparisons of precolonial and colonial taxes reveal that, whereas head and land taxes under Gia Long and Minh Mang in the nineteenth century had taken between 3 and 5.5 percent of a man's rice yield per hectare, the colonial government in 1937 took between 16 and 18 percent.[40] In the eight year period of 1888–96, the colonial regime raised taxes as follows: head tax for registered villagers, 14 to 40 centimes; head tax for nonregistered, 0 to 40 centimes; rice-land tax, increased 50 percent; indirect taxes, doubled.[41] Summing up the evidence for Cochinchina, Osborne states that "all commentators agree that the substitution of French for Vietnamese brought an increase in the tax burden of the rural population."[42]

The precise dimensions of the growing tax burden are difficult to establish. It is enough for our purposes to know that they increased considerably and that their growth was not offset by any compensating improvement in the capacity of the cultivator to pay them. In fact, the overwhelming weight of evidence suggests just the opposite: that the average per capita consumption of rice had been tending to decline since

39. Ngo Vinh Long, "Before the August Revolution: The Living Conditions of the Vietnamese Peasants Under the French," pp. 64–65. This is an earlier version of the book later published as *Before the Revolution*.

40. Ibid., p. 68. Although the disparity Long computes would not have been nearly so dramatic if 1928 (when much higher rice prices prevailed) had been chosen for comparison, the gap is not too misleading considering the many additional taxes created by the colonial regime.

41. Chesneaux, *Contribution à l'histoire de la nation vietnamienne*, p. 145.

42. Milton E. Osborne, *The French Presence in Cochinchina and Cambodia: Rule and Response 1859–1905* (Ithaca: Cornell University Press, 1969), p. 84.

1913, especially in Tonkin and Annam.[43] Thus the peasant was caught in the vice of a generally rising tax claim and a declining capacity to pay.

As usual, however, a concern with average misses the main feature of peasant taxation in Vietnam as in Burma. First, the peasant, alas, does not receive an average income out of which he pays his annual taxes. How intolerable a tax is judged is thus not an abstract question but is tied inevitably to the sacrifices it imposes in a given year. The connection is forcefully illustrated in the following popular song from Vietnam.

After the flood, the fields are lifeless
and take on a frightening appearance.
The sugar cane was withered.
One mau [of land] yielded barely two small baskets of paddy
but the state didn't consider this.
Rates were raised more and more,
taxes were heavier and heavier.[44]

To ask how fixed land taxes bear down on a peasant is to ask how his food supply varies—and that is an *annual* question. The fact that the Tonkinese and Annamite peasant lives close to the margin and must pay large taxes establishes what we might call a tendency toward collision. The actual collisions are proximately caused by such factors as oscillations in crop yields, prices, and the availability of credit, which oppose the tax claim of the state (or the rent of the landlord) to the family subsistence of the peasantry.

*Head Tax*

The amount of the head tax varied slightly for each of the three regions of Vietnam and was raised in each region from time to time.[45] In Tonkin, the tax of .50 piastres was raised to 2.5 piastres for the adult males on the village rolls and .4 piastres for the previously untaxed "*non-inscrites*" (*ngoai tich*). By 1920 all male citizens owed 2.5 piastres per annum except those employed by the colonial government. The tax in Annam by 1928 was also 2.5 piastres for all adult males. Following a tax

43. See Henri Lanoue, "L'Industrilisation de l'Indochine, 21 Nov. 1938," *Bulletin de la Société d'Études et d'Informations Économiques,* cited at length in Chesneaux, *Contribution à l'histoire,* chap. 9, and note 1, chap. 3, of this book for additional sources.
44. Nguyen Hong Giap, "La condition des paysans au Viet-Nam pendant le periode coloniale (1884–1945) à travers les chansons populaires" (thèse, 3e cycle, University of Paris, 1971), p. 47.
45. The amount of the head tax is in each case taken from the data in Long, "Before the August Revolution," chap. 3, pp. 59–80, except where otherwise cited.

revision in 1937 the rate appears to have been slightly over 4 piastres in
Tonkin, 3.95 in Annam, and 4.50 in Cochinchina. As in Burma, the tax
was due in cash by a given date.

These last cash figures naturally tell us very little about the head tax
burden unless related to real income. Using the 1937 paddy price
figures, average tenancy sizes, and average yields, Ngo Vinh Long estimates that the tax took at least 20 percent of the net income of both
sharecroppers and smallholders in Tonkin and Annam and 10 percent
of the after-rent income of the larger tenancies found in Cochinchina.[46]
Though the burden was obviously great, these figures seem excessive as
averages.[47] The main point, however, is that the concept of "average
burden" can again tell us relatively little. Head taxes represented, to
change the metaphor, a kind of fixed economic sandbar over which the
household economy had to navigate; if the water level was high due to
high prices and good crops, it represented no great obstacle; if the water
level was low, however, it might block passage altogether. The sandbar
becomes of consuming political interest in low water years when it may
jut above the surface. In this sense, the range of variation in water level is
more important than any average.

As important as the size of the tax was the new comprehensiveness
with which it was imposed. The flexibility in the traditional system lay
primarily in the village's capacity to understate its population and
thereby reduce its tax liability. When the French took over Annam and
Tonkin, at least two-thirds of the adult males of most villages had
escaped the tax rolls.[48] The introduction of the modern colonial state, its
censuses and fiscal agents, gradually whittled this administrative latitude
down to negligible proportions.[49] In many cases it meant that a substantial proportion of the village poor were for the first time effectively taxed
by the state. By requiring the head tax receipt as a form of personal

46. Ibid., pp. 61–62.
47. First, they include only rice production as income, while in some areas, particularly
Tonkin, secondary occupations might be as important as paddy-growing for much of the
agrarian population. Second, the use of 1937 rice prices as a basis of calculation is
representative of the 1930s, but hardly of the 1920s when prices were roughly twice as
high. Calculations from 1927 prices would thus reduce the average burden to about half
the level suggested by Long.
48. Long, p. 60.
49. A study of a fishing village on the southern Annam coast revealed an official
population that was 75 percent of the real population. This is a far smaller disparity than
Long reports for the traditional village, and there is even some reason to believe this
isolated village may have been able to escape the close official scrutiny given to villages in
the main rice growing areas. Gustave Langrand, *Vie sociale et religieuse en Annam* (Lille,
1945).

identification for a variety of purposes, the French made it increasingly difficult for the villager to avoid payment.

Colonial power at the village level not only assured the collection of the head tax, it assured overcollection. Backed by the colonial apparatus, local notables frequently collected more than was due and pocketed the difference. The rapaciousness of local officials was a constant administrative complaint—"All the information we have consistently underlines their [notables and mandarins] mercilessness and corruption"[50]—and abuses were the norm. The week before taxes had to be remitted was occasionally a period of outright terror. Belongings were seized and auctioned on the spot, recalcitrants were beaten, while others were jailed until their families came forward to pay the tax.[51] The gratuitous exactions of mandarins and notables left a rich vein of bitterness in the popular culture as the following folksong indicates.

> They ransack everywhere
> in the house and in the kitchen,
> they take all the baskets, large and small,
> they empty all the jars, huge or tiny . . .
> from those who have neither water buffalo or cattle
> they grab even the sickles and blunt knives.[52]

The mandarins themselves were experienced not so much as agents of the state but as plunderers.

> Oh my dear children, remember this saying:
> those who steal by night are the brigands,
> those who steal by day are the mandarins.[53]

It is impossible to guess the extent of overcollection, but the practice was widespread and pressed most heavily on modest villagers whose complaints would not be heard at higher levels.

Though the tax was, in absolute terms, slightly higher for the Cochinchinese peasant, it was far more of a subsistence threat to the poor Tonkinese or Annamite peasant, for whom even a small tax could provoke a family financial crisis. In Annam the problem was compounded. Not only was the Annamite generally the poorest peasant in Vietnam but, owing to his greater dependence on rainfall, his yields were the most variable in the nation. Thus, crises could almost be

50. Chesneaux, *Contribution à l'histoire de la nation vietnamienne*, p. 191.
51. See the texts by Nguyen Cong Hoan, Ngo Tat To, and Hoang Dao, translated by Long in "Before the August Revolution."
52. Nguyen Hong Giap, "La Condition des paysans," p. 116.
53. Ibid., p. 73.

predicted in a statistical sense whenever a crop failure in Annam or (somewhat rarer) in Tonkin raised the human cost of paying the tax to painful levels.

## Land Taxes

The form of the land tax in Vietnam was comparable to that in Burma. That is, it was a fixed tax assessed annually per hectare according to soil classification and it fostered the same inequities, taking far more in bad years and extracting as much proportionally from the marginal smallholder as from the large landowner. The tax was also, as in Burma, collected with increasing rigor. As cadastral surveys proceeded apace, there was less likelihood that small patches here and there would be overlooked. Finally, remissions that were inadequate in Burma were even more exceptional in Vietnam. Land rates seem to have been collected implacably even if crops were entirely lost.[54]

Working from average yield figures, Long has estimated that the land tax amounted to roughly 10 percent of the per hectare yield throughout Vietnam.[55] It therefore cut far more deeply into the subsistence resources of the smallholder in Tonkin or Annam, most of whom had much less than a hectare of land, than it did into the income of the 3–5 hectare smallholder in Cochinchina. In bad years, which were frequent in Annam, many villagers seem to have been forced to abandon their tiny plot of village land to meet tax arrears and to seek work on nearby plantations.[56] A Vietnamese novelist, Hoang Dao, described this process at work:

> Thus, in years of poor harvests, small landowners—who comprise the majority of the [landholding] population—are forced to sell their land at very low prices. The result is that rich people who lend money at high interest are gradually taking over all the land in the village.[57]

## Alcohol and Salt Monopolies

The place of rice wine in the consumption pattern of the Vietnamese peasantry was comparable to the role of beer in the life of the English working class. It was a major consumption item and most households either distilled a portion of their harvest themselves or, more likely, bought a comparable amount from nearby villages which specialized in

54. Gran, *Vietnam and the Capitalist Route*, chap. 7.

55. Long, "Before the August Revolution," Table 10, p. 68.

56. Yves Henry, L'Economie agricole, pp. 43–44.

57. Hoang Dao, *Mud and Stagnant Water*, quoted in Long, "Before the August Revolution," pp. 66–67.

its production. Beyond its social and nutritional significance, rice wine was also a central component of many ritual celebrations.

The French alcohol monopoly and tax in Vietnam thus represented a fixed charge on a major item of local consumption. Many Vietnamese distillers were forced out of business by the licensing of producers who were, for the most part, now French and Chinese. Shortly after 1900 the sale of rice wine was centralized as the colonial authorities purchased the output of licensed distilleries at a fixed price and then sold it to the public (through Chinese retailers). The price rise was enormous.[58] A litre of rice wine that had cost roughly 5 to 6 centimes at the time of conquest cost 29 centimes by 1906. In fiscal terms, however, the huge price increase failed to produce a comparable growth in revenue. It is certain that the discrepancy was due to a lively black market, taking advantage of the new profits to be made, rather than to any reduction in consumption. Determined to increase lagging sales receipts, colonial officials intensified the search for illegal distilling plants and offered generous rewards to local informers. At the same time they hit upon the ingenious device of forced sales which required each locality to purchase a volume of rice wine corresponding to what the officials assumed to be standard consumption patterns. In this way, the revenue from the alcohol monopoly was assured and could be enlarged by price increases or population growth.

Defiance of the alcohol monopoly was widespread and seemed to enjoy the "universal complicity of the population."[59] The origin of this defiance lies not only in the burdens of monopolistic prices and the profits available to black-marketeers, but also in the resentment provoked by this infringement of a traditional right. Like the Pennsylvania farmers who launched the Whiskey Rebellion when they were denied the right to make liquor from their own corn, the Vietnamese were indignant at having to pay an imposed price for a product that they considered inferior to what they could ferment locally.[60] To circumvent the state monopoly and buy from traditional suppliers represented the exercise of a popular traditional privilege. The monopoly was especially offensive to the smallholder as it amounted in practice to a second tax, over and above the land rates, on the rice he produced. It was naturally an even greater blow to the substantial artisan class that distilled rice wine, for it either deprived them of their livelihood or exposed them to fines and imprisonment.

58. Long, p. 63.

59. Pierre Gourou, *The Peasants of the Tonkin Delta* (New Haven: Human Relations Area Files Press, 1955), vol. 2, pp. 526–27.

60. Long, "Before the August Revolution," p. 64.

The enforcement of the unpopular rice wine monopoly was as provocative as its principle. Fiscal inspectors and informers scoured the countryside in their frequently successful search for illegal distillers. The offenders who were, from the villagers' perspective, quite within their rights, were hauled off to jail or saddled with ruinous fines. Long cites the case of a small hamlet in Thanh Hoa, Tonkin, whose entire rice lands were confiscated and sold when the inhabitants could not raise the fines imposed for local distilling.[61] Since the violation of the monopoly was more or less universal, its enforcement tended to be capricious or selective according to the motives of local officials. Prosecution frequently seems to have been pressed against factional enemies within the village while those allied with the dominant elite were left untouched.[62] For the cultivator the rice wine monopoly was at the same time a new and fixed financial burden, an abridgement of a natural right, and a cynical tool in the hands of local officials.

The practice of licensing and monopoly pricing extended in Vietnam, as in Burma, to the production and distribution of salt as well. Given the importance of salt in the Southeast Asian diet, the increase in price represented a substantial new burden. Not only was salt necessary to replace normal daily loss in such a hot climate, but salt was also a major ingredient in the preservation of dried fish and in fermented condiments (nuoc-mam in Vietnam, ngapi in Burma) that constituted staples in the local diet.

The imposition of the monopoly meant, in many areas, cutting off the local population from nearby sources of supply that had been far cheaper. They found that the price increased almost fivefold between 1892 and 1907. Although there was a black market in salt as in rice wine, this offered only limited and sporadic relief for the peasantry in the main rice districts. What is certain is that the cost of salt stirred as much resentment among the villagers as its infamous counterpart in France, la gabelle, had stirred among the French peasantry centuries earlier.

The salt tax was, in terms of its effect on peasant household expenses, virtually another head tax.[63] That is, since the annual family's consumption of salt was even more inelastic than their consumption of rice wine, consumption was not cut back appreciably even though the cost was raised; thus the salt revenue constituted a fixed charge against oscillating peasant incomes.[64]

61. Ibid., p. 65. The account is taken from the introduction to a novel by Hgô Tât Tô.
62. Gran, Vietnam and the Capitalist Road, p. 388.
63. Couper estimates that in Burma the average family consumed 3.6 lbs. of salt per annum which amounted to a tax payment of 1.5 rupees, or roughly one-third the amount they paid in head taxes. The Couper Report, p. 50.
64. I have not mentioned numerous other taxes that were either entirely new or raised

*Portents*

Well before the truly revolutionary explosion in 1930, tax protests, whether they took the form of traditional petitioning of mandarins or attacks on revenue officials, seem to have become a permanent feature of agrarian Vietnam.[65] They could be expected following poor harvests or in villages where officials were particularly rapacious. Not surprisingly, the largest outbreak prior to 1930 followed the 1907 credit crisis and the shortage of cash in Vietnam.[66] It began more or less peacefully in Central Vietnam (Annam) with peasants presenting grievances against excessive corvée labor and an increase in the head tax that had just been imposed. Over 300 gathered at Faï-Fo (near Tourane) to demand lighter head taxes and less corvée. Thousands of others gathered in Quang-Ngai, Annam, before the spring harvests and near Hué to voice similar complaints. Despite the efforts of nationalist mandarins to give the movements central direction, they retained their localist character. The *jacqueries* which developed here and there show clearly the direction of the peasant's anger. In Binh Dinh collectors of taxes and collaborating notables were attacked. Elsewhere revenue officials were also primary targets followed by mandarins and their secretaries. The repression that followed extinguished large-scale defiance until 1930 when an economic crisis once again made what might have seemed like small taxes unbearable.

---

to new levels and that also represented a charge, directly or indirectly, against subsistence commodities. Among them were taxes on *nuoc-mam* itself, on wood, carts, wells, ponds, boats, and fish.

65. Gran, *Vietnam and the Capitalist Road*, p. 215.

66. Details taken from Chesneaux, *Contribution a l'histoire*, chap. 10, and Marr, *Anti-Colonial Movements*, chap. 8.

# 5 The Depression Rebellions

The depression delivered the coup de grâce to an agrarian order already weakened by structural changes well before 1930. Signs of trouble ahead were not lacking. Colonial officials recognized that rice production per capita had been declining for some time, that the terms of tenancy were stiffening, that the indebtedness of smallholders and tenants was growing, and that taxes bore heavily on the peasantry in poor years. Concern, if not action, was widespread about the rising proportion of rural landless, while tax protests and rent boycotts were common following poor harvests.

The export boom of the 1920s, however, shielded the peasantry, and therefore the colonial regimes, from the full effects of the new structural threat to subsistence security. As long as the price of rice climbed, it meant that the cost in rice of fixed tax charges and debts was somewhat less burdensome. It meant that credit remained available as a short-term strategy. It meant, finally, that a variety of employment opportunities were created in agriculture, commerce, and industry and in the plantation sector that, to some extent, replaced the loss of traditional safety valves.

With the onset of the depression, all these buffers were removed and the menace to peasant subsistence routines assumed new proportions. One way of appreciating what happened is to examine the effect of the depression on the flows of cash income into and out of the household budget.[1] The incoming stream of cash income is largely derived from the sale of a portion of the crops (often in the form of a crop loan that is repaid in kind) or from wage labor within the village or in the outside economy. This stream of cash income is potentially very unstable, depending on the strength of the labor and primary commodity markets. During the depression the cash flow from the sale of rice, for example, was reduced to half or one-fourth its former size—or, alternatively, it took from two to four times the amount of rice to purchase the same amount of cash. For nonconsumable export crops, the reduction was much more dramatic. The flow of income from wage labor was similarly affected. Wage rates dropped by more than half and the volume of employment opportunities was reduced to a trickle, throwing a large portion of rural and urban wage laborers back on the slender subsistence resources of the village.

---

1. This conceptualization is taken from Boeke, *The Structure of the Netherlands Indian Economy*, chap V, who applies it to the village unit in Java.

The stream of cash flowing out of the household was more varied and, alas, more stable. On the one hand, there were the subsistence commodities such as cloth, kerosene, or wood (if not available locally), salt, fish, and occasionally vegetables. The prices of such goods, with the important exception of salt, did tend to decline in proportion with the drop in rice prices. On the other hand, there were the relentless major claims of head taxes, land rates, debts, and land rent which either remained unchanged or declined only slightly.[2]

The crushing effect of the depression on the income of tenants is strikingly evident from the typical case, below, of a family budget, taken from the Settlement Report of Insein, Lower Burma, in 1930.[3] If anything, it understates the peasants' difficulties inasmuch as the price of rice fell much further by 1934. The figures of tenant income and

|  | Revenue | Expenses |
|---|---|---|
| Gross value of produce of 33.44 acres at 41 baskets per acre at price of Rs 110 per 100 baskets | 1,488 | |
| Deduct: cost of cultivation paid in kind at Rs 14.48 per acre | | 478 |
| Deduct: advance from landlord of Rs 150 at 2% per month for 8 months (need 5.23 per acre in cash cultivation costs), thus 5.23 × 33.44 | | 174 |
| Deduct: Repayment of *sabape* loan (Rs 25 given in cash and paid back with interest in baskets of paddy) | | 55 |
| Deduct: Rent at Rs 15.51 per acre or 35% | | 512 |
| Deduct: Seed grain set aside for next planting at 3/4 basket per acre | | 27 |
| | 1,488 | 1,246 |
| Balance | 242 | |

2. The number of French civil officials had doubled between 1911 and 1925 and the general budget of the colony had grown more than twofold from 43 million piastres in 1914 to 88 million piastres in 1927. Chesneaux, *Contribution à l'histoire de la nation vietnamienne*, p. 195.

3. *Report of the Land and Agriculture Committee*, Part I, pp. 10–11.

expenses are reported for a large tenancy of 33.44 acres and are typical of the results collected from a sample of 107 tenants. No allowance has yet been made for the subsistence needs of the extended cultivating family which the settlement officer figured as follows:

|                                        | Rupees |
|----------------------------------------|--------|
| 2 men at Rs 5.75 each per month        | 138    |
| 2 women at Rs 5 each per month         | 120    |
| 2 children at Rs 2.50 each per month   | 60     |
|                                        | 318    |
| Deduct balance                         | 242    |
| Subsistence deficit                    | −76    |

Only the minimal subsistence expenses have been calculated here. If we were to add the expenses for clothing, repairs to the house, tools, ceremonial and religious outlays, and cash consumption items (chillies, matches, kerosene, *ngapi*), the deficit would be far larger. It is nonetheless abundantly clear that the tenancy system no longer met the subsistence needs of the rural population

The collapse of the commodity and labor markets, affecting the income side of the household ledger, was an impersonal event for which it was difficult to find a guilty party.[4] The outside claimants for this reduced income, by contrast, were hardly impersonal; they were extra-village moneylenders, landowners, and the state.[5] Their demands, though unchanged in absolute terms, were now pressed on a peasantry that was virtually without resources. To the extent that they extracted what was owed them—from a peasantry with its back to the wall—to that extent they lost whatever slim claim they might have had to compliance and risked provoking the resistance of a peasantry defending its right to subsistence.

The "scissors crisis" of agrarian income is reflected in painful detail for Lower Burma in the reports of settlement officers. The illustration in Table 6 is of a small landowner of 100 acres who let the land at a rent of

4. Except insofar as most populations see the government in particular and elites in general as responsible for maintaining an order that provides physical security and customary subsistence patterns. In this sense, the economic crisis may subjectively have represented a loss of the "mandate of heaven" for the colonial regime even though it was hardly directly responsible. Precolonial states, it should be recalled, *did* intervene to control market forces and prevent the export of grain—steps that the colonial regimes refused to take. See Adas, *The Burma Delta*, p. 23, and James C. Ingram, *Economic Change in Thailand*, 2nd ed. (Stanford: Stanford University Press, 1971), chaps. 1–3.

5. In the case of landowners this was less true for Upper Burma, Tonkin, and Annam where many of them remained within the village.

Table 6. Fluctuation in Proceeds, Net Income, and Land Revenue Burden, 1924–1937

| Year | Rent in baskets | Gross proceeds, rupees | Land revenue | Net income | Percentage of land revenue to gross proceeds | Percentage increase of land revenue |
|---|---|---|---|---|---|---|
| 1924–25 | 1,200 | 2,400 | 350 | 2,050 | 14.6 | Normal |
| 1931–32 | 800 | 450 | 300 | 150 | 66.6 | 356.2% of normal |
| 1936–37 | 1,000 | 1,000 | 333 | 668 | 33.4 | 129.4% of normal |

12 baskets per acre in 1924-25, 8 baskets per acre in 1931-32, and 10 baskets per acre in 1936-37.[6] One may readily infer the situation of both tenants and smallholders from the difficulties of this landlord. For the smallholder the effective increase in the burden of land revenue was enormous and more than wiped out his profits. For the tenant, if we assume stable yields, the decline in gross cash income due to the fall in rice prices from 1924 to 1931 was of the same order as the decline in gross cash income for the landowner—that is, 81 percent.[7] Only a small portion of tenants received any remissions at all, and those were trivial in comparison with the decline in rice prices.[8]

The state, however, was above all attentive to its own needs. In Hanth-awaddy District during the same period, the settlement officer proposed new rates that would have reduced the revenue yield by 19½ percent and thereby reduced, by a small fraction, the new inequities. His recommendations were rejected in favor of a small *increase* in land rates in order to, as officials put it, "reduce, so far as possible, the heavy fall in revenue demand which the decreased value of the crop has made inevitable."[9] The priorities of the colonial state were crystal clear.

Much the same logic prevailed in Vietnam. For Cochinchina, for example, the relative burden of the body tax and land rates may be roughly gauged by plotting collections against the fall in paddy prices from 1919 through 1934 (see Figure 3). The year 1919 is taken as a base year of 100 and the movements of tax collections and prices are computed on that basis. The decline of paddy market may be taken as a rough indication of the tenant's cash position and thus the distance between paddy prices and the tax receipts represents something of the magnitude of their growing real claim on peasant income. Taken together, the trend lines in Figure 3 show both the relative stability of the state's tax claim as compared to the health of the rural economy and the glaring contrast between income and fiscal demands in the depression. If anything, the contrast understates the difficulties of the cultivator for he lost virtually all of his other opportunities to raise cash, whether from minor cash crops or from casual wage labor.

Despite the situation of the cultivator, the landowner and the state pressed their claims on him for at least two reasons. First, the claimants themselves were in trouble. Landowners and moneylenders (often the same people) were commonly in debt and courted ruin themselves

6. *Revision Settlement of Bassein,* excerpt from "Memorandum by Messrs. Dawson's Bank, Ltd.," p. 11.

7. Ibid.

8. Ibid., p. 49.

9. *Third Revision Settlement of Hanthawaddy,* p. 12.

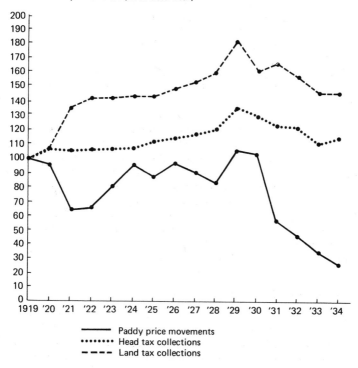

Figure 3. Cochinchina: Paddy Price, Head Tax and Land Tax Revenue, 1919–1934 (1919 Base Year)

——— Paddy price movements
••••••• Head tax collections
– – – – Land tax collections

*Source.* Figure 3 was computed from the following sources: Paddy prices, *Annuaire Statistique de l'Indochine 1941–43,* p. 305; tax data, J. Boyer, "Les impots directs en Indochine," *Revue indochinoise juridique et économique* 7 (1939), 497, 492. The head tax figures include only the portion allocated to the general budget for Cochinchina; an amount roughly three times as large went for local and provincial budgets.

unless they could collect from their tenants and debtors (often the same people as well). The state, for its part, had lost a great deal of its revenue from excise taxes and customs duties and thus risked having to dismiss a large portion of its personnel and to dismantle much of the institutional framework that had developed over three decades. Thus the situation became something of a "zero-sum" struggle for survival between the state and the landholding-moneylending class on one hand and the peasantry on the other. Second, the colonial state had the institutional and coercive means both to enforce its claim to revenue and to enforce the contractual rights of creditors and landowners.

The exact configuration of the pressure on peasant subsistence varied by region. In Tonkin, Annam, and Upper Burma where sharecropping was common, and where the small class of rural workers were often paid in kind, the collapse of the cash economy was somewhat less catastrophic. The tenant or laborer still received the same proportion of the harvest or the same amount of rice. In these poor subsistence areas the problem of taxes was by far the dominant one. By contrast, in somewhat richer, more commercialized areas of Lower Burma and Cochinchina where debts and fixed (or even cash) rents were more common, the claims of the landowning-creditor strata (particularly when they were also foreigners) stirred almost as much resentment as the tax load. Overall the tax issue dominated. The head tax was collected from all, often at the same time, while the rent and debts were more variable from region to region and from owner to owner.

## Cochinchina: "La Terreur Rouge"[10]

The chronological link between the drop in the price of rice and expressions of peasant resistance is striking. In April 1930 the price began its headlong plunge, and by the beginning of May the colonial government was faced with an unprecedented rash of protests and violence in Cochinchina and Annam.[11]

The depression meant an unavoidable loss of revenue from indirect taxes, notably customs duties, which formed a large share of Cochinchina's annual revenue. Thus, total tax receipts fell from 22.5 million

10. The term used to describe the unrest and rebellion in Cochinchina and Annam in 1930–31.

11. For the beginnings of rural unrest, see Annex 15, "Relevé des manifestations de masse provoquées ou organisées par le P.C.I. du 1er mai 1930 au 31 Décembre, 1931," in Gouvernement Générale de l'Indochine, Direction des Affaires Politiques et de la Sûreté Générale, *Contribution à l'histoire des movements politiques de l'Indochine Française*, vol. 4, *Le Parti Communiste Indochinois (1925–1933)*.

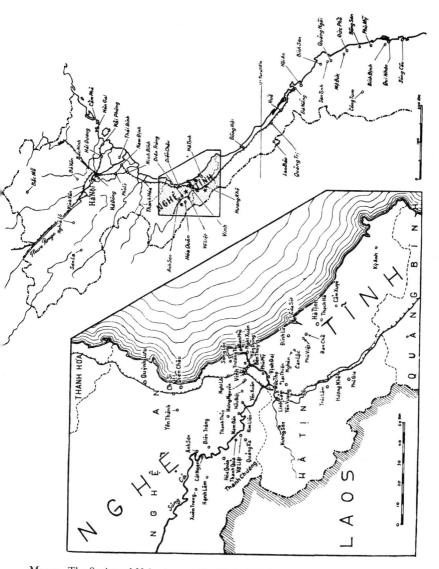

Map 3    The Soviets of Nghe-An and Ha-Tinh, 1930-31. Source: Adapted from Tran Huy Lieu, *Les Soviets du Nghe-Tinh de 1930-31 au Viet-Nam* (Hanoi: Editions en Langues Etrangères, 1960). Used by permission.

piastres in 1929 to 21.4 million in 1930 and to 17.3 million in 1931.[12] To minimize the loss, colonial officials leaned more heavily on the collection of head taxes (roughly seven piastres per adult male) which were not vulnerable to the level of economic activity. Despite growing unemployment, lower wages, the disappearance of credit, and floods in the trans-Bassac region, the colony actually managed to raise its 1931 head tax receipts by 70,000 piastres over the previous year. The cold logic of the colonial fiscal system thus placed a growing reliance on the most regressive form of taxation at precisely the moment when the poorest taxpayers were least able to part with the money.

Colonial officials were not unaware that both fixed land rates and fixed head taxes worked an enormous hardship on poor cultivators in bad years. Like their English counterparts in Burma, however, they also appreciated that, however oppressive fixed taxes were, they were nonetheless the most stable, regular form of colonial revenue. A proposal to tax only wealthier classes and eliminate the *impôt personnel* was explicitly rejected in 1932 by a financial advisor who pointed out correctly that it would mean a large loss of revenue since the poor were so much more numerous than the rich.[13] Efforts to tie the land rates to the price of paddy and hence to the ability of smallholders to pay was rejected for identical reasons. As a financial advisor noted, "The local administration [Cochinchina] was afraid of the *instability* of the yield of such an important tax."[14] Given the choice between guaranteeing its income or that of its subject population, the colonial regime naturally preferred the former.

At tax time, forced auctions of peasant belongings and animals were more frequent as local notables and mandarins sought to raise the sum for which they were held responsible. More peasants were jailed or beaten until they produced the required amount. It was at this time as

12. These data and much of the following information on Cochinchina and Annam come from documents contained in the *Archives d'Outre Mer* in Paris, classified under *Indochine: Nouveaux Fonds* by carton and dossier number. Hereafter, all such citations include the notation *A.O.M. Indochine NF,* followed by two numbers that refer to the carton and dossier, respectively. These budget figures and those immediately below for head tax receipts are taken from "Rapport fait par M. Moretti concernant la situation financière du budget local, Cochinchine, 28 May 1932," pp. 10–21, *A.O.M. Indochine NF:* 285–2490.

13. "Rapport fait par M. Moretti concernant le réglementation des impôt directs au Tonkin, 18 February 1932," p. 27, *A.O.M. Indochine NF:* 285–2490. The justice of the capitation tax was supported by another official in the same report on the basis that it represented a tax on the manifest benefits of living in an "organized society" from which all profited. Ibid., p. 23.

14. "Rapport fait par M. Moretti concernant la situation financière du budget local, Cochinchine, 28 May 1932," p. 30, *A.O.M. Indochine NF:* 285–2490.

well that many marginal smallholders fell into the tenant or laborer class as they were forced to sell their paddy or garden land.[15] Some administrators seized a portion of the tenant's or smallholder's crop in lieu of the head tax.[16] The new levels of coercion hardly lend themselves to quantitative treatment, particularly since many abuses were never officially recorded. Judging by newspaper reports and by the volume of peasant action, however, tax collection in the countryside became more and more a matter of threats and violence.[17]

> There is no need to disguise the fact that, nevertheless, *the collection of these taxes is due to the direct action of the province chiefs and their militia*. The means of coercion which they possess evidently account for much of the satisfying results they achieve, and it must not be concluded from the collections that the burden of taxes is easily borne by the population.[18]

The cost of attempting to maintain the same volume of head taxes from a rural population even more penurious than usual was the direct resort to force.

The tax claim of the state in Cochinchina had implications for the peasant's relation to the landowner as well as to the state. In many of the newly settled provinces it had been customary for the large landowner to advance his tenants the cash for their head tax in addition to production costs. The decline in the rice price, however, touched off a far greater decline in his net income while he also faced his anxious creditors and land taxes that now loomed larger. As a result, he put an abrupt end to such advances. The tax squeeze, in this sense, not only pitted the cultivator against the state, but also precipitated a deepening crisis in landlord-tenant relations. At a minimum, landlords refused to provide working capital or loans; "others demonstrated a growing intransigence; trapped themselves, they pressured their tenants to the maximum. Their behavior was the negation of the solidarity with the cultivator which they proclaimed or even of a working complementarity."[19] Thus assailed by taxes on the one hand and desperate landlords on the other, peasants fought what amounted to a defensive war on two fronts.

When they could, peasants avoided paying taxes. The popular at-

15. Long, *Before the Revolution*, especially the translations of Hoang Dao and Hguyen Cong Hoan, pp. 179–218.

16. Gran, *Vietnam and the Capitalist Road*, p. 412.

17. See *La Tribune indochinoise, La Lutte*, and *Le Paysan de Cochinchine* in the period May through August 1930.

18. Bernard, *Le Problème économique indochinois*, p. 160, emphasis added.

19. Brocheux, "Grands propriétaires," p. 71.

titude seemed to reflect the subsistence ethic—the notion that claims to resources were legitimate, if at all, only after local subsistence needs were satisfied. It was for this reason, presumably, that *"une véritable mystique de non-paiement"* swept the countryside and Vietnamese refused to pay taxes or debts *"parce que c'était la crise."* [20] This simple remedy was undoubtedly successful for some, because the number who paid their head tax in fact declined by 20 percent.[21] What is striking, however, is not that the colonial state let 20 percent of its subjects slip through its net but that it managed to collect from the other 80 percent.

As for the majority who could not escape paying, or suffering the consequences of default, their response was often more active. First, at what we might call the prepolitical level, there was a great deal of self-help outside the law. Tenants and laborers often confiscated the major part of the crop before the harvest or attacked the granaries of local landowners. Attempts to stop them met stiff resistance—so much so, that many landowners left home each night for nearby towns where they could sleep under the protection of the colonial militia, a pattern that was to become a way of life after 1945.[22] Banditry and theft, an integral part of Cochinchina's frontier history, were increasingly common. In a portion of Soc-Trang which had also suffered crop losses, bands of 50 to 100 peasants attacked junks taking rice from their region and divided it among themselves.[23] This case, and many others, seem clearly to merit the label of *social* banditry. That is, such acts were popular inasmuch as they removed rice from the wealthy and redistributed it to the poor, and they corresponded with the notion that local production must, above all, feed the local population.

Explicitly political acts, whether formal protests or violence, were also increasingly common. Police records list 54 mass demonstrations, marches, or attacks between May 1930 and June 1931, most of them in the countryside. The official descriptions often speak vaguely of *"un rassemblement séditieux,"* or, more often, of simply *"un rassemblement de 600 indigènes."* [24] Two characteristics of these events are clear. First, they were truly mass actions rarely involving fewer than 200 people and occasionally as many as 1,000 to 2,000. Second, and most important, the majority of actions reported involved either a protest of, or a direct attack on, the tax system of the colonial state. Demonstrations in the

20. Melin, *L'Endettement agraire,* p. 3.

21. Gran, *Vietnam and the Capitalist Road,* p. 412.

22. *Le Parti Communiste Indochinois* (1925–1933), *Documents,* vol. 4, *Contribution à l'histoire des mouvements politiques de l'Indochine Française* (Hanoi, 1924), p. 32.

23. Chesneaux, *Contribution à l'histoire,* p. 215.

24. *Le Parti Communiste Indochinois (1925–1933),* Annexe 15, pp. 124–28.

initial month often took the form of mass presentations of tax grievances directly to authorities. Both the form and content of these gatherings were traditional and outwardly deferential. For example:

> 2nd May, 1930—A gathering of 200 inhabitants in front of the district office of Cho-Moi (Long-Xuyen province) who demand a delay for paying their tax. The demonstrators disperse after being assured that their request will be transmitted to higher authority.[25]

Elsewhere in Long Xuyen, in Sadec, in Cantho, and in Cholon, peasants gathered at district headquarters to demand a reduction in the tax or a delay in its collection.[26] On a few occasions, at least, it appears that petitions for delays were granted on the spot, thus encouraging similar demands for leniency in neighboring districts. Before long the protesters began calling for a reduction of head taxes or their abolition. Demands for the distribution of paddy stocks held by large landlords, an end to market taxes, the return of land confiscated by fraud, and the imposition of controls on rice prices were also heard. The head tax, however, was the central unifying issue. At this stage the crowds were typically peaceful and generally dispersed after gaining an official hearing.

As their financial plight worsened and as tax relief seemed remote, peasants turned to violent direct action. Their actions and objectives, though spread over several provinces and covering nearly a year, were remarkably similar. If the militia did not prevent them, the angry peasants headed straight for the village or district office, which they destroyed together with all its records. The most common entries in the police record thus read, *"déstruction des archives," "incendie de la maison communale," "pillage de la maison communale," "la mise à sac de la maison communale," "les archives sont brulées."* Lacking the means to attack the police and militia of the colonial regime, the peasantry assaulted its administrative presence. That administrative presence, within the village was typically the *maison communale* where the records for the head tax, the land tax, and the corvée were kept. By destroying those records, peasants hoped to destroy the state; by destroying the state, they hoped to destroy taxes. Thus the disturbances in Cochinchina passed from deferential petitioning in the tradition of Confucianism to an insurrection along anarchist lines.

The leadership of the fledgling Communist Party was instrumental in

25. Ibid., p. 124.
26. *Troubles en Cochinchine, mai-juin 1930, Le Rapport,* pp. 3–20, and *Les Faits,* pp. 4–5, *A.O.M. Indochine NF:* 327–2641.

organizing many of the larger peasant demonstrations in the initial period of unrest, although the destruction of land and tax records was virtually a peasant tradition in colonial Vietnam.

> the communists plundered and systematically destroyed the communal buildings in many provinces of N. Annam and in Cochinchina. In destroying the records of the village, the civil registers, survey records, tax rolls, etc., they sought to give the peasant the illusion that the Communist party was liberating him from taxes and service.[27]

Later on, however, the insurrections took on even more autonomous features as the well-informed French police rounded up much of the party cadre. The absence of coordinated political leadership is perhaps what gave the unrest in Cochinchina a sporadic, localist character and helps explain why it was so easily crushed. What is critical for our purpose, however, is that even when party cadres were instrumental in organizing mass action, they were obliged to organize that action around the concrete grievances of rural cultivators. Those grievances led directly to demands for an end to taxes and for the seizure and distribution of rice from the landlords' granaries.[28] While the party may have lent a certain coherence to the initial protests, it hardly needed to instruct peasants about the objects of their anger.

Following the repressive campaign by French authorities, an uneasy calm returned to the countryside. The calm was deceptive for, on the heels of the election of the Blum government in France in 1936, when political action again seemed possible, new disturbances broke out. In this second stage of protest the terms of tenancy were attacked directly. Peasants refused to pay rents, refused to clear out when evicted by landlords, and, when they felt that land which they had cleared had been taken from them by legal manipulation, they reoccupied it. The form of the protest is instructive for it reveals the peasant conception of what an equitable tenancy contract would involve.

> Others only agree to hand over to the landlord half of the remaining paddy after deducting the amount they consider indispensable for their nourishment and that of their family during the coming year, the seed paddy for the coming planting season, clothing and

27. *Le Parti Communiste Indochinois (1925–1933),* p. 32.

28. For the growing rural proletariat of Cochinchina the issues were somewhat different. Thus, workers at the notorious Michelin rubber plantation at Dau Tieng, Thudaumot, demonstrated when they found that, owing to the low price of rubber, their wages would be cut along with their rice ration. See "Incidents à Michelin," 10 février 1930, *A.O.M. Indochine NF:* 225–1839.

maintenance for the members of their families and their dependents, and, finally, the food for their plow animals.[29]

Here is a movement which, like the precapitalist food riots described by
Eric Rudé, displays an elaborate and discriminating sense of equity and
rights.[30] Despite a certain amount of renewed effort by colonial officials to
pass tenancy legislation and warnings to large landowners to mend their
ways, the same agrarian relations remained in force with portentous
implications for southern Vietnam's postwar history.

## THE SOVIETS OF NGHE-AN AND HA-TINH

Events in the northern Annam provinces of Nghe-An and Ha-Tinh
began at almost precisely the same time and escalated in roughly the
same manner as they had in Cochinchina. The main difference was that
the rebels in Nghe-An and Ha-Tinh actually succeeded in taking power.
By the end of September they had taken over the most populated
sections of Nghe-An and neighboring districts in Ha-Tinh. They established what amounted to autonomous village republics and held out
against tremendous military and economic pressure for as long as nine
months until finally crushed.

Roughly 2,000 Vietnamese were killed before the rebellion was over;
most of them fell in the course of large demonstrations that were
bombed or fired upon by colonial forces. For a brief moment, however,
the rebels of Nghe-An and Ha-Tinh actually managed to create an
agrarian order that reflected their values. This tragic experience vividly
illustrated what peasants hated most in the colonial order and the kind
of society they wished to recover.[31]

### The Vulnerability and Explosiveness of Northern Annam

In most respects, the peasantry of Northern Annam was even more
poorly equipped to survive the financial rigors of the depression than
the peasantry of Cochinchina. Inhabiting the poorest region of the

29. Brocheux, "Grands propriétaires," p. 69.

30. Eric Rudé, *The Crowd in History: A Study of Popular Disturbances in France and England
1730–1848* (New York: Wiley, 1964).

31. A wealth of important data on this revolt was gathered by La Commission d'enquête
sur les evenements du Nord Annam, hereafter referred to as the Morché Commission,
after its chairman. The report and all the evidence gathered by the Commission are
available in the *Archives d'Outre Mer, Indochine Nouveaux Fonds*. I have also found the study
by Tran Huy Lieu, *Les Soviets du Nghe-Tinh de 1930–31 au Viet-Nam* (Hanoi: Foreign
Languages Pubiishing House, 1960), very informative, although the evidence seems to me
to indicate a more modest role for the Communist Party than he would permit. See also
one party militant's account, "A Highlight of the Movement," by Hguyen Duy Trinh in *In
the Enemy's Net: Memoirs from the Revolution* (Hanoi: Foreign Language Publishing House,
1962), pp. 9–42.

colony in the narrow lowlands between the sea and the mountains, the Annamese were on a permanent tightrope just above the subsistence level. The caloric value of their diet was the lowest in the country.[32] Even in a good year Annam exported no grain and in bad years the population was fed from the surplus of Cochinchina or Tonkin.

Within this ensemble of dearth, the provinces of Nghe-An and Ha-Tinh were cursed with the most undependable rainfall and hence the most undependable harvests in Annam.[33] It is this combination of marginal subsistence agriculture together with a vulnerability to ecological disaster that made Nghe-Tinh such a volatile region. Hunger was a normal part of provincial life, as an average of three out of six harvests were partly or entirely lost. When one poor harvest came on the heels of another, hunger passed into famine. "In 1906 and 1907," the Director of Agricultural Services recalled, "I saw people dying of hunger on the roads and villages fighting one another to dig up potatoes."[34] An attempted rebellion led by dissident scholars (*lettrés*) in the midst of this famine was, in fact, a lineal ancestor of the 1930-31 revolt. As recently as 1925, the failure of two successive harvests had provoked another famine in Ha-Tinh. "The misery was so bad five years ago that I found people dead from hunger along the roads in Ha-Tinh province."[35] Life was not simply hard in the Nghe-Tinh area; it was perilous. Anyone over 30 could recall at least two occasions when physical survival itself was at stake.

Nghe-Tinh had a continuous historical reputation for dissidence and revolt that extended well back before French control. Its rugged geography made it a natural home for rebellion, while a high concentration of local scholars and dynastic pretenders provided a ready leadership. In this same area in 1874, a celebrated revolt of scholar-gentry broke out against the French. Two of its leaders were, in fact, from Thanh Chuong district of Nghe-An which was to play a leading role in the 1930 uprising.[36] The concentration of dissident elites in this region is perhaps the result of a long tradition of settlement by mandarin families hoping to take advantage of the Nghe-An regional examination site.

32. Henry, *Economie agricole*, pp. 40–48.

33. Castagnol, "Monographie agricole de la Province de Nghe An," *Bulletin Economique de l'Indochine* 33° (Novembre 1930-B), 823, 828, *A.O.M. Indochine NF:* 336–3694. See also Gourou, Le Sol en Indochine, pp. 77–78, 114, and the enormous variation in rainfall which he reports.

34. "Déclaration de M. Gilbert," Directeur des Services Agricole, to Morché Commission, 18 July 1931, *A.O.M. Indochine NF:* 332–2684, *Dossier de Hué.*

35. "Déclaration de M. Cotin," industrialist, to Morché Commission, *A.O.M. Indochine NF:* 333–2689.

36. Woodside, *Community and Revolution*, p. 231.

From the French point of view, dissidence in Nghe-Tinh was not only an elite tradition but a popular custom as well. Colonial officials were tempted to see rebelliousness as an inherited feature of regional character. "The populations of Nghe-An, Ha-Tinh, and Quang Ngai have always shown themselves to be particularly hostile to the established authority."[37] Their "love of plotting" was noted as was their "proud and undisciplined character."[38] An ex-public works official, who had spent 20 years in Tonkin and 12 in Annam, contrasted the local inhabitants' behavior with that of the more docile Tonkinese: "They are stubborn, arrogant, and crafty. One remark to a coolie and all the others walk off the construction site."[39]

The region of Nghe-Tinh was thus politically explosive for a variety of reasons. Its physical isolation from the great centers of population had always posed severe problems of political control. Its distinct culture and scholarly tradition supplied an indigenous leadership that was resistant to outside interference. Finally, and most important, its poverty and capricious climate made for a turbulent population that had every reason to defy claims on its tenuous subsistence.

## Narrowing the Margin

The claims on the income of the Nghe-Tinh peasantry tended to increase throughout the early twentieth century despite the penury and instability of its economy. The percentage of landless grew and the terms of tenancy stiffened. Already by the 1920s many of Northern Annam's dwarf-sized tenancies could no longer provide a subsistence even in good years, and much of the rural population took on secondary occupations such as woodcutting, plantation labor, and petty trade to make ends meet.[40] Communal land that had once relieved the plight of the village poor had fallen increasingly into the hands of local notables and mandarins. The most onerous form of taxation, the head tax or *impôt personnel*, had gradually risen and fewer and fewer villagers managed to keep their names off the village tax rolls. Actual collections, moreover, were substantially higher than the law required, because of the extortion of mandarins, notables, and their subordinates. As the take from the

37. *Rapport de la Commission d'enquête sur les evenements du Nord Annam* (Morché Commission Report), p. 54, *A.O.M. Indochine NF:* 212–1597.

38. *Morché Commission Report*, p. 54.

39. "Déclaration de M. Dulcé," Municipal Counselor of Vinh, to Morché Commission, 27 June 1931, *A.O.M. Indochine NF:* 333–2686.

40. "Given the proximity of the Annamite range, many of them find, in the mountains, several resources which allow them to live during periods of crises." Henry, *Economie agricole*, p. 46.

rural population grew and rigidified, the structural probability of conflict was magnified. A bad crop or two would be enough to spark a crisis.

## Landowners and Rural Poor

Demographic pressure on the land in Nghe-An, Ha-Tinh, and Quang Ngai (also touched by the revolt) amounted to a case study in Malthusian economics. Not only were crop yields small and uncertain but the amount of rice land per capita (.144, .153, and .150 hectares for the three provinces, respectively) were among the very lowest of the sixteen provinces of Annam.[41] In Nghe-An, nearly three-quarters of those who owned land had *less* than half a hectare and their *average* holding must have been no more than one-fourth of a hectare (or roughly one-half acre). Most of this class, unable to subsist on its holdings alone, was obliged to sharecrop or work for wages on the land of others. In Ha-Tinh marginal smallholders also predominated (65 percent) and faced the same options.

As is evident from Table 7, large landowners constituted a very small portion of the rural population. Their economic and social importance, however, was enormous. They employed the bulk of the rural wage labor and let many tenancies. They frequently controlled much more land than they owned directly, by virtue of the debts owed them by smallholders. Finally, there is some reason to believe that the scattering of holdings and the deceptive registration of titles may have concealed a greater concentration of ownership than the official figures indicate.[42]

Table 7. Distribution of Land in Nghe-An and Ha-Tinh[43]

| | *Size of holding in hectares* | | | | | |
| --- | --- | --- | --- | --- | --- | --- |
| | *0–.5* | *.5–2.5* | *2.5–5* | *5–25* | *25–50* | *50 & over* |
| *Nghe-An* | | | | | | |
| No. of owners | 74,650 | 21,676 | 4,356 | 1,082 | 90 | 8 |
| % of owners | 73.2 | 21.3 | 4.3 | 1.1 | .09 | .007 |
| *Ha-Tinh* | | | | | | |
| No. of owners | 46,924 | 19,035 | 4,462 | 1,070 | 20 | 6 |
| % of owners | 65.6 | 26.6 | 6.2 | 1.5 | .02 | .008 |

41. Henry, *Economie agricole*, p. 23.

42. Castagnol, "Monographie agricole de la Province de Nghe An," p. 838, notes, "While the morselization of landholding is very pronounced, there exists a fairly large proportion of large landowners, but their lands are made up of scattered parcels."

43. Ibid., pp. 123, 124.

Despite Northern Annam's reputation as a land of marginal small-holders, the impact of population growth, the seizure of communal land, and agrarian indebtedness had created a large class of landless. This was most strikingly the case in the areas of Nghe-An (Nam Dan, Anh Son, and Thanh Chuong) bordering the Song Ca river which constituted the heartland of the rebellion. In Nam Dan, for example, 90 percent of the families had no land whatever. In Thanh Chuong the proportion of landless had reached 60 percent.[44] The declarations made before the Commission of Inquiry into the revolt emphasize the precarious subsistence of this class:

> The soil is poor. The villages have little communal land. The poor people are at the mercy of the rich landowners who exploit them without pity.[45]

> They [the landless] rent their services to the rich. They live from hand to mouth and die of hunger in periods of scarcity.[46]

The desperate condition of the landless, as implied above, resulted not simply from their poverty but from increasingly stiff terms of tenancy and farm labor. Although the link between landowner and tenant or laborer was not quite the cash nexus it had become in Cochinchina, it was clearly moving in that direction. Even a small shift in that direction was an immediate threat to the livelihood of the Annamite cultivator. The wages of farm laborers, for example, varied less and less with the price of rice and other necessities.[47] "There is no doubt that the land-owners of Annam are unreasonably inflexible with the workers whom they employ and to whom they allow a salary barely sufficient to keep them alive."[48] Sharecroppers, for their part, were only rarely given a larger share of the harvest following a poor crop. "The peasant who toils hard must give half his crop to the rich landowner. This is tolerable when the harvest is good. But when it is bad, it is misery."[49] Whatever protective

44. For Nam Dan, see "Déclaration de Tran Huu Sa," Provincial Counselor of Nam Dan, *A.O.M. Indochine NF:* 333–2686, *Dossier de Vinh.* For Thanh Chuong, "Déclaration de Dinh Bat Truong," provincial counselor of Thanh Chuong, *A.O.M. Indochine NF:* 333–2686.

45. "Déclaration de Nguyen Van Tinh," retired mandarin, *A.O.M. Indochine NF:* 334–2689, *Dossier de Vinh,* Pièces Annexes.

46. "Déclaration de Nguyen Duc Ly," *A.O.M. Indochine NF:* 333–2686.

47. Ibid., p. 3. "The daily worker's wage is not proportional to the price of food commodities."

48. *Morché Commission Report,* p. 51, *A.O.M. Indochine NF:* 212–1597.

49. "Déclaration de Nguyen Luong Binh," Sub-district chief of Son Tinh, Quang Ngai, *A.O.M. Indochine NF:* 335–2691, *Dossier de Quang Ngai,* p. 2. Judging from the folk songs of

value traditional forms of tenancy and labor had once provided were
fast disappearing.

The steady loss of communal land to corrupt mandarins and village
notables was eliminating another traditional form of social insurance.
Villages that had held as much as 50 percent of their land in common a
few decades ago had lost most of it to private ownership.[50] A candid
explanation was given by the French Résident Supérieur in Annam, Le
Fol, for his helplessness before this land grab:

> There are abuses which belong in the category of those committed
> by the natives against their own compatriots. There is no doubt that
> the notables abuse their power in order to help themselves to the
> lion's share of communal property. The government doesn't inter-
> vene in the commune which is the Annamite social unit. *We have
> these alternatives: either to let the notables be and the revolutionary leaders
> will exploit us for the abuses for which the notables are responsible, or
> intervene and we will then guarantee ourselves the hostility of the well-to-do
> population, the only group which is actually interested in the maintenance of
> order.* I believe for that reason it is preferable not to intervene in the
> redivision of communal rice land.[51]

This is as good a description as one could hope for of the dilemma
confronting the colonial regime at the village level, and of the choices
consciously made.

*Taxes*

The perennial deficit of Annam was one of the major fiscal headaches
of colonial governors. Taxes barely sufficed to meet the salary payroll
alone in the protectorate, which was kept afloat by grants and loans from
Cochinchina and France. As a result the Resident of France at Hué was
under unremitting pressure to raise local revenue yields and to pare
expenses to the bone.

Raising taxes in Annam meant, above all, raising the capitation and
land rates. These two measures were not only among the most regressive
features of the colonial fiscal regime but they accounted for the lion's

---

the region and from what happened elsewhere, it appears that the rich stopped lending
money in 1930 as well. Nguyen Hong Giap, *La Condition des paysans,* p. 40.

50. For the disappearance of local common lands, see the various declarations in *A.O.M.
Indochine NF:* 333–2686, and the "Déclaration de Nguyen Duc Ly," Member of the
People's Chamber of Representatives for Nghe An, in ibid.

51. "Déclaration de M. Le Fol," 6 June 1931, *A.O.M. Indochine NF:* 332–2684, *Dossier de
Hué,* p. 16.

share of the protectorate's revenue. The officials concerned were aware that there was already "too great a disparity in the taxes paid by the poor which bear too heavily on them and the taxes paid by the rich which could be raised."[52] Nevertheless, they were apprehensive, and with good reason, that a graduated head tax would be impossible to administer and would open the way to new excesses of corruption by local officials. They also knew that the more inelastic the tax regime, the more reliable its yield.

The head tax was a great burden for the poor. In 1928, the basic rate was set at 2.50 piastres for all on the tax rolls and a large number of partial exemptions for the very poorest (who had paid only .40 piastres) were eliminated. Moreover, the rate of 2.50 piastres was only the base rate, to which a number of surtaxes had been added (*centièmes additionnels*) which might vary anywhere from .26 to .88 piastres according to the locality.[53] Most of these surtaxes were imposed to support local state schools attended, for the most part, by the children of the well-to-do and thus bitterly resented by poorer taxpayers.[54] Assuming that the average tax was three piastres, we can appreciate the sacrifice this represented for laborers by comparing it to daily earnings. Wages in Nghe-An and Ha-Tinh in the late 1920s varied between roughly 10 and 15 centimes per day plus food; the tax would thus represent a minimum of 20 days' earnings and perhaps as much as 30 days. For a sharecropper, following a mediocre or poor harvest, the burden would have been no less onerous.

Even these figures do not do justice to the weight of personal taxes as they were administered by mandarins and notables. Local officials were in the habit of adding all sorts of illegal charges which they then pocketed. A peasant who owed 2.80 piastres, for example, would in all likelihood have to pay as much as four piastres before he emerged with a stamped tax receipt.[55] Corruption of this kind was so universal that the

52. *Morché Commission Report,* p. 74.

53. *Budget Annam,* "Rapport de M. Demongin, Inspecteur Générale des Colonies, Chef de Mission, Régime fiscal," and, in that report, the "Rapport fait par M. Chastenet de Gery," pp. 6–8.

54. *Morché Commission Report,* p. 72. For an excellent discussion of school taxes and educational issues generally, see Gail P. Kelly, "Educational Policy in Colonial Vietnam" (Ph.D. dissertation, University of Wisconsin–Madison, 1975). The *fonds de concours,* as the school taxes were known, supported both a district "franco-indigène" school and, by 1926, also a compulsory local primary school along the same lines. Apart from the expense, the local schools were a threat to village scholars who had taught in the Sino-vietnamese tradition.

55. "Déclaration de M. Dulcé," p. 5.

effect was to raise the actual take by at least 50 percent and in some villages far more than that.[56]

Despite the knowledge that the *impôt personnel* was the most hated tax in its arsenal, the protectorate government nevertheless extended its coverage to indigents who had been exempt and made certain that fewer adult males escaped the village rolls. From a fiscal perspective, the results were satisfying: in 1927 the head tax yielded 1,376,566 piastres; in 1931, 2,230,910 piastres.[57] From a human perspective, the results were catastrophic. In 1931 Northern Annam was in the midst of its worst famine of the twentieth century. The tax in that year was, in the literal sense of the word, murderous.

Taxes on land, the second pillar of regional revenue, followed the same inexorable logic. In 1923 the tax on all categories of land was raised by 30 percent.[58] In 1929, a missionary from Ha-Tinh told of a similar increase that distraught villagers attempted in vain to have revoked.[59] Another strategy that brought in new revenue was to simply reclassify all lands into the next higher soil category and hence the next higher tax bracket. This had been done in 1907 and again in the 1920s. Such reclassifications, of course, had nothing to do with changes in yield but were purely matters of fiscal convenience. "Thus, in the province of Vinh [Nghe-An], to meet certain expenses, the successor of M. Châtel raised all the paddy lands by one category."[60] The land tax system as it evolved was keyed above all to the revenue needs of the colonial budget. Its annual take was unrelated to actual crop yields or to the price of rice and was thus increasingly out of line with the ability of smallholders to pay. Receipts from 1926 through 1930 show a modest upward trend (see Table 8).

Again, the meaning of these figures must be seen in the context of the four disastrous harvests from late 1929 through the first half of 1931 and the credit crisis of the depression. The state's claim in 1930 and 1931 was collected from a smallholding population with its back to the wall.

The salt monopoly represented yet another fiscal boon for the state and a heavy burden on peasant household budgets. Salt supplies for a family of ten, that had cost no more than 10 centimes annually in the

56. "Déclaration de Le Thuoc," ex-school director in Vinh, born in Ha-Tinh, *A.O.M. Indochine NF:* 335–2693.

57. "Rapport fait par M. Chastenet de Gery," p. 10.

58. Ibid., p. 18.

59. "Déclaration de R. P. Cherriers," missionary in Van Hanh, Ha-Tinh, for 20 years, *A.O.M. Indochine NF:* 334–2689.

60. "Déclaration de M. Ferey," plantation owner at Song Con, Ha-Tinh, *A.O.M. Indochine NF:* 334–2689.

Table 8. Land Tax (*Impôt Foncière*) Receipts—Annam[61]

| Year | Receipts |
|------|----------|
| 1926 | 2,245,958 |
| 1927 | 2,553,244 |
| 1928 | 2,563,168 |
| 1929 | 2,606,736 |
| 1930 | 2,650,807 |
| 1931 | 2,478,000 (est.) |

1890s, cost 10.80 piastres by 1930, according to one witness.[62] Here again colonial officials were willing to ignore the salt monopoly's regressive impact in view of its steady yield. Résident Le Fol in Annam was again candid about his priorities: "I recognize the unpopularity of the salt system. It offers, however, great advantages from a fiscal point of view."[63]

Finally, there were a host of petty regulations and tax charges that were both regressive and annoying. Market fees, boat taxes, and small-scale extortion connected with routine administration fell especially heavily on the landless for whom small-scale marketing was often a vital sideline. Of all these petty charges, however, the imposition of strict forest regulations was the most resented. The forests of Annam had traditionally served as an informal source of economic relief for the poorest villagers who made charcoal or cut wood during slack seasons to sell at nearby markets. Forest agents used the intricate regulations and taxes at their disposal to levy fines at will and line their own pockets.[64]

61. "Rapport fait par M. Chastenet de Gery," p. 13. These figures include a small amount of urban real estate taxes. Figures from earlier in the 1920s would undoubtedly show the effects of the major increase in 1923.

62. "Déclaration de Nguyen Duc Ly," p. 4. See also the progression of the receipts of the salt monopoly in Indochina, *Rapport sur la Régie du sel en Indochine*, 23 June 1930, *A.O.M. Indochine NF:* 282–2481, p. 1. Using Henry's wage labor data, the 10.80 piastres works out to be the equivalent of from 70 to 108 days of wage labor. Even for a family of ten, however, that seems an impossibly high figure.

63. "Déclaration de M. Le Fol," Resident of France in Annam, 6 June 1931, *A.O.M. Indochine NF:* 332–2684, p. 13.

64. See *Morché Commission Report*, pp. 75–76. The popular anger at forest agents is illustrated by this remark by a municipal counselor in Vinh: "In order not to be harassed by the forest administration it is necessary to be on good terms with its agents. You know that lim [a kind of hardwood] can only float on rafts of bamboo. The forest posts tax these bamboos as a tithe. There is corruption. The natives meet with dishonest agents. They say, when they see one of them driving the latest model car, 'There goes the car made of wood.' " "Déclaration de M. Mouton," *A.O.M. Indochine NF:* 333–2686.

Their interference with wood gathering on village lands that had always been open to the peasantry was interpreted as an attack on traditional subsistence rights. "If they [peasants] accept the tax for state forests, they do not understand the intervention of the state in village forests."[65] While the sums involved may have been minimal, the taxes and fines threatened an important option for the most destitute.

## Economic Crisis and Famine

The effect of demographic pressure alone on the hostile natural environment of Annam constituted a real and present danger to the survival of the peasantry. This danger was compounded by worsening terms of tenancy and a colonial state with a remorseless appetite for revenue. Annam's agrarian economy was simply too poor and too tenuous to be expected to yield up, year after year, the rents and taxes imposed upon it.

As it happened, the clash came in 1930 in the wake of the world economic crisis and the worst famine in local memory. When the state nonetheless pressed ahead with its claim, there was little choice but to resist. The result was the most massive popular revolt the colony had witnessed. It was hardly a revolt of rising expectations; it was rather a revolt of desperation.

Annam was particularly hard-hit by the depression. Many of the marginal cash earning opportunities in transportation and petty trade were reduced or swept away altogether. The prices of cash crops such as hemp, tobacco, tea, sesame and other oil plants, sugar, and ground nuts fell dramatically, and with them fell the incomes of many smallholders along the Song Ca valley where the revolt was strongest.

The unemployment generated by the economic crisis also appeared to be more severe in Annam than elsewhere in Indochina.[66] Mines and plantations cut their work forces and the colony itself suspended work on public roads. The impact was notably severe in Nghe-An which had been for some time a net exporter of labor throughout Annam, to Cochinchina, and to Laos. "All the coolies without work," an official declared, "flowed back to Nghe-An."[67] At the same time, the depression dealt a nearly fatal blow to the province's slender but vital industrial

65. "Déclaration de Nguyen Van Thin," p. 2.

66. See the unemployment figures provided in "Annexes à la note periodique du ler trimestre 1933," in *Les Associations Anti-françaises et la propagande communiste en Indochine, A.O.M. Indochine NF:* 323–2625. While the unemployment totals in Tonkin were slightly higher, its population was much greater.

67. "Déclaration de M. Rigault," Delegate from Annam to the Colonial Council, 10 June 1931, *A.O.M. Indochine NF:* 332–2684, p. 4.

base. Much of the rural population near Vinh and its neighboring port of Benthuy had become dependent, directly or indirectly, on the employment and remittances generated by the match factory, saw mills, airport construction, bottling plant, locomotive yards, and electricity-generating facilities in the area.[68] The crisis led to a series of wholesale dismissals and salary cuts in these industries, which in turn provoked bitter strikes. The valley of the Song Ca (Nam Dan, Thanh Chuong, and Anh Son) was once again most directly affected as it represented the natural labor hinterland for the Vinh area. There is little doubt, though precise figures are lacking, that the slump in trade also reduced the cash incomes of many rural families in Nghe-An for whom secondary occupations were important.

On top of this difficult situation came a famine which even in a land of scarcity was almost without precedent. This dominating fact was, for many local observers, the key to the revolt. In testifying before the Commission of Inquiry the most experienced agronomist in the colony, Yves Henry, claimed that "The main reason for the troubled situation in Nghe-An and Ha-Tinh has to do with poor harvests. For two years the land has produced nothing. Four harvests have been devastated."[69] In the fall of 1929 low rainfall delayed the transplanting, and when the crop was finally in the paddy fields floods destroyed most of it. Both crops in 1930 were almost totally lost as the drought continued unabated. The spring crop in 1931 was completely destroyed both by drought and by what is known as the "Laotian dry wind" which prevented the rice from flowering. Sharecroppers were left with virtually no rice at all; half of nothing is nothing. Landowners stopped extending loans that had been used to pay taxes or purchase rice and the price of rice climbed toward famine levels.[70] By the time the second crop failed in early 1930, the unmistakable signs of famine and resistance began to make their appearance.

As the stocks of rice dwindled, peasants turned toward cheaper foods such as millet, beans, corn, potatoes, and various root crops for their daily fare. Gradually, other outriders of famine appeared. The poor

68. As nearly as I can estimate, these enterprises alone employed something like 2,500 workers, to say nothing of their indirect income and employment effects. See, for example, "Evenements de Vinh, Rapport sur le 12 Septembre," 31 December 1930, *A.O.M. Indochine NF:* 325–2634. Elsewhere it is mentioned frequently that the labor force for many of these plants was heavily recruited from villages along the Song Ca.

69. "Déclaration de Yves Henry," 11 August 1931, *A.O.M. Indochine NF:* 335–2693, *Dossier de Hanoi,* p. 2.

70. See "Déclaration de Nguyen Duc Ly," p. 3, and for the rice market in early 1930, "Discours de M. René Robin," Resident in au Tonkin, 6 October 1931, *A.O.M. Indochine NF:* 332–2680.

were driven to the forest where they dug up edible wild roots.[71] We can see in this process a kind of evolutionary retreat back through stages of food production. As lowland rice failed, peasants fell back on the products of highland slash-and-burn agriculture; as those crops in turn became scarce, they resorted to the primitive techniques of forest gatherers.[72]

The debilitating signs of hunger touched an ever-widening spectrum of the rural population. A Vietnamese official declared that 90 of every 100 villagers in Nam Dan (Nghe-An) suffered from hunger.[73] To be sure, hunger was no stranger to the Annam countryside; it was a normal state of affairs for many in the months before a new harvest. But this hunger was different. When asked if villagers were hungry, an Inspector of Agricultural Services replied, "Yes. Before people said *doi lam* [very hungry] and now they say *doi chêt* [*faim à mourir*, starvation]."[74]

Doctors who visited the countryside were struck by the physical evidence of malnutrition. In the village of Xuan-Nguyen in the Yen Thanh district of Nghe-An, a medical aide treated many cases of skin ulcers, dysentery, and anemia and noted that 100 villagers needed food while 40 others were in immediate danger of starving. In the same village, the poor had sold everything—buffaloes, rice land, their houses, and even household altars—to raise money for food.[75] The testimony of physicians who treated villagers speaks for itself.

> I found that famine existed in these villages [Yen Thanh]. I noticed that many individuals had the swollen stomach which is the mark of famine.[76]

> I had never seen such a sight as that at the *soupes populaires* [in Anh Son, Nghe-An and in Ky An, Ha-Tinh]: thousands of walking skeletons with absolutely nothing to eat, true cadavers whose ribs jut out under the skin.[77]

71. "Déclaration de M. Mouton."

72. To this day the same process can be observed in Annam in periods of dearth. See, for example, Patrice de Beer, "Où va le Viet-Nam," *Le Monde*, May 8, 1974, p. 8.

73. "Déclaration de Tran Huu Sa."

74. "Déclaration de M. Roule," Inspector of Farm Services at Vinh, *A.O.M. Indochine NF:* 333–2686.

75. "Éxtrait de rapports confidentiels en date 1 et 3 Octobre, 1930: Rapport de tournée au village de Xuan-Nguyen," *A.O.M. Indochine NF:* 334–2688.

76. "Déclaration de Dr. Lemoine," Physician, Director of the Hospital in Vinh, *A.O.M. Indochine NF:* 333–2686.

77. "Déclaration de Médecin Générale Gaide," Inspector of Sanitation and Medical Services, *A.O.M. Indochine NF:* 335–2693.

The documents assembled by the Commission of Inquiry give evidence of malnutrition and famine in at least five of Nghe-An's nine districts as well as in the district of Ha-Tinh most active in the revolt. There can be little doubt that by May 1930 much of Nghe-An's peasantry was nearing the end of its resources. In this context, the central events of the rebellion—the refusal to pay the head tax and the expropriation of rice—must be seen as straightforward acts of desperation.[78]

*The Heartland of the Revolt*

At one time or another the rebellion in Northern Annam touched virtually all of Nghe-An, much of northern Ha-Tinh, and parts of Quang Ngai. The veritable heartland of the revolt, however—the area which mounted the most massive and determined resistance—was the densely populated valley of the Song Ca river to the west and northwest of Vinh. Following the course of the river upstream from the provincial capital, one passes through, on the Nghe-An side, first Nam Dan and then Thanh Chuong. Further north lies Anh Son, also a rebel stronghold. Nam Dan occupies a special place in Vietnamese history both for its tradition of radicalism and for being the birthplace of the two greatest nationalist heroes of the twentieth century, Phan Boi Chau and Ho Chi Minh. Together with Thanh Chuong, Nam Dan was won over entirely to the rebel cause. As a confidential report in early October 1930 warned, "The two districts of Thanh Chuong and Nam Dan are in a state of total dissidence and veritable anarchy."[79] This state of affairs was to continue for almost a year.

The members of the Commission of Inquiry were at a loss to explain why the revolt should have centered here. By regional standards, at least, the valley's soil seemed to be rich and fertile; one might even call these districts "relatively prosperous."[80] Poorer areas such as Quynh Luu in Nghe-An and Ky An in Ha-Tinh had, by contrast, been less totally committed to the uprising. For this reason the commission tended to discount economic hardship as the motive for the rebellion and to concentrate instead on communist agitation.

The commission's cavalier rejection of any economic interpretation seems to me unwarranted for a number of reasons. First, in terms of average rice yield per unit of land, only Anh Son is clearly in a privileged position compared to the rest of the province. Thanh Chuong and Nam Dan figure fourth and fifth, respectively, in a list of eight Nghe-An

78. See the discussion of rebellion and hunger in Chapter 6.
79. "Éxtrait de rapport confidentiels en date 1 et 3 Octobre, 1930."
80. *Morché Commission Report*, p. 49.

districts ranked by rice yield per hectare.[81] The most complete study of local agriculture available at the time, in fact, went out of its way to emphasize the poor soil and low yields of Nam Dan.[82] If the heartland of the rebellion did not have the worst yields of the province, neither did it have, Anh Son excepted, anything like the best.

Second, there is an ecological distinctiveness to each of these three districts that is of capital importance. If we divide the province by soil types, we find that all three have clayey soil while the soils in the rest of Nghe-An tend to be sandy.[83] The critical feature of clayey soil is that it is far more sensitive to variations in rainfall than sandy soils. As the Inspector for Agricultural Services for Nghe-An explained, "Clayey soils are preferable when there is plenty of water. But their yield is poorer than sandy soils when there is a drought."[84] Once again averages are misleading. The clay soils of these districts might have had an average yield over a ten-year period which compared favorably with that of sandy soils. But the averages would conceal their special vulnerability to drought and thus the greater possibility of complete crop failures. A drought, of course, is precisely what Northern Annam experienced and it is likely that the resulting crop losses were even more severe in these districts than elsewhere in the province. From this perspective, the tenuousness of the Song Ca valley's rural economy was an extreme version of both Annam's and Nghe-An's problem. Within Indochina, Annam had the most ecologically precarious economy—that is, the one most prone to subsistence crises. Within Annam, Nghe-An in turn had the most variable rainfall and hence the most tenuous food supply. Within Nghe-An itself, the clayey soils of Nam Dan, Thanh Chuong, and Anh Son compounded the already huge risks of a disastrous harvest.

The quality of their soils was not the only reason why the districts along the Song Ca were particularly disaster-prone. They were as vulnerable to the depression as they were to drought. Particularly in Nam Dan and Thanh Chuong, a sizeable acreage was devoted to nonedible cash crops such as tobacco, tea, and hemp.[85] The market for these crops collapsed with the economic crisis and what little could be harvested sold for virtually nothing. No figures are available to indicate how decisive this loss was, but there is little doubt that it cut deeply into the cash income of the peasantry at a time when the price of subsistence foods

81. "Renseignements sur le Nghe-An," *A.O.M. Indochine NF:* 334–2688, p. 10.

82. Castagnol, "Monographie agricole de la Province de Nghe An," pp. 833–37.

83. "Déclaration de M. Roule," p. 2.

84. Ibid. Clayey soil hardens to a rock-like consistency in drought, which makes the preparation of the soil for transplanting virtually impossible.

85. Castagnol, "Monographie agricole de la Province de Nghe An," pp. 828–33.

was climbing. The social structure of this region added further to its difficulties. Since a larger share of the rural population was without land, it was particularly exposed to the impact of the depression on wages, employment, and the availability of credit.[86] Finally, in this context, the marked dependence of Nam Dan and Thanh Chuong on the urban market and employment provided by the town of Vinh made their economy all the more tenuous.

The reason for the tenacity of the rebellion in these districts thus lies not so much in their poverty, though they were certainly poor, but rather in their distinctive double susceptibility to drought and to the fluctuations of the wider economy. Had their economy been poor but stable, the inflexible demands of landowners and the state, while onerous, might have been less of an immediate threat. As it was, however, the caprices of weather and prices could, from one year to the next, plunge them into such a crisis that taxes and share rents menaced survival itself.

Sharecropping arrangements were exacting but they were not appreciably worse in 1930 than they had been in 1929. Mandarins were as corrupt as ever, but not much more so in 1930 than in 1929. Taxes, however, *had* become more onerous in 1930 than they had been in the late 1920s. Faced with a decline in the yield of indirect taxes that varied automatically with the level of economic activity, the colonial regime minimized its losses by stepping up the collection of its depression-proof taxes, notably the head tax. The results in the three rebellious provinces were ominous (see Table 9). By 1931, the colonial treasury had suc-

Table 9. *Impôt Personnel*, 1927 and 1931[87]

| Province | No. on tax rolls 1927 | Collections 1927 | No. on tax rolls 1931 | Collections 1931 |
|---|---|---|---|---|
| Nghe-An | 69,480 | 136,005 | 82,402 | 215,202 |
| Ha-Tinh | 54,398 | 107,172 | 64,839 | 164,745 |
| Quang Ngai | 46,183 | 89,475 | 57,100 | 147,090 |
| Totals | 170,061 | 332,652 | 204,341 | 527,037 |
| % Increase | | | 14.3 | 58.4 |

86. *Morché Commission Report*, p. 50.

87. "Rapport fait par M. Chastenet de Gery," p. 10. The totals and percentages are computed from the report's figures. A small proportion of the increase, for Nghe-An at least, may have come from laborers returning home from elsewhere in Indochina. The bulk of the increase, however, can be explained by the fiscal needs of the protectorate.

ceeded in augmenting the tax rolls by nearly 15 percent and the receipts by almost 60 percent. The peasants of Nghe-Tinh would have been hard put to pay this tax bill under the best of circumstances.

The circumstances, however, were not the best but the worst. The bottom had dropped out of the Nghe-Tinh economy and its crops had failed. Missionaries in the region stressed the convergence of tax collections and famine as the proximate cause of the rebellion.

> Since 1930 three harvests have been lost and the fourth, that of the tenth month, appears in jeopardy. The collection of taxes was abruptly made at the moment when the population was ruined by drought. In order to pay, the inhabitants have had to sell off all their property.[88]

Another missionary told of villagers who were forced to sell their belongings, their buffaloes, and even their communal land at whatever price they could get in order to raise the cash for the tax. Speaking of the rebel call to resist taxes, he added by way of understatement, "When one doesn't have enough to eat, one doesn't pay taxes willingly."[89]

It is this conjunction of steady and rising demands on the peasant surplus together with a crisis in agrarian income and food supply that made the explosion unavoidable. Sooner or later, this conjunction was an entirely *predictable* consequence of the ecological givens of Annam's agrarian economy and the rigid fiscal claims imposed by the state.

THE COURSE OF THE REBELLION

The first signs of widespread rural discontent took the form of large demonstrations in June, July, and August of 1930. They were mostly confined, as they had been in Cochinchina, to large-scale petitioning for tax relief. Typically, a mass of peasants would congregate outside a district office to petition for a reduction or delay in taxes. Taking advantage of the latent threat they generally posed for outnumbered officials, they often forced mandarins to sign the petition themselves before forwarding it. Head taxes were most at issue but other state-imposed burdens were not ignored. In one case, 1,000 petitioners sacked a government rice-wine storehouse. In Quynh Luu (Nghe-An), 600 peasants petitioned for a reduction of salt prices and managed to coerce a French officer and a customs official into appending their names. Growing in size and boldness, these demonstrations culminated

88. "Déclaration de R. P. Derribes."
89. "Déclaration de R. P. Dalaine," Director General of the Xa-Doai Seminary, Xa-Doai, *A.O.M. Indochine NF*: 333–2686.

in early September in a march of "many thousands" in the district capital of Nam Dan where the alcohol tax office was destroyed and a terrified mandarin was made to sign a tax petition.[90]

In one form or another the resistance to taxes, and especially to the head tax, dominated the first half of the rebellion. In Nghe-An alone 32 major demonstrations are listed in the official account of the uprisings and a great majority of the crowds involved either demanded that the head tax be reduced, delayed, or revoked or else seized and burned the local tax records.[91] The size of these crowds was imposing. There were seldom less than 200, while the larger gatherings brought together as many as 20,000.[92] The resistance to taxes took other forms as well. A missionary in Nghe-An reported that five or six villages in his area "decided not to pay the taxes and took everything that they had into the mountains."[93] Elsewhere, the poor simply refused to pay.

> In a fairly large number of villages [Ha-Tinh] the head tax, in particular, was not paid by the poor who were on the tax rolls; the landowners or the village [presumably the notables in this case] have been obliged to make good the default of the landless who are supported by communist leaders; this was also the occasion for large gatherings and fights.[94]

90. *Annexe No. 15, Le Parti Communiste Indochinois (1925–1933)*, p. 130. Lieu sets the date as September 2 and the number of participants at 20,000. Lieu, *Les Soviets du Nghe-Tinh*, p. 24.

91. "Relevé chronologique des évenements, Nghe An, Novembre 1929 à Juin 1931," *A.O.M. Indochine NF*: 334–2688.

92. It was in the course of these large assemblies and marches, two of which were actually bombed from the air, that most of the casualties occurred. Typically, a crowd would besiege an administrative center defended by a few militia who, feeling threatened by the crowd (which, if armed at all, was armed with sticks and knives), opened fire. With few exceptions the crowd fled leaving their fallen comrades behind while the militia forces were unscathed. As peasants realized the consequences of such large gatherings, they became far less common.

93. "Déclaration de R. P. Gonnet," missionary at Botda, Nghe-An, *A.O.M. Indochine NF*: 333–2686, p. 2. There is a classic Southeast Asian pattern involved here. When a rebellion begins, the peasantry is likely to head for the hills while elites move into the district and provincial towns to seek the protection of the state. It is as if the tenuous bonds that unite civil society at the village level become unraveled. The peasantry seeks safety by moving out of range to a more primitive but more independent life, while the elites, who depend ultimately on the coercive power of the state, flee toward the center. We can see in this process a reversal of the long historical movement that served to establish the lowland rice kingdoms and the state.

94. "Weekly Report to the Inspector of Political Affairs at Thanh Hoa from Inspector Lagrèze, 31 May 1931," *A.O.M. Indochine NF*: 335–2690. The appeal of redistributive norms is evident in the effort to get the well-to-do to shoulder the major share of the tax burden in bad times.

In many other villages the local notables and headmen were threatened with death if they attempted to collect taxes from the poor.[95] To the poor the government was known, above all, as a tax collector and it was as tax collector that it was attacked.

By mid-September, as the tempo of violence grew, the colonial regime was losing its grip in Northern Annam. "During the course of September, mandarins and notables sought refuge in the district headquarters leaving entire districts without any representation of colonial authority."[96] Taking advantage of the vacuum, the peasants of Nghe-An began pulling down the edifice of the colonial state. "It is as a true jacquerie—that one can grasp the peasant rebellion. The archives of the villages, lists of civilians, land records and tax rolls were destroyed by cultivators who believed that by doing so they would free their land of any taxes."[97] The motives were much the same as those in Cochinchina, but the relative weakness of the state in Annam allowed the action to be carried further. Most administrative offices and their tax rolls were destroyed, post offices and railroad stations and schools were burned, alcohol warehouses plundered, collaborating officials assassinated, forest guard posts destroyed, rice stores seized, and at least one salt convoy attacked.[98] It would be hard to imagine a more comprehensive attack on the colonial state.

The elimination of taxes and of those who collected them appears, from what evidence there is, to have supplied the initial popular motive for participation. The Communist Party of the province also recognized taxes as the paramount issue. In the provincial program, drawn up in great haste after the peasantry had already seized much of the province, the first substantive point calls for "the abolition of all colonial taxes: head tax, market taxes, toll roads, salt tax, etc."[99] It would be convenient to have more direct evidence of peasant sentiments but, as with most

95. *Morché Commission Report*, Part 2, "L'action répressive," pp. 29–48.

96. Lieu, *Les Soviets du Nghe-Tinh*, p. 26.

97. André Dumarest, *La Formation de classes sociales en pays annamites* (Lyon: P. Ferréal Imprimerie, 1935). See also, Chesneaux, *Contribution à l'histoire de la nation vietnamienne*, p. 214.

98. When the local *dinh* or communal building is attacked, it is often difficult to tell whether the immediate target is the tax and administrative records or the school, for the simple reason that both were often located in the *dinh*. Most often it appears that the tax records were the principal objective. We know, however, that the surtax (*fonds de concours*) for education was bitterly resented and that the district school in Thanh Chuong and at least two schools in Nam Dan were sacked and burned. See the declaration by the Director General of Public Education in Indochina, *Dossier de Hanoi*, Pièces Annexes, *A.O.M. Indochine NF*: 336–2694.

99. Lieu, *Les Soviets du Nghe-Tinh*, p. 27.

peasant movements, we must largely infer what the participants thought from what they did. Although the French police interrogated hundreds of peasants after the rebellion was crushed, they rarely bothered to ask why they had joined in—perhaps participation was so general that it seemed a senseless question. On one of those rare occasions when the question was asked, however, the role of taxes seems first and foremost. "We heard that the communists were for reducing all taxes, had the right to make their salt, their alcohol, and enjoyed a complete liberty in their public and private actions."[100] By his use of "we" it seems that the cultivator being interrogated is referring not only to his own motives but to those of his fellow villagers as well.

The executions and pillaging that accompanied the assault on the colonial tax system were linked, particularly in the first months of the revolt, to the same ethos. Just as the burning of tax lists expressed the determination to serve local subsistence claims before those of the state, many of the assassinations and pillages seemed directly motivated by the belief that the wealthy and those in authority had an obligation to share their resources with the poor in times of dearth—and, failing that, the poor then had the right to take what they needed by force.

Thus, a good many assassinations were traceable directly to the failure of the local official/notable to respect the redistributive norms of village life. In a village near Vinh in May 1931, for example, eleven notables were denounced and executed with the enthusiastic approval of assembled villagers. They were accused of having "crushed" the people with taxes and, beyond that, of being "egotistical"—"You have not wanted to divide your property with us; you wanted to obtain rank in the mandarinate; you must die today."[101] Earlier in Xuan-Lieu (Nghe-An), a local official was assassinated for refusing to share what were common resources. "Han-Khom the victim, my first cousin, who held the communal paddy, did not wish to loan it to villagers who were his enemies."[102] The popular character of many killings is frequently underlined by the participation of sizable numbers of villagers in the decision and in its execution.[103]

100. Gouvernement Général de l'Indochine, Direction des Affaires Politiques et de la Sûreté Générale, *Contribution à l'histoire des mouvements politiques de l'Indochine française*, vol. 5, *La Terreur rouge in Annam, 1930–31*, p. 215. Hereafter referred to as *La Terreur rouge en Annam, 1930–31*. There were a few other responses to this question but they tended to be deferential; e.g., "I joined because X joined," or, vaguer, "I am poor, I let myself be brought along in the hope of getting something out of joining," p. 214.

101. *La Terreur rouge en Annam, 1930–31*, p. 237.

102. Ibid., p. 283.

103. In the spring of 1931, after a disastrous harvest and as the military pressure around the rebel area grew, the character of the violence changed. Increasingly, the

From all accounts, however, the most common collective act during the second half of the insurrection was the seizure of grain from the better-off for distribution to the peasants. Sharecroppers, facing the prospect of handing over half of their drought-stricken harvest, often took it all. In five villages in Ha Tinh, 38 sharecroppers refused to pay their share rents and seized the harvest. Most of them were share tenants of the same large landlord who owned over 100 hectares of paddy fields.[104] Elsewhere, local notables and landowners were forced to sell the contents of their granaries cheaply to the village poor. When they refused it was pillaged—or, from the peasants' point of view, it was confiscated and distributed. As a French officer bluntly put it, "They pillage because they are hungry."[105] The hauls of rice were sometimes so large—10 tons, 30 tons, 50 tons—as late as the spring of 1931 that one is led to believe that there were indeed a fair number of substantial landholders in the region.[106] No doubt the implicit justification for the seizure of grain was the right to subsistence—the notion that it was intolerable that some should hoard grain while others went hungry. Such plunder, particularly after the fall crop failure, touched even modest landowners despite the justified fears of provincial party leaders that it jeopardized the broad coalition the party hoped to build. "The policy, the implementation of which provoked the most enthusiasm among peasants, was the confiscation of paddy from the rich and its distribution to people affected by the famine."[107]

The quasi-public character of these seizures was manifest in the usual practice of hauling the spoils to the communal building of the hamlet where they were then divided among poor villagers. Reporting on the course of the rebellion in Ha Tinh, an Inspector of Political Affairs emphasized the attention to probity that characterized the collection and distribution of food.

> Small bands have instructions to hold wealthy people for ransom
> . . . in a way that I would not call pillaging. It is not a question of

---

victims of assassinations were villagers suspected of collaborating with the enemy. The incidence of attacks on Catholic villages and churches increased. The search for food and desperate efforts to assure the physical security of local militants took precedence over earlier objectives.

104. "Weekly Report to the Inspector of Political Affairs at Thanh Hoa from Inspector Lagrèze, 31 May 1931."

105. For some examples of the amounts of rice seized, see *Morché Commission Report*, "L'action repressive," p. 25.

106. "Déclaration de Capitain Doucin," Delegate from Do Luong, *A.O.M. Indochine NF*: 333–2686.

107. Lieu, *Les Soviets du Nghe-Tinh*, p. 29.

acts of piracy accompanied by violence. . . . They thus look for stocks of paddy which excite the envy of people in need, which are then taken in an orderly fashion (*correctement*) and distributed.[108]

In terms of the moral norms of the subsistence ethic, there is no question that the peasantry was taking the *law* into its own hands. This discriminating sense of what was required makes a mockery of the term jacquerie as applied to the Nghe-Tinh rebellion.[109] Those who violated these norms ran great risks as the following case, also from Ha-Tinh, indicates. "When the members of the self-defense group carried out the seizures of paddy from the big owners of the area, they divided the take among themselves without sharing any with the members of other party groups. The actions of Rong made everybody angry."[110] Rong was publicly condemned at a meeting of some 300 villagers and executed.

As the famine deepened and military repression continued, the rebellion began to fall apart. Most of its leaders had been tracked down and arrested or killed. Mandarins and a reinforced militia were once again installed in the uneasy countryside. A modest food relief program was begun and hungry villagers were required to accept certificates of submission before they qualified for the food line. By the summer of 1931 the work of repression had all but crushed the rebellion. Colonial order was reestablished but, as the official report itself noted, "the calm will be the sigh of fear and not the calm of peace."[111]

There is little doubt that the rebellion would not have taken on quite the dimensions of size and cohesiveness that it attained had it not been for the role of the Communist party. While the precise role of the party does not materially affect the argument I am making, the connection between the "official" revolutionary party and the peasantry is instructive.

On the one hand, the party was stronger in Annam than elsewhere in Vietnam, and within Annam it was particularly strong in Nghe-An and its principal city, Vinh. French intelligence information indicated that, at the time of the uprising, there were about 300 active party members in

108. "Weekly Report to the Inspector of Political Affairs at Thanh Hoa from Inspector Lagrèze, 20 April 1931."
109. In fact, the *original* jacquerie from which the term itself is derived hardly fits the blind fury which the word has come to imply. From the elite perspective, insurrection is almost always equated with banditry, criminality, or senseless violence and thus the term jacquerie serves an ideological purpose. For a short description of the Jacques in the sixteenth century, see Rodney Hilton, *Bond Men Made Free* (London: Temple, Smith, 1973).
110. *La Terreur rouge en Annam*, p. 186.
111. *Morché Commission Report*, "L'action repressive," p. 50.

the Nghe-Tinh area.[112] What is more significant perhaps is the social lineage of the Nghe-Tinh revolutionary intelligentsia. Most of them were from anti-French mandarin families in the area and a surprising number of them had been pupils or teachers at the Cao Xuan Duc primary school in Vinh.[113] They were in some sense the more secular successors of a long regional tradition of anticolonial dissidents—what Woodside has called "the mandarin proletarians." There is ample evidence in tracts, banners, and reports of meetings that many of these party members were active in the rebellion. In fact, it is unlikely that some of the larger demonstrations, involving as many as 20,000 participants, would have occurred at all without the kind of extralocal leadership that only the party could provide. At the village level there is evidence of party initiative behind the establishment of some of the local "Xo-viets."

On the other hand, it seems abundantly clear that the insurrection had a momentum of its own and a spontaneity that was either heedless of the party or left it trailing far behind. The Indochina Communist Party (ICP) Central Committee sent a directive to the Annam branch immediately before the formation of the soviets in which it failed to mention them at all and went out of its way, in another directive, to single out the "adventuristic" policies of the Annam party.[114] Only in October when the insurrection was at high tide did the General Affairs Commission of the ICP see fit to endorse armed struggle as a means to power. Are we dealing then with a regional party initiative? Perhaps, but the word "party" is a misleading term for a body that was in considerable disarray—having recently effected a tenuous reconciliation between two factions. The Regional Committee's official journal was, as late as October 5, 1930, still cautioning against violence because neither the party nor the masses were prepared![115] Even the Nghe-An provincial party lagged behind.[116] At best, then, only a portion of the local party backed the revolt at the outset and we cannot ignore the possibility that noncommunist *lettrés* and others may have provided some initial impetus. What seems most likely is that some party elements elected to join and support an incipient uprising.

It is clear, in any event, that the party adopted the program of the peasantry and not the other way around. That program began with the

112. William J. Duiker, *The Rise of Nationalism in Vietnam, 1900–1941* (Ithaca: Cornell University Press, 1976) p. 222, n. 11.

113. Communication from Alexander Woodside.

114. Duiker, *The Rise of Nationalism*, p. 222.

115. Ibid., p. 230.

116. See above, n. 99.

opposition to taxes in the context of a depression and famine. Without that raw material a thousand party militants would have toiled in vain. In the struggle against taxes, the interests of the party and the impoverished peasantry coincided. But when it came to the second plank of the peasant program, the equitable distribution of food, the party emphatically denounced the campaigns against rich peasants, middle peasants, and small notables as *"une politique d'aventures."*[117] Here the party and the peasantry parted ways. While the party leaders were undoubtedly correct in seeing the need for a broad coalition of classes, the confiscation of food from the relatively well-to-do was nevertheless an integral, if violent, form of traditional redistributive norms. At this point, poor peasants were acting on their own and, as the official report concluded, "the leaders appear to have been overwhelmed by their subordinates."[118]

## LOWER BURMA—THE SAYA SAN REBELLION

It was not sheer coincidence that the British colonial regime in Lower Burma should have faced, in the same year, an explosion of peasant violence that was also without precedent. The Saya San Rebellion, which erupted in December 1930, swept through large portions of the north, central, and east central Irrawaddy Delta and extended as far as the Shan States in the northeast. Although its course was quite different in each district it lasted until roughly June 1931. Its popular character is beyond doubt; about 9,000 rebels were arrested or captured, 3,000 killed or wounded, and 350 convicted and hanged.[119] The official report remarked on the number of headmen and monks who took leading roles.

The main distinguishing feature of the Saya San insurgency, compared with the risings in Cochinchina and Annam, lay in its leadership rather than in its social base. Exhorting a peasantry with virtually the same grievances as in Vietnam, Saya San nevertheless drew explicitly on the millennarian tradition of folk Buddhism for his ideology. He claimed to be both the *Setkya-min* (the avenging king of Burman legend) and the *Buddha Yaza* (the divinely sent creator of a Buddhist utopia). Ample use was made of oaths, amulets, and a host of traditional for-

117. Lieu, *Les Soviets du Nghe-Tinh*, pp. 43–44, 53. In the last stages of the revolt there were also attacks on Catholic communities, factional struggles, and assaults on those with French education. This last pattern, expressing the "little tradition's" suspicion of outsiders and alien education may have further undermined party influence.

118. *Morché Commission Report*, "L'action repressive," p. 10.

119. E. Sarkisyanz, *Buddhist Backgrounds of the Burmese Revolution* (The Hague: Martinus Nijhoff, 1965), pp. 157–59.

mulas (particularly tattooing) which guaranteed invulnerability to modern arms. In ideological terms Saya San was undoubtedly more closely aligned with the "little tradition" of his peasant followers than were the party leaders in Annam who struggled, with little success, against "superstitions and anachronistic customs."[120]

What made Saya San's rebellion a true *levée en masse*, however, was not his closeness to the folk tradition alone but the subsistence crisis of the peasantry to which he appealed. Twentieth-century Burmese history was, after all, rich in would-be *setkya-min*. Such prophetic figures had aroused the suspicions of colonial officials in 1906, in 1910, in 1912 (when a millennarian pretender amassed 20,000 rural followers), and again in 1924–26.[121] These movements, however, were easily repressed, withered of their own accord, or else stilled government suspicions by settling quietly into the tapestry of local sects.

Saya San, by contrast, had at his instant disposal a peasantry whose fortunes, though deteriorating throughout the past decade, had just taken a dramatic turn for the worse. As in Vietnam, the collapse of the paddy price effectively tripled the real burden of head taxes, land taxes and debts, thus threatening subsistence routines. Employment in the urban sector was out of the question in the context of massive layoffs. Defaulting Burmese tenants had no sources of credit and were often replaced by Indians; remaining smallholders were faced with the imminent loss of their land (often to Chettiar moneylenders); and above all in December 1930, as Saya San reminded his followers, the collection of the capitation tax was at hand. In short, the crisis threatened to precipitate a large portion of Lower Burma's peasantry over social and economic thresholds from which a recovery was unlikely.

The distress of the Lower Burma cultivator was a direct consequence of the collapse of rice prices and the attendant collapse of credit. He was caught in a "scissors crisis" much like that faced by his counterpart in Cochinchina. Smallholders, unable to meet their debts or to borrow more, lost their land by the thousands. The tenant, who had "never been very secure," was now much worse off because "the system he had hitherto adopted of annual borrowings and repayments, has completely broken down with the fall in prices."[122] Not only were landlords no

120. The last point in the seven-point program of the Nghe-An provincial party resolution. Lieu, *Les Soviets du Nghe-Tinh*, p. 27.

121. There were many similar movements toward the end of the nineteenth century and doubtless many smaller scale *setkya-min* in the twentieth who never reached the threshold that would provoke official notice or action. Sarkisyanz, *Buddhist Backgrounds of the Burmese Revolution*, pp. 150–59.

122. *Revision Settlement of Hanthawaddy, 1930–33*, p. 38.

longer extending loans, but the modest fall in rents was nothing like the fall in paddy prices so that the tenant cultivator was unable "to obtain a decent living wage."[123] Floundering landlords continued "to take all they can get in good years as well as bad years."[124] A growing clamor for rent reductions met stiff resistance and, in turn, provoked widespread fraud and rent boycotts. Defaulting tenants were turned off their plots. Wage laborers were hardest hit as wages plummeted and employment evaporated. One settlement officer found that this growing class "has suffered most and is at present living from hand to mouth."[125]

It was not a question of outright starvation, as in Annam. Rather, it meant a massive and collective decline in a standard of living and an economic security which had for some time been deteriorating. It meant for many a precipitate fall from smallholding or tenancy into the ranks of day laborers. It meant for tenants a dramatic worsening of their terms of exchange with landowners as rents held steady against their diminishing income and customary production credit was revoked.

The common denominator, the rallying cry, that brought the Burmese peasantry to the banner of Saya San was the resistance to the capitation tax in a crisis. To be sure, there were other related issues as well: Indian tenants and wage laborers were attacked, forestry posts were burned, Karen Christians were assaulted, and land records destroyed. But it was the capitation tax—the immediate problem faced by all cultivators—which provided the detonator for the uprising.

In its analysis of the revolt the official colonial report takes notice of the relation between the economic crisis and the capitation tax:

> There is plenty of oral evidence to show that Saya San and his lieutenants, in their efforts to raise the countryside in open rebellion, had taken pains to exploit the dislike of taxes in general and of capitation and *thathameda* taxes in particular. . . . there is no dispute that all classes of agriculturists have been hit terribly hard by the disastrous fall in the price of paddy which began about the time of the first outbreak, but which took a serious turn only several months afterward: and there is no doubt that the insurrection owed some of its strength to all these factors and that the economic distress of 1931 undoubtedly fanned the flames.[126]

123. Ibid., p. 41.
124. Ibid., p. 4.
125. Ibid., p. 25.
126. Government of Burma, *The Origin and Causes of the Burma Rebellion (1930–1932)*, p. 43. Except where otherwise noted, the following material on the rebellion is drawn from this extensive official report.

And yet the report concludes that "the rebellion must be regarded as primarily political rather than economic in origin."[127] The contradiction, however, is only apparent. By "political," the authors meant to emphasize that Saya San had been planning his insurrection well before the depression and that he intended not only to eliminate taxes but to sweep the British out and occupy the throne himself. In this limited sense the report is accurate; Saya San's intentions were at least as revolutionary as those of the party leaders in Annam.

Judging by the evidence of the report, however, what galvanized Saya San's rank and file supporters was the combination of an economic crisis and fixed taxes. As the past chairman of a committee sent by the General Council of Buddhist Associations to inquire into "excesses in the collection of the capitation and *thathameda* taxes," Saya San had seen for himself the resentment stirred by their forced collection even before the depression.[128] He had found a potent source of discontent and his new association had as its first two purposes:

a) to resist the forcible collection of the capitation and *thathameda* taxes; and
b) to offer civil resistance against oppressive forest laws which deprived villagers of the free use of bamboo and timber for domestic purposes.[129]

In view of the unprecedented scope of colonial taxation, a document seized in connection with the revolt was not perhaps entirely facetious when it claimed that everything but flower pots was taxed.[130]

The initial purpose of the *galon* (a mythical bird of great strength) *athins* (associations), which were to form the tenuous organizational grid for the revolt, was in every case resistance by force to the collection of the head tax. "Reference was made during this visit [of a rebel leader to Saya San in December 1930] to the projected formation of a 'galon' party, the object of which was stated to be to resist the collection of the capitation

127. Ibid., p. 2.

128. Ibid., p. 10. The report recognizes this dislike of taxes as well and refers to it in terms of "the hereditary disposition of the Tharrawaddy people to violence, lawlessness and contempt of authority" or "the rooted antipathy to pay taxes which has been a marked feature of Tharrawaddy District for some years past." It seems that Tharrawaddy was the "Nghe-An of Burma."

129. Ibid. The Samin movement in Java around the turn of the century evoked the same themes. See Benda and Castles, "The Samin Movement," and The Siauw Giap, "The Samin and Samat Movements: Two Examples of Peasant Resistance," *Revue du Sud-Est Asiatique* 67:2 (1967), 304–10 and 68:1 (1968), 107–13.

130. Government of Burma, *Burma Rebellion*, p. 26.

tax by the government."[131] At the same time a confederate in Henzada—an ex-monk named U Yazeinda—who formed many such village associations "urged non-payment of the capitation tax and said that he had the medicines which would render the villagers proof against the assaults of Government officials. *No member of our athin who has been tattooed will have to pay the capitation tax.*"[132]

Once the paddy market began to tumble, moreover, Saya San was quick to seize on the anger stirred by the increase in the real burden of taxes. The link is explicit in his appeals to villagers. In Tharrawaddy in early December 1930,

> Saya San *discussed the question of taxes and the general depression of the paddy market.* He exhorted his hearers not to pay the capitation tax but to rise in rebellion. He suggested the looting of headmen's guns, the cutting of telegraph wires, sabotage on the railway and active resistance to government forces.[133]

At about the same time, in addressing followers from many districts, the connection was made even more sharply.

> Saya San said that the time for the collection of taxes was then approaching fast. He recalled the oppression of the villagers by the military in connection with the collection of the capitation tax in Tharrawaddy District in the past and said that *the paddy and rice market was very poor this year and the poor people had been confronted with great trouble and misery and that they should rebel to escape capitation and other taxes.*[134]

The further weakening of the paddy market in early 1931 must have given peasants greater reason for resisting taxes, while the initial successes of the insurgents provided some hope of victory.

What was the nature of the millennium Saya San promised? Above all, it was defined by what it would extirpate rather than what it would create. As in the anarchist credo, the destruction of the existing state was to be the main constitutive act of the revolution. The first order of business was to kill all government servants from the governor down to the hamlet headman.[135] Once this was accomplished, the truly outstanding feature of the new order was that it would be a world without taxes.

131. Ibid., p. 23.
132. Ibid., p. 25. Emphasis added.
133. Ibid., p. 4. Emphasis added. The appeal to a defensive war for local autonomy is remarkably similar to the pattern of the Nghe-Tinh uprising.
134. Ibid., p. 5. Emphasis added.
135. Only a very few such assassinations actually took place.

The reconquest of the country was the means to this end. Saya San told his Tharrawaddy followers, "that they must fight the Government in order to recover the country and get exemption from the payment of taxes."[136] Later, in Thayetmyo, he explained to villagers that "the object of the movement was to regain Burma and promised that if he succeeds, he would become king and reduce or remit taxes." His principal subordinate in Prome saw the coming kingship of his leader in identical terms, "Only when Burma is governed by Burmans, taxation will not be heavy. The Burmans are now getting poor on account of heavy taxation. When we get back our country, debts due to Chettiar moneylenders will also not have to be paid." This vision of the millennium may have been negative but, in the context of the depression, the hope of a life without taxes was already the stuff of which utopias were made. In the master's own words again, "When we recover Burma I will declare myself King and exempt you from payment of taxes. *You will then be able to live in peace.*"[137]

In Henzada, Saya San's local commander, U Yazeinda, made it clear in his harangues to the local population that the principal appeal in the formation of *athins* was resistance to the capitation tax.

> There are many Athins in Tharrawaddy to oppose the British government. Don't pay the capitation tax. It has nothing to do with them. . . . capitation tax is levied only in Burma. The British government is unlawfully ruling the country by levying capitation tax which does not exist in other countries. If the people unite, government will be unable to do anything.[138]

As in Northern Annam, the Saya San rising, once launched, developed into a series of local rebellions that took an independent course of their own. In each case, events tended to reflect the nature of local grievances; in one place Indians might be singled out; in another, local headmen might be put to flight, in another the Forestry Service buildings might be burned. In Pegu and Thayetmyo Districts, rebels are reported to have frequently stormed headmens' houses, seized the "tax tickets" and burned them, "so that people might not have to pay taxes to the Government."[139] In Yamethin, Upper Burma,

136. Ibid., p. 15. The following two quotes are from ibid., pp. 31 and 34, respectively.
137. Ibid., p. 31. It was also a traditional practice of Southeast Asian monarchs, particularly those who had to win their thrones, to exempt individuals, villages, and even districts from taxes as a reward for their support.
138. Ibid., p. 25. One of the advantages of tattooing was to commit members of the *athins* to fight to the end since they would be irrevocably marked as insurgents in any event.
139. Ibid., pp. 31, 38. It is probable that this practice was even more general, as in Nghe-An and Ha-Tinh, but since such information was incidental to the main purpose of the report it is mentioned only in passing.

When passing through villages, the party cried out that taxes should not be paid if demanded and they declared themselves to be rebels (*thabons*), thereby making it manifest that their aim and object was to resist and overawe or fight the Government with a view to obtaining postponement or reduction of taxes.[140]

Another rebel band in Tharrawaddy

"then passed through Kyatgale village shouting out not to pay the capitation tax, not to sell paddy [presumably the paddy that would be sold to meet the tax claim], and to pray for the rebels' victory."[141]

In terms of its local appeal and the motives of rank-and-file participants, the Lower Burma Rebellion of 1930–32 thus comes as close to being a tax rebellion, albeit with millennial overtones, as any uprising in Southeast Asia. An end to taxes, and in particular the hated capitation tax, was both the secular gospel of the *galon athins* formed by Saya San and the main piece of legislation in the millennium he promised. It is the leitmotif in the words and deeds of his legions. That a fiscal measure of only minor importance for colonial revenue should have become the very symbol of state oppression is remarkable and instructive. Two qualities in particular seem to have made it the object of such righteous indignation and of such desperate resistance against overwhelming odds. First, it was a unifying issue par excellence. Wherever they lived, whether they were smallholders, tenants, or laborers, the capitation tax was the single material claim that weighed on all of them at a given, regular time. Second, and equally important, as the most rigid tax in the colonial revenue system, its impact on the cultivator's subsistence livelihood oscillated wildly with crop yields and paddy prices. In this context, the depression, representing the market-equivalent of a massive crop failure, transformed an onerous burden into a clear and present danger to the peasantry's already tenuous subsistence arrangements.

Before it was over the rebellion had touched 12 (of 20) districts in Burma. It had begun on December 22, 1930, nine days before the collection of the capitation tax and one day after the cultivators of Tharrawaddy had had their petition for a reduction or postponement of the tax refused by the Acting Governor.[142] The outcome was never in doubt as poorly armed rebels, trusting in their amulets and tattoos, fell in waves before the Lewis guns of the British Indian Army. It took one-and-a-half years and two imported divisions to flush out the resistance which continued until mid-1932. Three thousand rebels had

140. Ibid., p. 30.
141. Ibid., p. 14.
142. Ba U, *My Burma: The Autobiography of a President* (New York: Taplinger, 1959), p. 103.

perished in the attempt and Saya San himself, who had "refused to say anything in his own defense . . . went up to the scaffold with his head erect."[143]

The theme of tax resistance was not unique to the colonial peasantry. On the contrary, the "little tradition" of Southeast Asia is rich with evidence of the avoidance of corvée labor and grain levies. The effective question is thus not so much whether the state's claim is seen as legitimate but rather the degree of resentment and rage it provokes. To ask this question is to ask what impact a tax claim has on the central elements of peasant economic and social arrangements. The practical consequences of a tax are not, as we have seen, a linear function of the proportion of income that it draws from the peasant household. A 3 percent tax may not greatly affect a family's social status, production patterns or consumption habits in a good year, but may rupture them decisively following a bad year. It is the difference, to return to Tawney, between being up to your neck in water and drowning.

It is thus possible to specify the most exploitative and hence, other things being equal, most explosive mix of peasant economic conditions and state fiscal systems. The closer to the subsistence threshold and the more variable (whether due to nature or to the price system) the peasant's real income, the more likely any claim will be, and will be experienced as, exploitative and menacing. The more invariable the tax is—both across seasons and peasant classes—the more likely it will constitute, sooner or later, a direct threat to subsistence routines.

The probability of conflict was therefore built into the "traffic patterns" of the colonial state's tax system and the economy of its rural subjects. Resistance to head taxes prior to 1930 in Burma and Vietnam and also in Indonesia and the Philippines (the *cedula*) were straws in the wind.[144] The probabilities of a head-on collision, however, had grown enormously in the first three decades of the twentieth century for at least two reasons. First, the peasantry now faced a vastly more powerful state that had the wherewithal to make its claim to a stable revenue stick against almost any odds. Second, the avenues of retreat and protection previously available (for example, village redistribution, a land frontier, a buoyant demand for labor) were narrowing or had already been closed. What was new in 1930 was the suddenness and scope of the final collision, a massive collision made possible by the integrating force of the world market.

143. Ibid., pp. 109–10.
144. Selo Soemardjan, "The Influence of Social Structure on the Javanese Peasant Economy," in Clifton R. Wharton, Jr., ed., *Subsistence Agriculture and Economic Development* (Chicago: Aldine, 1969), p. 46.

# 6 Implications for the Analysis of Exploitation: Reciprocity and Subsistence as Justice

Most definitions of the peasant include at least two features. First, he is a rural cultivator whose production is oriented largely toward family consumption needs; this defines his central economic goal. Second, he is part of a larger society (including nonpeasant elites and the state) that makes claims upon him and this, in a sense, defines his potential human antagonists (or collaborators) in attaining that goal. I have argued that starting with the peasant's existential dilemma—his need for crisis subsistence insurance—we can deduce much of his conception of the decent landlord and the decent state, on the one hand, and his vision of the exploitative landlord or state on the other. The evidence within the Southeast Asian context indicates that structural change in the colonial period permitted elites and the state, to their short run profit, to increasingly violate the moral economy of the peasantry and become more exploitative. In Lower Burma and parts of Vietnam, as we saw, the particular configuration of demographic pressure, market fluctuations, and state action produced a flash point of actual rebellion.

Insofar as the subsistence problem of marginal cultivators is the lot of much of the world's peasantry and insofar as some of the same processes of change I have described are applicable outside Southeast Asia, parts of this argument may contribute to the study of peasant politics in general. In particular, it seems possible to say something about peasant standards of justice and equity—about what peasants consider a legitimate or illegitimate use of power. Although the variety of cultures, economic conditions, and historical experiences which shape peasants' attitudes makes such an enterprise hazardous, the analogous problems of subsistence, rents, and taxes for cultivators who occupy similar positions in the social structure are likely to foster a body of shared sentiments about justice and exploitation.

## STANDARDS OF EXPLOITATION

What is exploitation? What do we mean when we say that the state or landlords exploit peasants? Are some agrarian systems more exploitative than others? If so, how would one set about showing that this was the case?

At the core of the notion of exploitation is the idea "that some individuals, groups, or classes benefit unjustly or unfairly from the labor of, or at the expense of, others."[1] Embedded in this are at least two characteristics of exploitation that both socialist and nonsocialist schools of thought would accept. First, exploitation is to be seen as a *relationship* between individuals, groups, or institutions; the existence of an exploited party implies the existence of an exploiter. Second, exploitation is an *unfair* distribution of effort and rewards, in turn requiring some standard of distributive equity against which actual relationships may be judged. The existence of injustice implies a norm of justice. Beyond this small shared terrain, however, agreement evaporates and, particularly on the question of what the criteria of justice should be, there are almost as many answers as there are social scientists reckless enough to venture onto such treacherous conceptual ground.

Once the criterion for what constitutes a fair or equitable relationship has been provided, it becomes possible in principle to say something about *how* exploitative any particular relationship is by judging how far it departs from that standard. The problem, of course, is that others may not accept the standard as valid. For example, for those within the Marxist tradition, the labor theory of value supplies the conceptual basis for evaluating the level of exploitation. Inasmuch as all value flows ultimately from labor, the surplus value appropriated by the mere ownership of the means of production in the form of rent, profits, and interest provides a measure of exploitation. One hardly need subscribe to the labor theory of value, however, to see exploitation as an objective relationship that allows us to distinguish less exploitative from more exploitative situations. Is there not a difference, Barrington Moore asks, between a landlord who takes a third of the harvest and one who takes nine-tenths?[2] Under almost any conceivable definition of exploitation, then, some relationships are so much more massively unequal and coercive than others that they can easily be recognized as objectively more exploitative. Such stark contrasts in the human condition make an objective approach to exploitation very appealing.

Nevertheless, concepts of exploitation that begin deductively by creating an abstract standard of equity suffer from two inherent difficulties. The first is the degree of acceptance of the moral principles on which the criterion of justice is based. The labor theory of value is, after all, not the only touchstone available for building a theory of exploitation. To take an extreme example, marginalist economists in the laissez-faire tradition

1. Lewis L. Lorwin, "Exploitation," *Encyclopaedia of the Social Sciences*, vol. 6 (New York: Macmillan, 1931), p. 16.

2. Barrington Moore, Jr., *The Social Origins of Dictatorship and Democracy* (Boston: Beacon Press, 1966), p. 471. Moore's question assumes that the services the two hypothetical landlords provide to tenants are more or less comparable.

would equate the normative value of labor with the price it could fetch in the market—whatever that price happened to be. From this narrow perspective, only relationships founded on fraud or naked coercion—as distinct from market forces—could presumably be considered exploitative. Any a priori conception of justice thus presupposes a normative, if not an analytical, tradition. Those who operate outside that tradition will, if they accept the notion of exploitation at all, apply different standards. Ultimately, such disputes over what is exploitative and what is not are appeals to a normative tradition and not matters to be settled by empirical inquiry.

A second difficulty with deductively reached concepts of exploitation is far more serious because it compromises their analytical utility. This difficulty hinges on the fact that such theories rarely provide a conceptual link between an a priori notion of exploitation and the subjective feelings of the exploited. If the subjective feelings of the exploited can be shown to conform in all respects with the deductive standard, then of course the difficulty disappears. But in the absence of this conceptual bridge, any similarity between the level of exploitation as determined by the theory and the sense of exploitation among victims is largely fortuitous. This potential disparity is not a serious inconvenience if the goal of the theory is merely to classify situations as more or less unjust regardless of the views of participants. On the other hand, if it is hoped that that exploitation as uncovered by the theory and exploitation as felt by victims will have some relationship to each other, the inconvenience is far more serious.

One way of saving the theory when a disparity appears is by erecting another theory to explain the incongruity. This is precisely the function served by the concept of false consciousness. When the perceptions, assuming they can be accurately gauged, of workers or peasants whom the theory tells us are exploited fail to accord with their "objective situation," they are said to be in a state of false consciousness. The misapprehension of their true situation by some or all of the exploited provides the typical revolutionary party with one of its key tasks: to unmask the social myths or religious doctrines that prevent people from seeing things as they are.[3]

---

3. For the sake of consistency, the term false consciousness should also apply to cases where there is "objectively" no exploitation but where there is nonetheless a lively sense of social injustice among the population in question. Such situations are presumed to be rare, since the distorting values that lead to false consciousness are the products of the ideological hegemony of a ruling elite and thus tend to distort perceptions in the direction of an acceptance of the social order. See, for example, Frank Parkin, *Class Inequality and Political Order* (New York: Praeger, 1971), chap. 3.

The concept of false consciousness overlooks the very real possibility that the actor's "problem" is not simply one of misperception. It overlooks the possibility that he may, in fact, have his own durable standards of equity and exploitation—standards that lead him to judgments about his situation that are quite different from those of an outside observer equipped with a deductive theory. To put it bluntly, the actor may have his own moral economy. If this is the case, the failure of his views to accord with those of theory is not due to his inability to see things clearly, but to his values. Of course, one may choose to call these values a form of false consciousness as well. But, to the extent that they are rooted in the actor's existential needs, to the extent that they are resistant to efforts at "reeducation," to the extent that they continue to define the situation for him, it is they and not the theory which serve as reliable guides to his sentiments and behavior.

If the analytical goal of a theory of exploitation is to reveal something about the perceptions of the exploited—about *their* sense of exploitation, *their* notion of justice, *their* anger—it must begin not with an abstract normative standard but with the values of the real actors. Such an approach must start phenomenologically at the bottom and ask what the peasants' or workers' definition of the situation is. When a peasant considers 20 percent of his harvest a reasonable rent and 40 percent an unjust rent, how does he arrive at this judgment? What criterion of fairness does he use? On this basis it should be possible to construct the operational moral economy of a subordinate class.

Before proposing a standard of exploitation that I believe reflects the existential dilemma of peasants and their moral economy, the difficulties of deductive notions of justice may be illustrated with a few examples. In this case the examples are cast in terms of landlord-tenant relations. They could, with appropriate adjustments, be applied to peasant-state relations. Four potential standards of justice that tenants might apply to their situation are explained and then evaluated.

*Standard of Living*

Conceivably, the tenant's view of equity in exchange with a landlord might be a direct reflection of the tenant's standard of living. A system of tenancy that leaves the peasant relatively well-off would then be seen as generally benign while one that barely provided for his minimal needs would be seen as exploitative. This simplistic formulation is not without merit. For a man at the very edge of subsistence, the basket of grain taken by the landlord represents a far greater sacrifice than it would for a man with a modest surplus. One would expect the former to resent bitterly even a small rent while the latter would find a larger rent perhaps burdensome but not a direct threat to his family's survival. Conditions of tenancy which are thus at least tolerable for some may be intolerable for others. In this sense, it is hard to conceive of any standard of exploitation that is not related to the material conditions of peasant life—to the human consequences of a given claim on the resources of a tenant family.

Granting that a tenant's standard of living will necessarily color his vision of exploitation, it is unlikely to be his only guide. In addition, there is the relational aspect of exploitation to consider, since even tenants at the same level of penury may have markedly different relationships with their landlords. These differences are likely to influence their judgments as well. What happens, for example, when the conclusions a tenant might draw from his standard of living diverge from those he might draw from his exchange relationship with his landlord? Such situations are not historically rare. Imagine a near-famine in which landlords reduce the share of the harvest that they claim and open their granaries to hungry tenants. Here a probable decline in the standard of living is accompanied by an improvement in the terms of exchange between tenants and landlords.[4] The reverse situation is also conceivable in which the standard of living of tenants is improving (due perhaps to a buoyant market or to new wage earning opportunities), but their exchange relationship with their landlords is deteriorating.[5]

The standard of living of the peasantry, *taken alone,* seems an inadequate basis for a phenomenological theory of exploitation because it ignores the relational character of class linkage. It is true that we cannot expect to know whether a tenant will find a given claim on his resources tolerable or intolerable until we know how precarious his subsistence is. It is equally true, however, that a well-off tenant may find exploitative some claims which do not jeopardize his subsistence and that a poor tenant may find some claims tolerable. At a minimum, an adequate theory of exploitation must consider not only the tenant's standard of living but also the nature of the exchange that links him to the landlord.

*Next Best Alternative*

Another way to judge the legitimacy of the landlord-tenant relationship is to ask what the tenant stands to lose if the relationship ends. How

4. See, for example, Epstein, "Productive Efficiency and Customary Systems of Rewards," pp. 229–52.
5. This situation is often invoked to explain unrest among commercializing peasants prior to the French Revolution and among much of the European peasantry in the late fourteenth century when the nobility attempted to roll back the gains serfs had made after the plague had decimated their numbers and thereby increased the market price for labor.

much worse is his *next best alternative?* Here the argument is that the tenant is a realistic man: he compares the net advantages of his present tenancy with the net advantages, say, of becoming an agrarian wage laborer. The difference he perceives is a measure of how fortunate he is, of his relative preference for his present role over the next best alternative and, thus, an indication of the legitimacy he is likely to accord his status as a tenant.

If peasants actually applied this test of fairness, however, they would accord legitimacy to almost any conceivable relationship. For all except those at the very bottom of the social order there is a next best alternative which would be even more disadvantageous than their current situation. When the alternative to near-starvation is outright starvation, does this mean that the tenant finds near-starvation acceptable or legitimate? Obviously not. It may indicate how dependent he is on a relationship that at least keeps him alive, or how willing he may be to comply with its terms to avoid a worse fate, but dependency and compelled compliance are hardly the same as legitimacy. To reason otherwise would amount to equating what is just with whatever exists. The irreducible quality of human requirements for rest and nourishment, if nothing else, creates nearly universal limits to what is a legitimate claim on tenant labor and crops.

## Reciprocity or Equal Exchange

Many exchange theorists would claim that a landlord-tenant relationship, like any other human relationship, will be judged to be exploitative or not depending on whether it satisfies the norm of reciprocity.[6] In essence, the moral idea involved is that one should return "favors" out of gratitude and that, consequently, equal exchange defines a fair relationship. Landlord-tenant relations characterized by balanced reciprocity would, in this view, give rise to feelings of gratitude and legitimacy while unequal exchange favoring the landlord would give rise to moral indignation and injustice.

Assuming that the norm of reciprocity is a common moral standard, how can it be applied to landlord-tenant relations? The major problem centers around the definition of "equal exchange" that the norm requires. This is the familiar difficulty of comparing apples and oranges. How much protection, for example, would represent a value equal to 20 percent of a tenant's harvest?

One solution to this dilemma is to take the participant's—the

6. Among others, see Alvin W. Gouldner, "The Norm of Reciprocity: A Preliminary Statement," *American Sociological Review* 25:2 (April 1960).

tenant's—actions as a guide to his values. What portion of his harvest is he willing to hand over in return for the landlord's protection? The tenant is the best judge of how much he needs and values protection, and its importance to him can be measured by what he is willing to give up to get it. As Gouldner notes, the value of a service "varies with the intensity of need when the benefit is given."[7] This approach at least has the advantage of avoiding abstract standards of value and focusing instead on the values implied by concrete social choices.

The fatal shortcoming of this procedure, however, is that it confuses the choices that circumstances force on people with choices that they find legitimate. For a tenant on the point of starvation, the value of food will be enormous and he may be willing under the circumstances to surrender all his next harvest, his land, and perhaps even his children in order to survive. Assuming he pays the price exacted, one may wish to call this "equal exchange"—he presumably could have chosen to starve instead. But one can hardly imagine that a tenant would regard such an exchange as anything but sheer extortion. The value of food for the starving tenant is established by a degree of need that is *itself* a social product of the existing distribution of wealth and power. He may have little choice but to comply, but he is surely not obliged to accept as legitimate the social arrangements that force such inhuman choices upon him. To reason otherwise would be to fly in the face of common sense and to legitimize any and all of the degrading alternatives that a system of power may impose.

It is clear that the power of some and the vulnerability of others make for bargains that violate common standards of justice. If the exchange of equal values is taken as a touchstone of fairness, the actual bargains men are driven to cannot then be taken as an indication of value and, hence, of equity. A tenant's need for food may be a measure of his dependency and of the power those who control the supply of food can exercise over him, but it can never be a measure of the legitimacy of that power. Tenants, as others, have no trouble distinguishing what is just from what they must accept under duress. In other words, it must be assumed that there are genuinely normative standards of value in exchange that are to some degree independent of the actual alternatives available in a given context.

*Just Price and Legitimacy*

It may still be possible to take the concept of equal value in exchange as a basis for feelings about equity, provided that the notion of value is

7. Ibid., p. 171.

not derived from the "going rate" of exchange that circumstances impose. This is the position taken by Peter Blau in the following passage which is applicable in principle to landlord-tenant relations:

> But if the power to command services and compliance comes from the supply of needed benefits, its exercise may not be experienced as disadvantageous. If the benefits are greater than what the social norm of fairness leads subordinates to expect in return for their services and compliance, they will consider their position advantageous and express social approval of the ruling group which fortifies its power and legitimates its authority. If subordinates' expectations are barely met, they will neither feel exploited nor express firm legitimating approval of the group in power. If, however, the demands of the ruling group with a monopoly of vital resources far exceed what social norms define as fair and just, subordinates will feel exploited and will seize any opportunity to escape the ruling group's power or oppose it, inasmuch as their situation is basically no different from that of groups subject to coercive force.[8]

Blau distinguishes between actual rates of exchange and the norms governing fair value. The distance between the two becomes the criterion by which men judge the equity or injustice of a relationship. A surplus above fair value in exchange fosters a response of legitimation; a deficit provokes a sense of exploitation.

The justification for assuming that "social norms of fairness" exist apart from actual terms of exchange seems substantial. Durkheim reminds us that "in every society and in all ages, there exists a vague but lively sense of the value of the various services used in society and of the values of things that are the subject of exchange."[9] This "true" price "very rarely coincides with the real price, but these [real prices] cannot go beyond a certain range in any direction without seeming abnormal."[10] The existence of a "fair price" or "true value" is implicit whenever bargains that have been made under duress give offense. A man who surrenders his child for a loan or who sells his birthright for a mess of pottage are extreme examples. The needs of the weaker party have allowed the stronger to impose an exchange that violates the true value of things; the bargain is thus unjust and extortionary. Even contracts that have been freely consented to may not be considered fair if

8. Peter Blau, *Exchange and Power in Social Life* (New York: Wiley, 1961), p. 229.

9. Emile Durkheim, *Professional Ethics and Civic Morals* (London: Routledge and Kegan Paul, 1957), p. 209.

10. Ibid., p. 210.

one party has been driven to pay a price that offends a shared sense of fair value. Minimum wage laws, as Durkheim notes, arise from just such sentiments of fair value. They are designed precisely to preclude employers from taking advantage of their power to force "unjust" bargains.

Evidence for the notion of fair value comes not only from such reflections on moral sentiments but also from concrete historical movements. The venerable tradition of *taxation populaire* and hunger riots in France and England is a striking case in point. There was a shared popular notion of what constituted a fair price for bread that, when it was exceeded, provoked moral indignation and the seizure of markets. "The central action in this pattern is not the sack of granaries and the pilfering of grain and flour, but the action of 'setting the price.' "[11] It was not uncommon for "rioters" to pay what they regarded as a just price in lieu of the market price. Such crowds and agrarian rioters often saw themselves as law-givers (one group called itself "the regulators") who enforced a popular moral consensus.

In any particular agrarian order there is likely to be a similar moral consensus among tenants. Some balance between what tenants provide in goods and services to landlords and what they receive in return will be seen as reasonable and any substantial departure from that norm in the landlord's favor will appear exploitative. Naturally, such norms will vary from place to place and from one period to the next. Despite these variations, however, there are some constants. First, a single interclass dyad is being dealt with here that everywhere originates in an exchange of land-use rights for rent. Second, if only tenants near the subsistence level are involved, it is likely that the common problems of welfare and security that they all face may foster common moral expectations about landlord behavior.

Any viable analysis of exploitation must, then, encompass at least three elements. It must be attentive to the relational or exchange quality of social relations; it must seek out the shared human needs that social actors expect from these relationships; and, in this context, it must work from the actual notions of "fair value" that prevail.

## EXPLOITATION AS A MORAL PROBLEM

The discussion of the norm of fairness brings us directly up against the fact that our approach to exploitation has thus far been too one-sidedly materialistic. An analysis that begins, as this one has, with the givens of the peasant household budget, and deduces peasant needs and

11. Thompson, "The Moral Economy of the English Crowd in the Eighteenth Century," p. 108.

interests from them, runs the risk of what one writer has aptly called "methodological individualism."[12] That is, it risks treating the peasant purely as a kind of marketplace individualist who amorally ransacks his environment so as to reach his personal goal—that is, the stabilization of his subsistence arrangements. The individual and society are set apart from this perspective and society is simply the milieu in which he must act.

To be sure, the goal of assuring subsistence exists as an irreducible given in the lives of most peasants. But to stop there is to miss the critical social context of peasant action. It is to miss the central fact that the peasant is born into a society and culture that provide him with a fund of moral values, a set of concrete social relationships, a pattern of expectations about the behavior of others, and a sense of how those in his culture have proceeded to similar goals in the past. The same might be said for any goal of man in society. The need to mate, for example, might also be "given," but the forms of marriage, their meaning, and the mutual expectations of the spouses are essentially cultural and historical creations. To say that people are born into society is not to deny their capacity to create new forms and break old ones; it is merely to recall that they do not walk out on an empty stage and make up their lines at random.

We are thus in the presence of cultural values and forms in all peasant social action. A villager whose harvest has failed does not respond randomly. He has a clear idea of those from whom he might appropriately ask help and what he might justifiably expect from each. He acts, moreover, in the expectation that his social map is more or less accurate, that his notion of the structure of moral claims conforms with the sense of obligation felt by others. Similarly, the widespread confiscation of grain from wealthy landowners and its communal division in Nghe-An and Ha-Tinh can only have come from a widely shared sentiment of what was justifiable under the circumstances. When Saya San urged the cultivators of Lower Burma to refuse to pay the capitation tax, he was likewise appealing to a common perception of the conditions under which the tax claim of the state was inadmissible. His appeal rested on the new hardships such taxes imposed in the midst of a depression and on the fact that the British had taxed what the Burmese took to be free gifts of nature.

12. Hamza Alavi, "Peasant Classes and Primordial Loyalties," *Journal of Peasant Studies* 1:1 (October 1973), 22–62. Alavi is particularly criticizing the analysis of factions in anthropology but his point is applicable here too. His usage of the term, I should add, is somewhat different than its usage in social science methodology.

Woven into the tissue of peasant behavior, then, whether in normal local routines or in the violence of an uprising, is the structure of a shared moral universe, a common notion of what is just. It is this moral heritage that, in peasant revolts, selects certain targets rather than others, certain forms rather than others, and that makes possible a collective (though rarely coordinated) action born of moral outrage.

To speak of righteous anger is, in the same breath, to speak of standards of justice, or moral values. Thus we are not dealing merely with a theory of peasant income or a theory of "relative deprivation" when we treat the peasant's subsistence ethic. Such theories by themselves tell us only that the peasant has a problem. How the peasant perceives that problem, whom—if anyone—he sees as responsible for his plight, what he expects from those around him, how he reacts, are beyond the scope of any analysis centered exclusively on his level of material well-being.

How, then, can we understand the moral passion that is so obviously an integral part of the peasant revolts we have described? How can we grasp the peasant's sense of social justice? We can begin, I believe, with two moral principles that seem firmly embedded in both the social patterns and injunctions of peasant life: the *norm of reciprocity* and the *right to subsistence*. There is good reason for viewing both the norm of reciprocity and the right to subsistence as genuine moral components of the "little tradition." Reciprocity serves as a central moral formula for interpersonal conduct. The right to subsistence, in effect, defines the minimal needs that must be met for members of the community within the context of reciprocity. Both principles correspond to vital human needs within the peasant economy; both are embodied in many concrete social patterns that owe their strength and longevity to the force of moral approval or disapproval that villagers can bring to bear.

## RECIPROCITY AND THE BALANCE OF EXCHANGE

The moral principle of reciprocity permeates peasant life, and perhaps social life in general. It is based on the simple idea that one should help those who help him or (its minimalist formulation) at least not injure them.[13] More specifically, it means that a gift or service received creates, for the recipient, a reciprocal obligation to return a gift or service of at least comparable value at some future date. Durkheim claimed that this notion of equal exchange was a general moral principle to be found in all cultures. Many anthropologists, including Malinowski

13. Gouldner, "The Norm of Reciprocity," p. 171.

and Mauss, have found that reciprocity served as the basis for the structure of friendship and alliance in traditional societies.[14]

In the village economy of Southeast Asia the principle of reciprocity is at work in a host of activities. The *gotong-rojong* forms of mutual assistance in Java are a celebrated example of structured reciprocity and they are ritually reinforced by a neighborhood communal meal (the *selametan*) which marks crucial junctures in the life of peasant households. Reciprocity is seen as the basic moral principle underlying social action in village Thailand, both within the family and between families.[15] In the Philippines, the pattern of personal alliances has been interpreted largely by reference to reciprocity, or the notion "that every service received, solicited or not, demands a return," with feelings of shame (*hiya*) and obligation (*utang na loob*) providing the motivating force.[16] Reciprocity underlies the typical patterns of labor exchange during the transplanting or harvesting of wet rice as well as *rites de passage* celebrations, such as marriage feasts, when the ceremonial obligations of a family exceed their resources in labor or in kind. In each case the assisting family knows that it can expect a comparable return in services at some later date. This same principle often structures the exchange of food resources within a village. A family that is hard-pressed will expect help from others who have fared better and will expect to reciprocate when the situation is reversed.

Much of the need for reciprocity, clearly, is inherent in the agricultural and ceremonial cycle. It operates largely within the village settlement where the social pressures of the community reinforce the sentiments of obligation. Although the examples provided involve the exchange of identical services or goods, this is not necessarily always the case. What is required is rather the exchange of *comparable* values.

For our purposes, it is critical to understand that the obligation of reciprocity is a moral principle par excellence and that it applies as strongly to relationships between unequals as between equals. In peasant societies not yet permeated by class cleavage, these relationships com-

14. Bronislaw Malinowski, *Crime and Custom in Savage Society* (London: Paul, Trench, Trubner, 1932), pp. 30–50. See also Marcel Mauss, *The Gift: Forms and Functions of Exchange in Archaic Societies* (Glencoe: Free Press, 1954), passim. Mauss would claim that much of his analysis of "prestation" and the social links it creates could be applied to nontraditional societies as well. See also Cyril S. Belshaw, *Traditional Exchange and Modern Markets* (Englewood Cliffs, N.J.: Prentice-Hall, 1965).

15. See, for example, Herbert Phillips, *Thai Peasant Personality* (Berkeley and Los Angeles: University of California Press, 1965), and Lucien Hanks, *Rice and Man*, chap. 6.

16. See Frank Lynch, S.J., "Social Acceptance," in Lynch, ed., *Four Readings on Philippine Values* (Quezon City: Ateneo de Manila University Press, 1964), p. 21, and Mary Hollnsteiner, "Reciprocity in the Lowland Philippines," in ibid., pp. 22–49.

monly take the form of patron-client bonds. The extensive anthropological literature on these characteristic social ties between elites and their clients emphasizes the moral idea of reciprocity, of mutual rights and obligations, which gives them their social force.[17] Of course it is unlikely that the goods and services exchanged between patron and client will be identical, for the nature of the relationship is based on their differing needs. While the exact nature of the exchange will typically reflect the needs and resources of both patron and client over time, as a general rule the patron is expected to protect his client and provide for his material needs whereas the client reciprocates with his labor and his loyalty. The moral tone of the relationship is often reinforced by ceremonies of ritual kinship or other symbolic ties.

A great many, perhaps most, interpretations of rural class relations in Southeast Asia have relied upon the patron-client model of association to explain the pervasiveness of interclass followings and factions.[18] The normative model for the conduct of these relationships may be seen in

17. Given the burgeoning literature on this topic, an extensive bibliography here is out of the question. A few exemplary works are: George M. Foster, "The Dyadic Contract in Tzintzuntzan: Patron-Client Relationship," *American Anthropologist* 65 (1963), 1280–94; Eric Wolf, "Kinship, Friendship, and Patron-Client Relations," in M. Banton, ed., *The Social Anthropology of Complex Societies* (New York: Praeger, 1966); J. Campbell, *Honour, Family, and Patronage* (Oxford: Clarendon Press, 1964); Alex Weingrod, "Patrons, Patronage, and Political Parties," *Comparative Studies in Society and History* 19 (July 1968), 1142–58; Fredrik Barth, *Political Leadership Among the Swat Pathans*, London School of Economics Monographs on Social Anthropology, No. 19 (London, 1965). For a more complete bibliography, see Steffen Schmidt, James Scott, Carl Lande, and Laura Guasti, eds., *Friends, Followers, and Factions: A Reader on Political Clientelism* (forthcoming, University of California Press).

18. Carl Lande, the first to apply explicitly the patron-client model to Southeast Asian politics, found it an indispensable tool in explaining the absence of class-based voting and the alliances between "big people" and "little people" that characterized Philippine parties. Lande, *Leaders, Factions, and Parties: The Structure of Philippine Politics* (New Haven: Yale Southeast Asia Studies, Monograph No. 6, 1964). A careful study of village politics in Upper Burma by Nash concluded that a villager's basic political decision was to affiliate himself with a well-to-do patron who could protect and advance his interests. Manning Nash, *The Golden Road to Modernity*. Local politics in Malaya and Thailand has been explained in comparable terms. See, for example, M. G. Swift, *Malay Peasant Society in Jelebu*, and Herbert Phillips, *Thai Peasant Personality*, (Berkeley and Los Angeles: University of California Press, 1965). Even in rural Java where party labels suggest an ideological polarization, one major interpretation has emphasized the factional nature of *santri-abangan* cleavages, in which each party was led by rich peasants who brought along their kin, neighbors, and clients. Robert R. Jay, *Religion and Politics in Rural Central Java*, Cultural Report Series (New Haven: Yale University Southeast Asian Studies, 1963), pp. 98–99. On this also see Donald Hindley, *The Communist Party of Indonesia 1951–1963* (Berkeley and Los Angeles: University of California, 1966), chap. 14, and Rex Mortimer, "Class, Social Cleavage, and Indonesian Communism," *Indonesia* 8 (October 1969), 1–20.

the social pressures within the village, which operate to require the relatively well-off to use their resources in ways that benefit the poorer members of the community. By being liberal with his wealth, a villager acquires a reputation as a good man and at the same time surrounds himself with a grateful clientele which is at his disposal. There is a lively sense among clients as to what they may rightfully expect from the relationships and what may be required of them. When these expectations are met, the effect is to give moral sanction to the pattern of stratification. That is, differences in status are not illegitimate per se; their moral standing is contingent on how closely would-be patrons conform to the moral expectations of the community at large.

If the growth in permanent disparities in power opens the way to what we might call patronage, it also opens the way to exploitation. For it is such differences that allow the stronger party to take advantage of the needs of weaker parties and thus violate the norm of equivalent reciprocity. So long as the reciprocating parties are of more or less equal standing, the exchange tends to be balanced and stable. One smallholder, for example, is motivated to help his smallholding neighbor harvest since he himself will need the same assistance later. Neither can impose his will upon the other but must, in his own interest, be forthcoming if he hopes to continue to evoke the services he needs. Once substantial power differences are introduced, however, this "invisible hand" disappears and exploitation may enter. For inequalities in society mean, above all, unequal control over the scarce resources of the community, and it is this difference alone that provides one party with the bargaining or coercive strength to impose an unequal exchange, an exchange that violates a widely shared sense of fair value. Those who occupy the upper reaches of a stratification system are thus often in a position to unilaterally supply goods and services which those at the bottom need desperately for their survival and well-being. If they control much of the available land and food in the community, for example, they are able to impose terms on others that reflect their monopoly. The fact that demand for the food sources they control is, alas, highly inelastic, given human nutritional needs, allows them potentially to demand compliance with whatever price they impose.

Thus, the crucial question in rural class relations is whether the relationship of dependence is seen by clients as primarily collaborative and legitimate or as primarily exploitative. Here the issues of compliance and legitimacy are analytically distinct.[19] Given the principle of reciprocity, I

19. Empirically, of course, disapproving submission may be difficult to distinguish from approving submission if there are no opportunities for the expression of discontent. We will take up this issue in the following chapter.

believe that it is possible to make at least a rough distinction between equal and unequal exchange and to associate unequal exchange with sentiments of exploitation. One would expect, in this context, that any major shift in the balance of exchange between peasants and landlords or between peasants and the state—any major shift, that is, in the ratio of goods and services peasants provide to elites and the goods and services they receive in return—would be accompanied by a corresponding shift in the perceived legitimacy of the relationship. This criterion of judgment, it should be emphasized, it not merely an abstract standard by which an outside observer can ascertain whether exploitation exists; there is good reason to believe that it is a standard by which peasants themselves actually judge their relationships with others. The argument here follows the valuable insights of Barrington Moore and others who have demonstrated that popular conceptions of justice have a common objective core.[20] As Moore explains:

> An overlord who does not keep the peace, who takes away most of the peasant's good, seizes his women—as happened over wide areas of China in the nineteenth and twentieth centuries—is clearly exploitative. In between this situation and objective justice are all sorts of gradations where the ratio between services rendered and the surplus taken from peasants is open to dispute. Such disputes may intrigue philosophers. They are not likely to rip society apart. The thesis put forward here merely holds that the contributions of those who fight, rule, and pray must be obvious to the peasant, and the peasant's return payments must not be grossly out of proportion to the services received. *Folk conceptions of justice, to put the argument in still another way, do have a rational and realistic basis, and arrangements that depart from this basis are likely to need deception and force the more they do depart.*[21]

For the client or subordinate, the key element of evaluation is the ratio of services he receives to services he provides. But the client's ratio and the landlord's ratio are not necessarily mirror images; the patron's gain

20. Moore, *Social Origins of Dictatorship and Democracy*, pp. 453–83. His argument was advanced considerably by Sydel F. Silverman in "Exploitation in Rural Central Italy: Structure and Ideology in Stratification Study," *Comparative Studies in Society and History* 12 (1970), 327–39. On exchange theory and class relations, see also Peter Blau, *Exchange and Power in Social Life*, and Arthur Stinchcombe, "Agricultural Enterprise and Rural Class Relations," *American Journal of Sociology* 67 (1961–1962), 165–76.

21. Moore, *Social Origins of Dictatorship and Democracy*, p. 471, emphasis added. The same reasoning may be applied to the state. Thus, "collecting taxes, for example, would not be exploitation where the state and its rulers provided justice, protection, and in modern times decent public services." Moore, *Reflections on the Causes of Human Misery and Upon Certain Proposals to Eliminate Them* (Boston: Beacon Press, 1970), p. 53.

is not necessarily the client's loss. The opening of a new school, for example, may make it easier (less costly) for the landlord to assist his tenants' children in getting an education while not necessarily reducing the value of that service. Thus, the landlord's position in the exchange may be improved while the tenant's is not worsened. Under other circumstances, though, the two parties may be at loggerheads; a landlord who previously took 50 percent of the harvest and now takes 75 percent is gaining at the direct expense of his tenant.

The concept of balance employed here is not directly quantifiable. On the one hand, there is again the problem of what exchange rate to apply; how many baskets of grain are a fair payment for how much protection and subsistence insurance? On the other hand, there is the problem of indivisible elite services (such as the sponsoring of public works, schools, village festivals, collective charity) which are not unambiguously divisible into exchanges between individuals. Nevertheless, both the direction and approximate magnitude of a shift in the terms of trade can often be ascertained. Once the kinds of services and their frequency and volume have been specified in both directions, we have a rough picture of the existing pattern of exchange. If elites discontinue a service and the services of peasants remain unchanged, we know the balance has become less favorable for peasants. If elites demand more without providing more, we know that peasants are in a less advantageous position.[22]

Beyond changes in the nature and number of reciprocal services, the cost of a given service may shift. In an era when wage labor opportunities are expanding, a landowner's demand for free labor service from his tenants may become more onerous (have a higher opportunity cost) than before and hence affect the balance. The balance may be similarly altered by a change in the value of a given service. Thus, the value of physical protection was especially high in the chaos of the early feudal period in western Europe but declined later as invasions subsided and central states were created. Variations in the cost or value of a service can, in such cases, lead to a shift in the legitimacy of the exchange while the content of the exchange remains constant.

Any assessment of the balance of exchange must also consider, as peasants themselves must, the entire pattern of reciprocity. The more precapitalist the context, the more likely the exchange will involve a

22. These models in fact correspond roughly to two processes of agrarian change. The former is characteristic of a commercializing landowner class that reduces or terminates most services performed by the traditional aristocracy while continuing to squeeze peasants. The latter resembles the efforts of a declining rural aristocracy to survive by exacting each and every feudal privilege while being unable to maintain, let alone raise, their services to their retainers.

great variety of reciprocal services beyond the arrangements for cultivation and the division of the crop. A landlord's crisis help, influence, and protection may be more valuable in the peasant's estimation than a 5 or 10 percent increase in the share of the crop he must deliver. The disappearance of such services may thus jeopardize the legitimacy of agrarian elites even though landowners take less of the crop and peasant labor requirements are reduced.

This conceptualization of reciprocity runs into difficulty, of course, when we wish to know *how much* of a shift has taken place and not merely its direction, and also when we try to gauge the net effect of changes which push the balance in opposite directions. Precise calibration is out of the question but, as Moore notes, such ambiguous shifts are not likely to tear society apart. However, we, together with the peasants who experience them, can detect gross differences. In areas such as the Mekong Delta and Lower Burma, the unmistakable shift in the balance of exchange against peasants from 1910 to 1935 makes fine measurements hardly necessary.

All of this is not to say that norms of equity in the balance of exchange do not vary from culture to culture and over time. They most certainly do. What the nineteenth-century Chinese peasant might have considered a decent landlord would, to the contemporary Thai peasant, seem oppressive indeed. For this reason it would be dangerous, in the absence of the grossest differences, to draw conclusions about the relative legitimacy of agrarian elites in two distinct cultural and historical settings on the basis of the comparative balance of exchange between elites and peasants. Neither is the range of cultural variation infinite in this respect, for the exploitative nature of a landlord whose claim on the crop leaves his tenants hungry and who provides nothing in return is perfectly apparent in any setting. Within a *particular* cultural and historical context, any major shift in the balance of exchange is likely to have a corresponding impact on the legitimacy of the relationship.

The principle of reciprocity puts the problems of "false consciousness" and the role of "outside agitators" in a new perspective. Inasmuch as peasants have a sharp appreciation of their relations with rural elites, they have no difficulty in recognizing when more and more is required of them and less and less is given in return. Peasants are thus not much subject to "mystification" about class relations; they do not need outsiders to help them recognize a pattern of growing exploitation which they experience daily. This does not mean outsiders are inconsequential. On the contrary, they are often critical to peasant movements, not because they convince peasants that they are exploited but because, in the context of exploitation, they may provide the power, assistance, and supralocal organization that helps peasants *act*.[23] It is thus at the level of collective action that the typically small scale of peasant social life constitutes a disability, not at the level of assessing class relations.

The idea of a balance of reciprocity or a balance of exchange implies a continuum of possible links, ranging all the way from equality of exchange to unreciprocal relationships of pure coercion. Insofar as exchange relationships involve parties with unequal power, they are likely to be lopsided. Just how lopsided they are, however, is of great analytical interest—for the particular balance of reciprocity will make a great difference in both the quality and stability of class relations.

Three brief examples of landlord-tenant relations will serve to illustrate substantial disparities in the degree of reciprocity and, hence, in the degree of legitimacy that the landowner is accorded. All three are drawn in general terms from Central Luzon in the Philippines, and the order from less exploitative to more exploitative reflects an historical sequence as well as an analytical series.[24]

The men who created many of the new rice haciendas in Central Luzon in the early twentieth century established a pattern of tenancy arrangements which, while based on class inequalities, incorporated a considerable degree of reciprocity. Typically, they employed the *kasama* system of tenancy in which production costs and the crop itself were shared equally. The landholder might provide the price of seed, transplanting costs, and occasionally the use of a plow animal, while the costs of threshing and irrigation were divided equally. Most important, the landlord distributed rice at no interest between harvests and cash loans (at interest) that he did not insist on collecting after a poor harvest. Beyond the terms of tenancy itself, the *hacendero* normally made a personal contribution to a tenant family at times of birth, baptism, or marriage or when death or illness struck. Finally, the locally dominant landlords often provided services to the community as a whole that included organizing and contributing to local charities, public works, and festivals, settling local disputes, and acting as the representative of local interests to outside authority. For his part, the tenant supplied the balance of production costs and the labor on his plot, additional labor when the *hacendero* asked, and various services as a member of his landlord's local political faction.

The balance of exchange on such haciendas deteriorated noticeably in

23. "Outsiders" may often encourage local defiance merely by winning a victory that destroys for a time the miasma of elite power that had previously held peasants in check.

24. For a more extended discussion see Benedict J. Kerkvliet, "Peasant Society and Unrest Prior to the Huk Revolution in the Philippines," *Asian Studies* (Manila) 9 (August 1971), 164–213.

the 1920s and 1930s.[25] Landowners gravitated steadily away from their holdings toward the economic and social advantages of the provincial towns. Both their personal and timely assistance to needy tenants, and the collective services they had once maintained, diminished or disappeared with their physical withdrawal. Most important, the practice of loaning grain in the months prior to the new harvest was sharply curtailed. By any standard there had been a marked deterioration in the balance of reciprocity—an increase in exploitation. Tenants themselves remembered the older landlords as better men and referred to the older pattern of tenancy as more just. The change in the level of exploitation was, moreover, reflected in the rise of tenant agitation and violence.

Finally, if we move to pure rentier ownership that came to characterize portions of Central Luzon, the tenant-landlord relationship often became one of unvarnished exploitation. The owner typically provided nothing beyond the land, and that at a high and often invariable rent. He contributed nothing to production costs and transferred the risks of agriculture entirely to the shoulders of his tenant. In fact, the sum total of the relationship between the two was reduced to the annual appearance of the landowner or his agent to claim the rent—unless, of course, he required that it be brought directly to him.

This progression was not simply the replacement of big-hearted, sentimental landlords by cold-eyed, impersonal rent collectors; it was rather a reflection of the changing bargaining power of landlords vis-à-vis their tenants. Part of the change was demographic. Haciendas were created at a time when land was easily available and tenants could, if they wished, find opportunities elsewhere. Later, when the frontier was closed and population had grown, the landlord was in a position to take more and give less to tenants. Part of the change was political. The growth of state power with its guarantee of landed property put less and less of a premium on the creation of a strong local clientele as the means to power. In effect, then, the degree of reciprocity in landlord-tenant relations—the level of exploitation—was a function of the shifting balance of power in the countryside.

Each of these successive landlord-tenant systems is, in a reasonably demonstrable way, more exploitative than its predecessor. Looking at what the landlord does for the tenant and the tenant for the landlord, each exchange is progressively less favorable for the tenant while the last can hardly be described as an exchange at all. It would not be inappro-

25. The particular cases abstracted here are actually those of the same hacienda, first under the management of the founder from 1905–1924, and then under the management of his son from 1924–1936.

priate to call the early hacienda system a patron-client arrangement.
This term is merely a convenient shorthand for a vertical exchange
relationship that is characterized by a substantial degree of reciprocity
and provides a wide range of economic and social protection to dependents in return for their labor and support. Toward the more reciprocal
end of the spectrum, the *status* of the elite is more willingly granted and
the attitude of subordinates more closely approaches genuine *deference*.
Toward the less reciprocal end of the spectrum, by contrast, there is less
patronage and more force; status gives way to *power* and deference to
*submission*.

## SUBSISTENCE AS THE FUNDAMENTAL SOCIAL RIGHT

If the legitimacy of elites, in the eyes of peasants, were simply a direct
linear function of the balance of exchange, our task would be decep-
tively simple. The discontinuous character of human needs, however,
makes such an easy formula inconceivable and ignores the existence of
the physical and social thresholds in peasant life that were the starting
point of our analysis.

There is strong evidence that, along with reciprocity, the right to
subsistence is an active moral principle in the little tradition of the
village. It is certainly inherent in the preference for social arrangements
that minimize the danger of going under, discussed in Chapter 2. More
important, it is reflected in the social pressures on the relatively well-to-
do within the village to be open-handed toward their less fortunate
neighbors, pressures that are characteristic of Southeast Asian village
life. Insofar as power relations within the village permitted, these rights
to subsistence tended to be observed in the precapitalist agrarian order.
Attitudes toward systems of tenancy and the obligations of landlords in
both Lower Burma and Vietnam also turned on the duty of the landowner to provide for the minimum material needs of his tenants. We can
do no better than to recall the words of the sharecropper quoted earlier:
"A man of his means was supposed to loan his tenants rice and help
when times were hard. That's part of being a landlord."

The operating assumption of the "right to subsistence" is that all
members of a community have a presumptive right to a living so far as
local resources will allow. This subsistence claim is morally based on the
common notion of a hierarchy of human needs, with the means for
physical survival naturally taking priority over all other claims to village
wealth. In a purely logical sense, it is difficult to imagine how any
disparities in wealth and resources can be legitimated unless the right to

subsistence is given priority.[26] This right is surely the minimal claim that an individual makes on his society and it is perhaps for this reason that it has such moral force. "The necessities of life form the basis of the right to subsistence. . . . which may be characterized as recognizing the claim of every member of society to the commodities and services necessary to support existence in preference to the satisfaction of the less pressing wants of others."[27] Such a right thus implies not only the claim of the poor on the resources of the village itself but also their claim on the wealth of better-off villagers. In preindustrial Europe, as well, subsistence appears to have been the moral principle to which the poor appealed.

> For since man occupied an appointed place or degree in the body politic, every man had a claim on that body to provide him with the means of livelihood: Transactions or contracts that militated against his right to subsistence, however arrived at, were unjust and invalid. For most people, the ultimate appeal was to social, in contrast to economic, duty.[28]

The right to subsistence took concrete form in the doctrine of the "just price" tied to wages and in the practice of the Russian *mir* whose members redistributed land at regular intervals in accordance with family size. Pitt-Rivers, describing Andalusia, states the operating assumption of many of these practices: "The idea that he who has must give to him who has not is not only a precept of religion, but a moral imperative of the pueblo."[29]

Threats to the peasantry's right to subsistence are not, then, a direct linear function of the balance of reciprocity. We must begin, not with the balance of exchange alone, but with its effects on the life of the peasant household. If the balance of exchange is deteriorating but the material situation of the cultivator's family is stable or even improving, discontent may be evident but it is unlikely to provoke massive unrest. It is when a worsening balance of exchange menaces crucial elements of subsistence routines, when it stretches existing subsistence patterns to the breaking point, that we may expect explosions of rage and anger. No doubt these

26. See, in this context, the argument of Runciman, *Relative Deprivation and Social Justice*, p. 264.

27. Menger, *The Right to the Whole Produce of Labour*, pp. 9–10.

28. Alan Everitt, "The Marketing of Agricultural Produce," in Joan Thirsk, ed., *The Agrarian History of England and Wales, 1540–1640*, vol. 4 (London: Cambridge University Press, 1967), pp. 469–70.

29. Pitt-Rivers, *The People of the Sierra*, p. 62.

thresholds have a cultural dimension too, since they depend on what is necessary for the realization of minimum cultural decencies—for example, caring for elderly parents, celebrating crucial rituals—but they also have an objective dimension—for example, enough land to feed the family, subsistence help in case of crop failure or illness, minimum physical protection against outsiders. Exploitation is thus not a seamless web; each extra basket of rice the landlord or state takes does not make for an identical quantum of pain. The taxes that smallholders pay may finally reach a point where they must resist or give up the land. The contraction of gleaning rights and food loans may finally oblige a family to go hungry or leave the village. It is for this reason that claims on a cultivator's resources that vary with his capacity to pay are experienced as less exploitative than claims that are pressed without regard to his consumption needs.

There are also occasions on which the balance of exchange may actually remain the same but be experienced as vastly more oppressive. Peasants in nineteenth-century China, for example, found their customary rents suddenly intolerable when the handicraft employment, which had hitherto provided a margin of safety, evaporated.[30] Landlords were not taking any more, but the effect on subsistence of what they took was now catastrophic. The loss of common grazing land or a business depression that at one blow eliminates subsidiary employment may similarly make insupportable tenure arrangements that were in the past supportable. We must ask, as the peasant surely does, not only how much elites extract from him but what effects their claims have on the constituent elements of his life.

In each historical context, obviously, the social meaning of the right to subsistence and thus the obligations of the elite will vary considerably. Two aspects of this variation, however, merit special emphasis: (1) the positive as opposed to the negative formulation of elite obligations, and (2) the relation of the subsistence claim to the mode of livelihood.

1. The responsibilities of elites for peasant welfare can be stated in either maximal or minimal terms. Their most comprehensive terms assert the duty of elites to intervene to subsidize and assist peasants when, for whatever reason, their subsistence is in jeopardy. This formulation seems most appropriate to feudal systems of strong personal patronage where symbols of friendship (such as "compadre" ties) are a manifest component of the rhetoric of stratification. The hacienda systems of Central Luzon and of South America until the early twentieth century are cases in point. The less comprehensive or minimal formula-

30. Hsiao-tung Fei, *China's Gentry: Essays on Rural-Urban Relations* (Chicago: University of Chicago Press, 1953), pp. 116–18.

tion asserts only that the elite's claim to produce or labor must not jeopardize the peasant's right to subsistence. This version is perhaps most appropriate in the case of the peasant's historical relationship to the state and in the case also of his relation to landowners with whom personal bonds are tenuous. Frontier regions such as Cochinchina and Lower Burma would appear to fit this category.

2. Inasmuch as the moral claim of a right to subsistence derives in large part from an existential dilemma, it characterizes many sectors of the population for which subsistence is problematic. The actual content of that moral claim has, moreover, a direct relation to the claimant's sources of subsistence. Thus, for smallholding peasants, the claim might include continued access to the land, assistance from larger landholders during hard times, and remissions of taxes following a bad harvest. For a tenant it might involve a secure lease, similar help from the landlord in times of dearth, a reduction or elimination of rents and taxes after a poor season, and free access to common land and the forest. For an agricultural laborer its special features might be guaranteed employment, gleaning rights, a stable real wage, loans or assistance at times of need, and a tax load that varies with his capacity to pay. Finally, for a poor urban wage laborer, a price for bread or rice that was keyed to wage levels might be as important as steady work and the possibility of relief. While the right to subsistence may be typical of many social orders, its precise contours will necessarily vary with the specific context.

## TRADITION AND BREACHES OF STABLE EXCHANGE

Quite apart from the effect of subsistence thresholds on the legitimacy of class relationships, it is obvious that what we might call the force of custom has an independent influence of its own. From the perspective of the tenant, for example, there is a clear difference between a stable landlord-tenant relationship and one that is more impermanent and formless. Given similar balances of reciprocity, the traditional exchange is likely to have greater moral force. Its greater legitimacy seems to flow *not* simply from its antiquity but rather from the fact that its age represents a higher probability that its terms will be observed in the future. The tenant or serf assumes that his (land)lord will at least conform to the minimal traditions of reciprocity if he can and that local opinion will help guarantee the observance of traditional terms. If the tenant or client considers traditional reciprocity preferable to less traditional arrangements, his choice has some rational basis. Tradition helps confer legitimacy because it generally promises a higher level of performance according to expectations and because it is more durable and culturally sanctioned than less institutionalized forms of security.

In stable agrarian settings, then, the power relationships between elites and peasants may have produced a particular norm of reciprocity—a standard package of reciprocal rights and obligations— that acquires a moral force of its own. The resulting norms, so long as they provide basic protection and security, will be jealously defended against breaches that threaten the peasantry's existing level of benefits.[31] Sudden efforts to reset these norms to the disadvantage of the peasantry will be seen as violations of traditional obligations. Thus any balance of exchange above a certain minimum is likely to take on legitimacy over time, and even small movements away from a balance of reciprocity that will reduce peasant benefits are likely to give rise to a sense of exploitation which invokes tradition on its behalf. Whether or not this sense of exploitation takes the form of active resistance depends, of course, on a host of other factors including the coercive power of elites and the social organization of the peasantry.

The peasantry's defense of traditional reciprocity in such cases is no mindless reflex. It is motivated by the fear that a readjusted balance will work against them. A classic example of this situation is the English agricultural uprising in the 1830s when farm workers, whose bargaining position had eroded, invoked traditional local customs of hiring and employment against the commercial innovations of landowners.[32] If, on the other hand, elites realize that *their* bargaining power with peasants has deteriorated as, for example, was the case for much of the French rural aristocracy vis-à-vis a commercializing peasantry in the eighteenth century, it is *they* and not peasants who will be found invoking tradition. It is because the commercialization of agriculture so frequently works against the interest of poorer peasants that they are cast in the role of defending traditional rights and obligations and demanding the restoration of the status quo ante.

STRATIFICATION, OBLIGATIONS, AND RIGHTS

The principles of reciprocity and subsistence may also be viewed from the perspective of the general character of authority in society. Each stratification system generates its own myth or rationale to explain why some should be exalted above others. Such myths may be largely prescriptive: He is king because he is of divine birth, because he is the eldest son of the previous king, and so forth. Without exception, however, all

31. See, for example, Bloch, *French Rural History*, chap. 2.
32. Hobsbawm and Rudé, *Captain Swing*. In many respects this account is instructive for understanding peasant reactions to the breaches of exchange brought about by the green revolution in the past decade. Cf. Francine Frankel, *India's Green Revolution* (Princeton: Princeton University Press, 1971).

such justifications have a performance or service dimension as well. Thus, the king may be responsible for bringing rain, for the first ceremonial plowing that assures good crops, or for victoriously leading his people in battle. It is largely by reference to its contribution to the welfare of the group that power seeks to become authority—to legitimize itself. In his *Political Anthropology*, Georges Balandier views the notion of reciprocity and obligation as a universal corollary of any system of authority. "In a more general way, it might be said that power must justify itself by maintaining a state of collective security and prosperity. This is a price to be paid by those who hold it—a price that is never wholly paid."[33] Authority, as Balandier sees it, is necessary for the performance of collective social tasks and, in this functionalist sense, natural. The legitimacy of that authority, however, is contingent upon the performance of obligations for which it is held responsible.

These general obligations of power have practical consequences in society: kings might be killed if the crops failed to ripen; Russian priests, we are told, were beaten if the rains did not come;[34] and emperors lost "the mandate of heaven" when famine stalked the land. The tendency for the electorate to turn out any government that has presided over a sharp economic depression is, more speculatively perhaps, another case of the general obligations imposed upon power. Even the widest expressions of authority in society thus imply a normative structure of obligations for those who claim the society's privileges. These duties, which are often quite specific, in turn create a standard of performance by which the justice of inequalities may be judged. Failures to meet these obligations necessarily undermine the normative basis of power.

The critical point here is that in all but the most coercive systems of rural class relationships, there is some pattern of reciprocity, some pattern of *rights*, which peasants claim as the duty of those who control scarce resources. Such normative traditions are reflected in popular conceptions of what constitutes the "good" lord, the just king, the decent landlord. The justification of any hierarchy of status and power thus implies the creation of role obligations that carry moral weight. The acceptance of distinctions in status and wealth is in this sense always contingent and never absolute. A study of relations between farm workers and their employers in contemporary England concluded that, "As long as the former [landowner] conforms to the worker's image of 'the good farmer,' it seems that employer-employee relationships will remain

33. Georges Balandier, *Political Anthropology* (New York: Pantheon Books, 1971), p. 39.
34. Moore, *Reflections on the Causes of Human Misery*, pp. 53–54.

harmonious, however great the disparities of income and life-style."[35]

To say that there are norms in such power relationships is not to deny that, from a wider perspective, they may be exploitative. They often are. There is, however, no contradiction between the insistence on those remaining rights that exist within a constraining context and the recognition that the context is itself unfair. Many factory workers, for example, see the industrial system of authority and rewards as unjust and might support a fundamentally new structure of power if the opportunity presented itself. But this hardly prevents them from defending their existing rights and appealing to the established obligations of employers within the existing system. Similarly, peasants on Central Luzon haciendas in the 1930s were increasingly receptive to parties that called for the expropriation of the holdings of large landowners, but at the same time ferociously protected what they took to be their fundamental rights to food loans within the existing hacienda system.

For an agrarian system of stratification, then, as for any other system, it should be possible to establish the standards of reciprocity and fair return that prevail. The logical place to begin is with the respective needs and resources of the elite and of the subordinate population. In peasant society we are dealing with an exchange between wealth and power on the one hand and a near subsistence peasantry on the other, and the norms of obligation are set, to a great extent, by the existential needs of the lower class. The recurrent economic problem of peasant life is the ecological precariousness of the food supply; therefore, those who control the scarce resources of the society are responsible for the basic material requirements of their subordinates. *Here the norm of reciprocity and the right to subsistence are firmly joined. It is the right to subsistence that defines the key reciprocal duty of elites, the minimal obligation that they owe to those from whom they claim labor and grain.*

There is some reason to believe that this nexus of inequality and subordination within the context of the economic right to subsistence is a central feature of most precapitalist social orders. Tribal authority in Africa appears to have reflected this connection between dependence and rights.

> A subject could *demand* food and assistance from his chief in a time of need. . . . it is *his duty* to see that his "children" do not starve. Work in the chief's garden was a form of insurance against want. *If the chief did not make gifts to his people, they regarded him as a bad chief*, and exercised their final sanction of withdrawal to another chieftancy.[36]

35. Colin Bell and Howard Newby, "The Sources of Agricultural Workers' Images of Society," *Sociological Review* 21:2 (1973), 244.

36. William Watson, *Tribal Cohesion in a Money Economy: A Study of the Mambwe People of*

In fact, we find an identical logic behind the great French peasant uprising of 1538, the one from which the very term, "jacquerie", is derived. As Hilton notes, "the quick irritation that Jacques Bonhomme experienced . . . was nothing compared with his permanent rage against nobles whom he blamed, as a whole, for not having fulfilled their duty of protection which tradition and mutual obligation demanded of them."[37] Writing in the mid-nineteenth century, Friedrich Engels saw Irish landlord-tenant relations in much the same light.

> The landlord, whose tenant the peasant is, is still considered by the latter as a sort of clan chief who supervises the cultivation of the soil in the interest of all, is entitled to tribute from the peasant in the form of rent, but also has to assist the peasant in cases of need. Likewise, everyone in comfortable circumstances is considered under obligation to help his poorer neighbors whenever they are in distress. *Such assistance is not looked on as charity, it is what the poor clansman is entitled to by right* from his rich fellow clansman or clan chief.[38]

Much the same logic would appear to extend even to social systems in which the relationships of subordination owe their origin to straightforward acts of coercion. The masterful analysis of North American slavery by Eugene Genovese turns on precisely this theme of the rights of subordinate classes in the context of enforced dependence. Although we are not concerned with slavery here, Genovese's conclusion is instructive for it reveals the dynamics of what might be called the class dialectic of paternalism.

> The slaves had turned the dependency relationship to their own advantage. Their version of paternalistic dependency stressed reciprocity. . . . From their point of view, the genuine acts of kindness and material support to which they were by no means insensible, were in fact their due—payment, as it were, for services loyally rendered. . . . If the master had a duty to provide for his people and to behave like a decent human being, *then his duty had to become the slave's right.* Where the masters preferred to translate their own self-defined duties into privileges for their people—an utter absurdity the illogic of which the most servile slave could see through— the slaves understood duties to be duties. Because they knew that

*Northern Rhodesia* (Manchester: Rhodes Livingston Institute and Manchester University Press, 1958), p. 160, emphasis added.

37. Rodney Hilton, *Bond Men Made Free: Medieval Peasant Movements and the English Rising of 1381* (London: Temple Smith, 1973), p. 131.

38. Karl Marx and Friedrich Engels, *Ireland and the Irish Question* (Moscow: Progress Publishers, 1971), p. 341, emphasis added.

their masters depended on their labor . . . they felt that they had earned their masters' protection and care.[39]

At another level, in their religion and culture, slaves resisted their status as a permanently inferior caste, but within the context of white domination they nonetheless "drew their own lines, asserted rights, and preserved their self respect."[40]

We have only to look at late feudal society in the West to recognize the prototype of such structures of obligation. As Marc Bloch has shown, the feudal bond implied a diffuse and therefore comprehensive duty on the part of the lord to see that his men were protected and taken care of.[41]

His obligations were his men's *rights*, owed them as the repayment for their labor and compliance and stoutly defended against violation. As the growth of the state made sheer physical protection a less pressing need, the economic obligations of elites remained as a central justification of their role. The observance of these terms of exchange involved attention to the personal and familial needs of the subordinate peasantry, the tailoring of demands in labor and grain to annual conditions, and the provision of food in times of dearth. The moral force of these expectations is underlined by the anger and violence which their transgression generally provoked.

Essentially, this precapitalist normative order was based on the guarantee of *minimal social rights* in the absence of political or civil rights. Peasants expected of elites the generosity and assistance that they imposed within the village on their better-off neighbors; social rights were, in this sense, village morals writ large.[42]

It is well worth noting the striking differences between the normative base of this class system and that of nineteenth-century capitalism. These differences are nicely reflected in the evaluative questions asked by those who take the particular principle of stratification as given. From the capitalist perspective, the question most often asked of the system of

39. Eugene D. Genovese, *Roll, Jordan, Roll: The World the Slaves Made* (New York: Pantheon Books, 1974), pp. 146–47, emphasis added.

40. Ibid., p. 147.

41. "In the Frankish period, the majority of those who commended themselves sought from their new master something more than protection. Since this powerful man was at the same time a wealthy man, they also expected him to contribute to their support." *Feudal Society*, trans. L. A. Manyon, vol. 1, p. 163.

42. "Certain economic privileges (land rights, labour levies, market rights, etc.) and certain economic obligations (of generosity and assistance) are associated with the exercise of power and authority." Balandier, *Political Anthropology*, p. 34. Here again one sees the recognition of economic power as always contingent upon a responsibility for economic duties.

classes is the rate of mobility between them.[43] In traditional agrarian systems, by contrast, the important subjective question is not mobility between classes but rather the elite's performance of its obligations of assistance and protection—obligations that form the normative basis for relations of subordination. Before the rise of popular representation, then—which, not by coincidence, occurred at a time when social rights to subsistence were being swept away—the question was not "What are my chances of making it into the elite?"; it was "Is the elite doing its duty?" In traditional societies where most of the peasantry are not expected and do not expect to be part of the politically relevant public, the unwritten understanding that preserves these boundaries is that the elite political class will assure subsistence and protection to the nonparticipant lower classes. When these guarantees break down, the moral structure of exclusion loses the key element of its legitimacy.

The economic protection peasants require of elites in an avowedly paternalistic social order are often precisely those duties that the rhetoric of the ruling class itself accepts. In fact, the denial of political and civil rights is justified to the extent that the material interests of the peasantry are met by the elite's sense of *noblesse oblige*. The very logic that excludes lower-class participation adds moral force to the right to subsistence. Thus, it was typical for feudal elites to recognize their obligation to "do all that is necessary to ensure their [peasants'] being, in return for labor and attachment, properly fed, clothed, housed, spiritually edified, and innocently amused."[44] As late as 1859, the dependents of Lord Percy could compose a poem that was carefully, and perhaps cynically, worded to appeal to the feudal ethic.

> Those relics of the feudal yoke
> Still in the north remain unbroke.
> That social yoke, with one accord
> That binds the Peasant to his Lord.
> And Liberty, that idle vaunt,
> Is not the comfort that we want.
> It only serves to turn the head

43. The vast sociological literature on rates of mobility is a striking case in point, for it rarely inquires about class relationships.

44. Reinhard Bendix, *Nation-Building and Citizenship: Studies of Our Changing Social Order* (Garden City, N.Y.: Doubleday Anchor, 1969), p. 49. Identical arguments were, of course, an integral part of proslavery rhetoric, as Genovese notes. "Our slaves are our solemn trust and while we have a right to use and direct their labors, we are bound to feed, clothe, and protect them. Slavery is the duty and obligation of the slave to labor for the mutual benefit of both master and slave, under a warrant to the slave of protection, and a comfortable subsistence, under all circumstances." Genovese, *Roll, Jordan, Roll*, p. 76.

> But gives to none their daily bread.
> We want community of feeling
> And landlords kindly in their dealing.[45]

Lord Percy may or may not have lived up to his responsibilities. What is notable, though, is the invocation of social rights and its association with political dependence. The paradigm of the poem—dependence with security; liberty with insecurity—is almost perfectly echoed in the twentieth century by an old Vietnamese landlord, quoted earlier, recalling the good old days in the Mekong Delta.

> In the past, the relationship between the landlord and his tenants was paternalistic. The landlord considered the tenant as an inferior member of his extended family. When the tenant's father died, it was the *duty* of the landlord to give money to the tenant for the funeral; if his wife was pregnant, the landlord gave money for the birth; if he was in financial ruin the landlord gave assistance; *therefore* the tenant had to behave as an inferior member of the extended family.[46]

Such rosy pictures of benevolent landlords and nobles are images of how elites would have it seem, not necessarily how it was or is. We must not, however, for that reason miss the power of that rhetoric. It represents a standard of performance that elites, to justify their rule, apply to themselves—a standard of performance to which, by the same token, they can justly be held accountable by those whom they rule. If the elite claims deference on the basis of its contribution to peasant welfare, at the same time it provides a criterion by which it can be morally judged.

When the terms of reciprocity shift against peasants so as to threaten constituent elements of their livelihood, they may often act out of anger to restore their rights. Whether violence or rebellion occurs, of course, depends on a host of facilitating or inhibiting factors beyond the scope of this study, not the least of which is the power of elites to repress

45. F. M. L. Thompson, *English Landed Society in the Nineteenth Century* (London: Routledge and Kegan Paul, 1963), chap. 10.

46. Sansom, *The Economics of Insurgency*, p. 29. The rhetoric of mandarin authority contained the same paternalistic tones. Speaking of his trips to troubled villages early in the Nghe-Tinh uprising, one mandarin observed, "In coming ourselves to confer with the inhabitants, we consider them as being a part of our family, our conduct toward them is comparable to that of a father toward his children." Since the model behavior of the mandarin officialdom in Annam had long since ceased to bear any resemblance to the fatherly concern for peasant welfare that this Confucian image implies, most scholar officials were in flagrant violation of the principles on which they based their claim to status. The quotation is taken from a report by Le Tong-Doc (Ho Dac Khai), dated Vinh, May 30, 1930, p. 3, *Dossier de Vinh, Pièces Annexes, A.O.M. Indochine NF*: 334–2688.

dissent. Our interpretation of peasant anger, however, differs substantially from explanations of lower class unrest that stress frustration and relative deprivation, but I believe it accords better with the facts of most peasant rebellions.[47] The frustration theory of aggression begins with a stated *individual* goal that is being thwarted and the sum of individual frustrations, other things being equal, are then seen to represent the potential for violence. There is a deceptive simplicity here for any rebellion is, virtually by definition, an act of anger. The nature of that anger, however, makes all the difference in the world.

First, it is clear that one well-known variant of relative deprivation theory is not applicable to most peasant rebellions, including those we have studied. In that variant, the source of frustration arises from a group's comparison of its level of welfare with that of some reference group that is doing relatively better. Upwardly mobile groups, it appears, develop grievances of this kind when they are blocked from attaining the rewards to which they feel entitled. It is possible that one may find such sentiments prevailing in some peasant movements or, more likely still, among some participants. Yet the vast majority of peasant risings with which I am familiar are without doubt largely *defensive* efforts to protect sources of subsistence that are threatened or to restore them once they have been lost. Far from hoping to improve their relative position in the social stratification, peasant rebellions are typically desperate efforts to maintain subsistence arrangements that are under assault.

The bare economic facts of the peasant risings we have examined approximate what one theorist of rebellion has called "decremental deprivation."[48] In this case, the source of frustration is that more or less steady expectations are accompanied by a decline in the capacity to achieve these values. The effect of the depression on a peasantry whose income had certainly not improved in the past two decades might be viewed in these terms. As Gurr puts it, "men in these circumstances are angered by the loss of what they once had or thought they could have."[49]

The critical shortcoming of this explanation and of the frustration

47. For some well-known representatives of the relative deprivation school, see Ivo K. Feierbend, Rosalind L. Feierbend, and Betty A. Nesvold, "Social Change and Political Violence"; James C. Davies, "The J-Curve of Rising and Declining Satisfactions as a Cause for Some Great Revolutions and a Contained Rebellion"; and Ted Gurr, "A Comparative Study of Civil Strife"; all in Graham and Gurr, *Violence in America: A Staff Report*, vol. 2 (Washington, D.C.: U.S. Government Printing Office, 1969).

48. Ted Gurr, *Why Men Rebel* (Princeton: Princeton University Press, 1970), pp. 46–50.

49. Ibid., p. 46.

theory in general, however, is that by beginning with some crude "want-get ratio" they fail utterly to do justice to the moral indignation and righteous anger that characterize most peasant explosions. This failure is inherent in interpretations that begin either with individual goals or with objective welfare comparisons, because they ignore the social context of the peasant's actions—his expectations about his rights in society. The difference between indignation—which implies anger at injustice—and frustration or deprivation is nicely stated by Peter Lupsha:

> To be frustrated assumes no relational aspect vis-à-vis other actors or learned norms, except the existence of some blocking agent or agency. Thus, while the concept of indignation moves one immediately into questions of legitimacy and the "rightness" of actions, frustration is outside any such normative comparison. . . . To the extent it involves morals, indignation originates in and derives its meaning from the relation between individuals and society. Thus the individual's reaction of indignation depends on a learned standard (and is interpreted in terms of that standard) which lies outside of, and impinges creatively upon, his conception of moral and proper behavior and the underlying patterns of value deprivation and indulgence. Thus, the concept of indignation is linked directly to the cultural-philosophical underpinnings of society. For this reason, indignation seems particularly appropriate for explaining violence, as its logic locates it in that intersection of the psychological and the ethical where ideas of rightness and legitimacy originate.[50]

The peasant's idea of justice and legitimacy, our analysis suggests, is provided by the *norm of reciprocity* and the consequent elite obligation (that is, peasant right) to guarantee—or at least not infringe upon—the *subsistence claims* and arrangements of the peasantry. Thus, a central feature of the peasant's reaction to the violation of his rights is its moral character. By refusing to recognize the peasantry's basic social rights as its obligation, the elite thereby forfeits any rights it had to peasant

50. Peter Lupsha, "Explanation of Political Violence: Some Psychological Theories Versus Indignation," *Politics and Society* 3 (Fall 1971), 102. Barrington Moore also has expressed his dissatisfaction with the amoral conception of relative deprivation. "Thus the decay of legitimacy, as Max Weber used this term, captures the essence of this process far better than does desertion of the intellectuals or the current technical expression relative deprivation, which I find too narrow and materialistic." *Reflections on the Causes of Human Misery*, p. 171.

production and will, in effect, have dissolved the ¡
continued deference.[51] Defiance is now normatively¡
whose subsistence hangs in the balance faces mo¡
problem; he faces a *social failure*. This emphasis o
failure is central. It implies that the peasant as a political actor is more
than a statistical abstract of available calories and outgoing rent and tax
charges—more than a mere consumer, as it were, whose politics may be
deduced from his daily food intake. It confers on him, as we confer on
elite political actors as a matter of course, a history, a political consciousness, and a perception of the moral structure of his society. It implies
that his sense of what is just allows him to judge others as morally
responsible for his predicament and allows him to act, not just to restore
his subsistence but to claim his rights.

It is for this reason that so much peasant violence represents an
attempt to force elites to do what peasants see as their duty or, alternatively, to block their infringement of peasant rights. This effort to
restore customary interclass relations might justly be termed "violence in
defense of paternalism." It is also for this reason that the development of
capitalism, the commercialization of agrarian relations, and the growth
of a centralizing state represent the historical locus of peasant revolts in
the modern era. For, above all, these large historical forces cut through
the integument of subsistence customs and traditional social relations to
replace them with contracts, the market, and uniform laws. The effect,
as Wolf has noted, is to deny the peasant "his accustomed institutional
context to reduce his risks" and thus to promote the tensions that may
lead to rebellion.[52] The attempt to restore patterns of social and economic security that are about to be swept away is what gives to many
peasant movements their "backward looking" character and earns them
a bad or ambiguous reputation among Marxists.

> The outlook of other classes [petty bourgeoisie or peasants] is am-
> biguous or sterile because their existence is not based exclusively on
> their role in the capitalist system of production but is indissolubly
> linked with the vestiges of feudal society. Their aim, therefore, is
> not to advance capitalism or to transcend it, but to reverse its action
> or at least prevent it from developing fully. Their class interest

51. I believe that breaches in the normative structure of the village itself can be similarly
explained. That is, so long as the village as an institution actually provides crisis subsistence
insurance, it retains a core of legitimacy and hence the power to sanction the behavior of its
less well-off inhabitants. When it can no longer provide this guarantee, however, it loosens
the moral basis of the community and peasants feel freer to breach its norms. It goes
without saying that the relationship between the clergy and its peasant parishioners could
be analyzed along similar lines.

52. Wolf, *Peasant Wars of the Twentieth Century*, p. xv.

concentrates on symptoms of development and not on development itself.[53]

A few brief examples will illustrate this pattern. In the Central Luzon haciendas described earlier, the refusal of previously customary grain loans between harvests was met with protests and resistance. Tenants stole what they could from the landlord's stores and, when he retaliated with force, they often replied in kind by storming his granary and confiscating what they had previously had as a matter of right. Their action was designed to enact, unilaterally, a critical subsistence right which had been suddenly denied them. Their goal was not the elimination of landowners as a category but the restoration of more tolerable terms of exchange within the existing stratification. The ethic that guided these thefts is comparable to the feeling about the "rights of the poor" that Pitt-Rivers found in Andalusia. "For a poor man, when in need, to pilfer from the property of the rich or to pasture his goats illegally on one of the large properties is not considered immoral. It is a far greater wrong that some should go short when others have abundance."[54] When elites fail to use their property to assist the needy, they forfeit their right to deference and the "little tradition" condones taking what is needed as a matter of right.

The "Captain Swing" uprisings of English rural laborers in the 1830s, as described in Hobsbawm and Rudé's careful account, are also best seen as revolts in defense of customary rights.[55] They followed an agricultural depression after the Napoleonic Wars that suddenly deprived workers of many of the precapitalist subsistence guarantees they had previously enjoyed. "Instead of family, patronage, and custom, there was now the straightforward nexus of wages which bound the landless to the landed."[56] The rebels demanded "gifts" from prosperous farmers, the destruction of labor-replacing threshing machines, and steady employment. They wanted a return to older employment patterns and went so far as to ask for the reduction of tithes and taxes on landowners which, the latter claimed, had made the older hiring practices untenable. Like most rural revolts, it was an improvised and spontaneous reaction to a new subsistence threat. Amidst the violence "there is evidence that the laborers still accepted the ancient symbols of ancient ideals of stable hierarchy."[57] So sure were they of their moral rights that they always believed that the King and Parliament would back them.

53. Lukács, *History and Class Consciousness*, p. 59.
54. Pitt-Rivers, *People of the Sierra*, p. 178.
55. Hobsbawm and Rudé, *Captain Swing*.
56. Ibid., p. 15.
57. Ibid., p. 18.

"*Taxation populaire*" as it was known in France, was a classical and well-institutionalized enactment of similar popular rights.[58] It turned on the doctrine of a just price for bread and flour, which was that price that would allow the working poor to purchase their traditional ration. When the price shot above the acceptance level, an angry crowd often occupied the market, sold the staples at the "just price," and occasionally even handed over the proceeds to the merchants. The entire scenario was thus marked by a scrupulous sense of legitimate popular rights based on the community's responsibility for the right to subsistence.

All of these acts are predicated on the assumed obligation of both the well-to-do and local authorities to provide for the minimum welfare needs of the poor. The belief that the failure to honor this obligation dissolves the reciprocal claim to deference is nowhere better expressed than by the Diggers who seized common land during the English Civil War: "Rich men's hearts are hardened, they will not give us if we beg at their doors. If we steal, the law will end our lives, divers of the poor have starved to death already, and it were better for us that are living to die by the sword than by famine."[59]

There is a naive notion, current among social scientists, that really hungry people do not rebel because they lack the energy.[60] The origin of this notion perhaps lies in what were called the Minnesota Starvation Studies conducted during World War II to determine the psychological effects of the systematic denial of food. At some point in the process of starvation, it is undoubtedly true that lassitude sets in. Well before that point is reached, however, one may expect reasonable men to do whatever they can to lay their hands on food. In anything less than a concentration camp context, the coincidence of severe hunger with available stocks of food in the possession of landowners or the state is a call to action. There are instances, to be sure, where a collective famine exhausts the food resources of the society as a whole and in which the issue of hunger is thus not joined with the issue of injustice and the right of the poor to a subsistence from the means of the relatively well-to-do. But the onset of hunger in most societies, whether Annam or seventeenth-century England, leads not to listlessness but rather to rage. In 1648 the poor gathered on the roads to stop grain from going to market "and divided it among themselves before the owners' faces,

58. See, for example, Rudé, *The Crowd in History*, chaps. 1 and 3, and Thompson, "The Moral Economy of the English Crowd in the Eighteenth Century," for English parallels.

59. Christopher Hill, *The World Turned Upside Down: Radical Ideas during the English Revolution* (London: Viking Press, 1971), p. 100.

60. For an example of this Maslowian naiveté, see Mancur Olson, "Rapid Growth as a Destabilizing Force," *Journal of Economic History* 23 (December 1963), 529–52.

telling them that they could not starve."[61] A Leveller pamphlet explained, "Necessity dissolves all laws and government, and hunger will break stone walls."[62] The Digger Winstenley, who looked to the restoration of the commons and denounced the buying and selling of land and labor, operated from the same moral assumptions as the village creators of the Nghe-Tinh soviets when he proclaimed that it was the greatest sin "to lock up the treasuries of the earth in chests and houses . . . while others starve for want, to whom it belongs."[63]

The central goals envisioned by peasants are often limited—even if the means employed may be unlimited. They take up arms less often to destroy elites than to compel them to meet their moral obligations. Where a shred of the paternal normative structure remains, peasants often invoke it; where such a restoration is inconceivable, peasants often attempt to drive out the collectors of taxes and rents (or to move beyond their reach) and to reestablish an autonomous community. In those cases where the threat to subsistence routines seems cataclysmic and irresistible, the response appears more often to take on millennial and utopian overtones. Regardless of the particular form it takes, collective peasant violence is structured in part by a moral vision, derived from experience and tradition, of the mutual obligations of classes in society. The struggle for rights that have a basis in custom and tradition and that involve, in a literal sense, the most vital interests of its participants is likely to take on a moral tenacity which movements that envision the creation of new rights and liberties are unlikely to inspire. It is for this reason, perhaps, that:

> the chief social basis of radicalism has been the peasants and the smaller artisans in the towns. From these facts one may conclude that the wellsprings of human freedom lie not only where Marx saw them, in the aspirations of classes about to take power, but perhaps even more in the dying wail of a class over whom the wave of progress is about to roll.[64]

Only the moral vision of these classes and the moral indignation that it fosters can begin to explain why peasants may embark on revolt despite seemingly hopeless odds.

61. Hill, *The World Turned Upside Down*, p. 87.
62. Ibid.
63. Ibid., p. 266.
64. Moore, *The Social Origins of Dictatorship and Democracy*, p. 505.

# 7 Revolt, Survival, and Repression

Our inquiry has thus far focused on the nature of exploitation rather than the conditions that make for rebellion. Growing exploitation of the peasantry may well be a necessary cause of rebellion, but it is far from a sufficient cause. In describing the enlarged scope for exploitation by the state and landowners prior to the Nghe-An and Ha-Tinh soviets and the Saya San rising we do not mean to fall into post-hoc determinism and imply that, under such circumstances, revolt is inevitable. There is good reason, in fact, for holding that rebellion is one of the least likely consequences of exploitation. If exploitation alone were a necessary *and* sufficient condition of rebellion, much of Southeast Asia and the Third World would surely be in a semi-permanent state of civil war.

In this concluding chapter we can do no more than to suggest a few of the main conditions which, when combined with exploitation, seem to increase the likelihood of peasant revolts and those conditions that, despite exploitation, seem to reduce the possibility of rebellion. The structural context of revolt, the paths of survival and nonrevolt, and the anatomy of repression are, for this purpose, the central issues that merit attention.

The analysis of the first issue, the potential for rebellion, begins with the irreducible characteristics of rebellion itself. The fact that agrarian revolt involves substantial numbers of peasants acting simultaneously out of anger itself suggests what forms of exploitation are most explosive. At a minimum we would expect that an increase in exploitation that touches many peasants similarly, that is sudden, and that threatens existing subsistence arrangements would be especially volatile. This expectation is very much in keeping with our analysis of the peasant's subsistence dilemma which has emphasized the relative importance of the nature and timing of exploitation as well as its average level. As Barrington Moore notes:

> The timing of changes in the life of the peasantry, including the number of people simultaneously affected, are crucial factors in their own right. I suspect that they are more important than the material changes in food, shelter, clothing, except for very sudden and big ones. . . . what infuriates peasants (and not just peasants) is a new and sudden imposition or demand that strikes many people at once and that is a break with accepted rules and customs.[1]

1. Moore, *Social Origins of Dictatorship and Democracy*, p. 474. I have deleted two sentences

193

The scope and suddenness of the shock are important for three obvious reasons. Only a shock of substantial scope provides a large body of the peasantry with a collective reason to act. If the shock is also sudden it is more difficult to adapt to routinely or incrementally and is more likely to be a sharp moral departure from existing norms of reciprocity. Much of the potential for peasant rebellion must be understood, then, in terms of the structural vulnerability of the peasantry to the kinds of shocks in question. Accordingly, the treatment of the conditions of rebellion that follows both summarizes and places in a more general analytical context the earlier discussion of structural change in Southeast Asia. This analysis, I should add, is limited to rebellion. That is, I am not concerned with the broader question of peasant revolution, when a rebellion, in conjunction with other forces, actually succeeds in fundamentally changing the political order of the state. Such an analysis would require an examination of other classes and the international state system to which I cannot pretend to do justice here. Also excluded is the important question of the form that peasant rebellion takes (for example, secular versus millennial), which would demand a detailed discussion of cultural change and local social structures.

The question of rebellion raises a second issue that goes well beyond the confines of our earlier analysis. That issue concerns the reasons for the *absence* of revolt in the context of exploitation and misery. One cluster of explanations involves a host of adaptive or survival strategies that, for a time at least, stave off the immediate threat to subsistence. Some of these strategies are individual and often temporary (short-term migration). Some are collective (social banditry) and a few involve marginal opportunities created by elites in order to reduce the threat of

---

in the middle of this citation with which I would have to take issue. They read, "Economic deterioration by slow degrees can become accepted by its victims as part of the normal situation. Especially, where no alternative is clearly visible, more and more privation can gradually find acceptance in the peasants' standards of what is right and proper." I would distinguish much more sharply between what peasants consider "normal" and what they consider "right" as the two are by no means the same. It is true that slow changes are more absorbable (but not infinitely so) as peasants find a variety of means (labor intensification, short-term migration, etc.) to maintain their subsistence. It is also true that higher levels of exploitation are more tolerable to the extent that they contain a measure of subsistence crisis guarantees. Even a slow economic deterioration that is characterized by a more exploitative balance of exchange, however, is likely to be seen as exploitative, notwithstanding the fact that it has become normal. As I hope to show later, the perception of such situations as exploitative, despite the inability to change them, can often be detected in the symbolic and linguistic forms of the peasantry. I should add, however, that my quarrel here with Moore should be placed in the context of my great intellectual debt to him. I would hardly be in a position to take issue with him at all had I not learned so much from his discussion.

revolt (short-term employment, food relief). I believe that it is possible to identify some major determinants of the supply of these makeshift alternatives and thus to gauge when they are likely to militate most against revolt. The discussion here is speculative and is intended to identify the problems that merit research rather than to present definitive conclusions.

③ The third issue directs attention to the fact that the main deterrent to revolt is often not the survival alternatives open to the peasantry but rather the risks of rebellion. These risks are largely proportional to the coercive power of the state (and, of course, its willingness to use that power); the more overwhelming its power, the more likely the only alternative to an uncertain subsistence will be death.[2] In such situations I think it is possible, empirically, to distinguish a peasantry that submits only because it has no choice from a peasantry that would probably not revolt even if it had the choice.

## THE STRUCTURAL CONTEXT OF REBELLION

The major developments in the agrarian system of Southeast Asia in the early twentieth century reduced the subsistence margin of the peasantry, making it, as a class, increasingly vulnerable to subsistence threats. The new vulnerability took two forms. First, for at least large sections of the peasantry in Burma, Java, Vietnam, and the Philippines, the water level—to return to Tawney's metaphor—was rising in an absolute sense. The new subsistence problems often took tangible form in both the quantity and quality of food consumption. The effect of this narrowing margin was to greatly magnify the social and physical consequences of any sharp drop in yield or income.[3] Even in the rare cases

2. There are, of course, situations in which the alternative to rebellion is death in any case. In such a situation, rebellion may "make sense" no matter how hopeless the odds; one might as well die fighting to live as to succumb peacefully. The Warsaw ghetto uprising or the revolt at Treblinka constitute, in this sense, rebellions of hopelessness; knowing the odds were hopeless, the participants fought more to establish their resistance and to leave an historical record than with any expectation of survival. See the moving account by Emmanuel Ringelblum, *Notes from the Warsaw Ghetto* (New York: McGraw-Hill, 1958).

3. For these countries the evidence indicates no improvement in welfare levels and, in some cases, a decline in the postindependence period. See Douglas Paauw, "Economic Progress in Southeast Asia." *Journal of Asian Studies* 23:1 (November 1963), 69–91. Thus, the frequent association of rebellion with a setback following a substantial improvement in peasant welfare levels does not seem to describe the experience of the Southeast Asian peasantry. This is not to say that it is a priori excluded. It is conceivable, as noted earlier, to have an improvement in welfare levels of peasants along with an increase in the exploitativeness of elites or of the state. Such a threat to new levels of welfare that have gradually come to be taken as the subsistence norm might well spark a rebellion.

where the average water level may actually have fallen (Thailand, Cambodia, Malaysia), the amplitude of the waves rose so as often to increase the risk of drowning. As state and landowning elites steadied their take from the countryside and as village assistance weakened, the peasantry was exposed to more damaging shifts in income.

The more brittle and explosive agrarian structure was largely a product of the interaction of three forces: demographic change, production for the market, and the growth of the state. Demographic trends—the growth of population, the full occupation of arable land—undermined the bargaining power of the peasantry vis-à-vis those who controlled land. Production for the market, with its attendant risks and the competitive advantage it placed in the hands of those with capital, meant both new insecurities for smallholders and tenants and an expanding class of rural wage laborers who were totally dependent on market forces for their livelihood. The state, for its part, was both another claimant on peasant income and the guarantor of the new agrarian structure.[4] As a claimant, the state imposed a growing array of rigid fiscal claims on the peasantry. As guarantor of the price system and the disparities in power that the working of the price system fostered, its role was even more pivotal.[5] The coercive role of the state—its enforcement of contracts through the courts and its power to break peasant resistance—allowed landowners and moneylenders to wring the full advantage from their greater bargaining power.[6] The exploitative potential of demographic change and market production could only be fully realized within the context of a monopoly of coercion.

*The Nature of Collective Shocks*

Although the vulnerability of peasants in general to subsistence crises grew under the colonial transformation, some peasants were naturally more vulnerable than others. Such variations were in part individual and random. A large family with many nonworking dependents and little land was typically harder pressed to meet its subsistence requirements and thus was in a particularly risky position. With regard to agrarian revolts, however, the pattern of household insecurity is of less concern than patterns of collective insecurity that affect substantial numbers of

4. There is nothing inevitable here about the role of the state. In postcolonial North Vietnam and Burma the state intervened to redistribute land and to stabilize peasant income and security. Almost all postcolonial states have eliminated capitation taxes as a source of revenue.

5. Where the state is weak, this coercive force may reside in other institutions such as the private warlord armies that ruled large sections of China between the wars.

6. In the cases of Java and Vietnam, the institution of labor-repressive systems restricting movement had the effect of providing returns to plantation owners well above what their economic power alone would have indicated.

peasants. To explain why many cultivators launch on the course of rebellion, we must turn from questions of individual risk to the larger question of "public health." What are the conditions of vulnerability that make certain groups, areas, or classes collectively subject to ruin and that thereby provide a plausible basis for their common perceptions and reactions? Although such an ecology of geographical and social pressure points will naturally vary from society to society and over time, a few general principles of the distribution of risk can be established.

The general criterion of vulnerability is, not surprisingly, the variability of real income. Comparing two villages with the same average real income, the village with the sharpest fluctuations in income will naturally experience a greater frequency of subsistence crises. In this context it is necessary to delineate the major sources of income variability and examine their impact and range. Three important sources seem, from my reading of the Southeast Asian material, to deserve special emphasis: (1) natural yield fluctuations; (2) world market fluctuations; and (3) mono-crop price fluctuations. While this is hardly an exhaustive list, it can serve as a convenient point of departure for establishing those regions and sectors for which the claims of outsiders are most often likely to pose a direct subsistence threat.

ECOLOGICAL VULNERABILITY. The physical setting of certain areas subjects their inhabitants to fluctuations in yield of such amplitude that, even without the claims of elites, their survival is tenuous. If, in addition, incomes are generally low, any inflexible extraction by elites following a crop failure (or a series of them) is likely to have massive effects on peasant life. It is not surprising then that such areas often have a long historical record of rebellion and resistance to state authority. Northern Annam and the Khorat Plateau of Northeast Thailand have the least reliable rainfall in their respective countries and each has an impressive reputation as an area of resistance and rebellion. The *"esprit frondeur"* of Nghe-An, the classical cradle of revolt in Vietnam, was often remarked upon,[7] while Northeast Thailand continues to be a focus of opposition to the Bangkok regime. The fact that Northern Annam and Northeast Thailand are geographically somewhat isolated within their respective state systems might seem to provide another explanation for their traditions.[8] It is no coincidence that the great kingdoms of precolonial

7. *Parti communiste indochinois 1925–1933*, p. 33.
8. In the case of Northeast Thailand there is an ethnic and linguistic issue that adds to the friction inasmuch as a large part of the Khorat Plateau is a Lao cultural area—a provincial variant of the Thai tradition but with pronounced separatist tendencies. See Charles F. Keyes, *Isan: Regionalism in Northeast Thailand*, Cornell Thailand Project, Interim Report Series #10, Data Paper No. 65.

Southeast Asia were generally founded where the steady yields of irrigated rice provided a sounder economic base for a tax system. Few
traditional Southeast Asian states could have mustered the force required to regularly support a central court from the resources of more
tenuous agricultural areas. The fact that such areas are geographically
peripheral is thus due largely to their unpromising ecology—the factor
that helps account also for their rebellious traditions.[9] Banten in West
Java and the Dry Zone of Upper Burma might also be included in this
category. The association of uncertain yields and turbulent politics is
common outside the region as well: Northeast Brazil and the Levant
region of Spain, for example, seem to occupy comparable ecological and
political roles within their nations. To exaggerate somewhat, it may be
possible to infer quite a bit about the resistance of a region to the claims
of elites on the basis of the variability in its rainfall.[10]

Rainfall is, of course, but a single cause of large annual variations in
food supply. In irrigated regions there are also districts, such as Hanthawaddy in Lower Burma, in which the frequent danger of crop losses
(this time by flooding) fostered an insurrectionary tradition that was
most in evidence following a poor season. For other areas the more
unpredictable disasters of pests, crop disease, or the loss of plow animals
may create similar problems, but they are unlikely to give rise to the
*habits* of resistance that mark regions with permanent subsistence problems. The important point is simply that the consequences of a rigid
outside claim on a peasant product that is itself highly variable are
particularly massive. For this reason, areas of uncertain yield frequently
become focal points of resistance.

2 PRICE-SYSTEM VULNERABILITY. For more and more peasants in the colonial economy, however, the ability to meet the demands of outsiders
was as much a question of the health of the market as of the size of the
harvest. The effects on Cochinchina and Lower Burma of integration
into the world market have been dealt with at some length earlier, and
here I wish only to reiterate the potential for collective shocks that this

9. An unpromising ecology alone may be enough to spark a great amount of unrest, but
when it is joined with a dissident intelligentsia based in the region the combination will be
far more volatile. Thus the province of Quang Binh, south of Ha-Tinh, is no better off
than Nghe-An, nor is the province of Hung Yen, east of Hanoi, with its slogan: "drought
nine years of every ten, where the fifth month rice is burned and the harvest putrefies."
Neither of these provinces has quite the tumultuous history of Nghe-An and the difference would appear to lie in the readily available leadership for the insurrectionary tendencies of Nghe-An. I am indebted for this insight to Alexander Woodside.

10. The problem of the distribution of available water supplies in rain deficit areas is
also likely to constitute a major focus of political contention.

integration made possible. The extent of the market's penetration defined, as it were, a shock field: an area in which variations in income were often a function of market price and credit supply. Here the principle of unification was not the watershed or the rainfall area, but a shared price system.

The highly commercialized areas of Southeast Asia thus constituted an arena where prices and welfare levels were interdependent. Although average income might be higher than in traditional subsistence regions, the common basis of their prosperity was, at the same time, the basis of their common exposure to risk. The oppressiveness of rents and taxes and the availability of employment hinged less on crop fluctuations than on price fluctuations. Highly commercialized areas were thus liable to periodic "man-made" famines, and the key to the insurrectionary potential of such regions is the pattern of market shocks that suddenly make the fixed claims of outsiders an insupportable burden. The world economic crisis of 1930 and, to a lesser extent, that of 1907 were striking examples of how a market failure could increase the exploitative consequences of existing claims.

To focus on price fluctuations alone is to understate the vulnerability of an agrarian cash economy to subsistence crises. In the course of its development a commercialized economy tends both to strip away traditional structures of protection that characterized the earlier society and to create a floating labor force that is wholly dependent on the cash nexus. So long as the price of rice rose and the market for labor remained buoyant, the erosion of these traditional securities might occasion little alarm. It is indeed possible to imagine a willing complicity of the lower class in the commercialization of labor relations in the rare cases where it appears to benefit them. But when a crisis strikes there are fewer retreats for this population.

The extractable surplus from such regions in buoyant times is, furthermore, larger than that from noncommercialized areas. Both landowners and the state are likely to establish claims to the surplus in periods of relative prosperity which they are not at all inclined to reduce in a poor market. It is not simply a question of habits and appetites either. A period of commercial growth produces a substantial landholding and trading elite whose power is roughly proportional to its size and wealth. To the extent that it has grown robust, to that extent is it in a position to impose its will (either directly or through the state) in lean years. The situation of the state is somewhat comparable. In Burma and Vietnam the fiscal basis of the colonial regime rested predominantly in the more commercialized zones of the Irrawaddy Delta and the Mekong Delta where a disproportionate share of the state's revenue originated.

Built upon the rich pickings of this economy in the 1920s, the state was able to resist a reduction in the flow from its main financial artery in the hard times that began in 1930.

Finally, we must remember that in cash crop regions the elites themselves were firmly enmeshed in the market. A price failure or credit crisis hit them first. As the value of the crop they claimed and the capital value of their land plummeted and as their creditors closed in, they too faced ruin. Their very integration into the market impelled them to wring all they could out of their tenants and laborers in order to stay afloat. At the time, therefore, that the market reduces the tenants and laborers to penury, landowners are under the greatest temptation to press even harder and to eliminate any remaining vestiges of paternalism. For those at the bottom of the agrarian structure, the pressure of the market and the pressure of the elite are thus likely to coincide.

A commercialized countryside, then, represents an economic shock field in more than one respect. Not only is the well-being of the region as a whole contingent on world market forces but the lower classes, despite the fact that they may do well in the short run, are likely to provide a surplus value to elites and to the state that is adjusted upward in good times but is not readjusted downward when a slump threatens over-committed ruling groups.

MONO-CROP VULNERABILITY.   Within a larger commercialized area there are often subregions that are affected differently by various market stocks. Shifts in trading patterns or in relative crop prices may spell hardship for one area and opportunity for another. A crop area, in this context, defines a shock field of its own: it is dependent both on general market conditions and on the demand for its main product. In describing the ecology of agrarian revolt in seventeenth-century France and China, Roland Mousnier emphasizes the influence of crop areas and regional specialization in delineating the boundaries of discontent.[11] A collapse of the silk trade, for example, could plunge an entire area into economic chaos without seriously affecting other regions. The "Captain Swing" uprising in the 1830s, similarly, was sharply confined to the cereal growing areas in the south and east of England that were most threatened by the trade slump.[12] Other factors were also associated with the local intensity of the revolt, but the limits of the shock field were defined by cereal-growing, while the pastoral economy was relatively unscathed.

What is noteworthy here is that the development of agricultural

11. *Peasant Uprisings in Seventeenth-Century France, Russia, and China*, passim.
12. Hobsbawm and Rudé, *Captain Swing*, chap. 9.

specialization, of crop sectors, sets up a differential vulnerability to particular market forces. For any market shock, one can establish a likely pattern of repercussions for each agricultural sector. For much of Southeast Asia, of course, the overwhelming dominance of rice cultivation makes the notion of crop area coincide with much of the agrarian economy. The distinction is useful, however, for areas where plantation and smallholding cash crops such as rubber, tobacco, or sugar constitute a main source of livelihood. Being primarily grown for export rather than local consumption, these crops are particularly sensitive to violent price fluctuations. A sudden slump in price (the collapse of rubber prices following World War I) may well produce a sector-wide subsistence crisis and throw large numbers of rural laborers back into the subsistence economy. Within a commercialized economy, then, the incidence of exploitation depends heavily on exogenous shocks but these shocks are often so sector-specific that they require separate analysis.

A crop failure or a market crisis has the effect of suddenly making the current claims of elites far more onerous and/or of actually increasing those claims (or reducing services). As recipes for collective anger they do not necessarily point to a specific culprit. The identification of the culprit, the social direction in which anger is directed, depends in each case on the particular conjunction of pressures. For Annam, in the context of the depression, the continued collection of fixed taxes posed the most immediate threat to subsistence and the strikes in Vinh provided the opportunity to act. For a large rural wage force the immediate threat might stem from wage slashes or the dismissal of workers. For smallholders the continued demands of creditors might constitute the cutting edge of the crisis. The onset of an economic crisis thus directs attention to the pattern of existing claims on peasant resources, which may now represent a direct menace, and to the existing forms of economic security (for example, subsistence loans, permanent tenure). The pressure on subsistence routines created by a market or crop failure is translated into a pattern of anger and resistance in accordance with how it is socially transmitted.

## Revolt and Peasant Social Structure

This raises the important question of the social structure of the agrarian population that receives these shocks. Is it possible to show that their social composition makes some peasantries inherently more insurrection-prone than others? The answer is ambiguous and allows of no easy generalizations.

If we distinguish peasantries with strong communal traditions and few sharp internal class divisions (Annam, Tonkin, Upper Burma, East and

Central Java) from peasantries with weak communal traditions and sharper class divisions (Cochinchina, Lower Burma), it is possible to make a case that the former are more explosive. The argument is based on two lines of reasoning.[13] First, it follows that a more undifferentiated peasantry will experience economic shocks in a uniform fashion since structurally its members are more or less in the same boat. Thus a head tax would stir almost unanimous resentment in the Nghe-An village where the relatively even distribution of income makes the burden comparable for most villagers. The same measure in Cochinchina, with its far more variegated class structure, could be expected to have a less uniform impact. It might stir resentment but the sharpness of that resentment would vary with the different burden it imposed on wage laborers, tenants, and smallholders.

The second line of reasoning holds that communitarian structures not only receive shocks more uniformly but they also have, due to their traditional solidarity, a greater capacity for collective action. For such villages, it would seem, the organizational barriers to action are reduced simply because they have recourse to an existing structure of local cooperation that has remained intact; their "little tradition" is a ready-made vehicle of action. The pioneer villages of Cochinchina and Lower Burma, by contrast, are far more divided structurally and hence socially. There is no ready-made structure of communal authority (or it is far weaker) of which they can make use. Thus, the argument runs, the more communal the village structure, the easier it is for a village to collectively defend its interests.

This reasoning, while convincing as far as it goes, overlooks at least two factors that might lead to different conclusions. The *exposure* to shocks, for one thing, seems to be inversely related to the uniformity with which they are received. It is precisely the more differentiated and atomistic villages which, because they are most often found where commercial forces have been strongest, are most vulnerable to market disturbances. While their responses to these disturbances may be more problematic, their greater exposure may nevertheless make them more explosive. The second complication is that there is good reason to believe that the more communal structures are often able to "redistribute pain" in such a way as to avoid or postpone subsistence crises. A case in point is the Javanese village that, until at least the 1960s, retained enough communal elasticity to provide most of its inhabitants with a marginal subsistence niche. By the reshuffling of labor and tenancy

13. Moore, *Social Origins of Dictatorship and Democracy*, p. 475, appears to argue along these lines.

rights, it alleviated the immediate subsistence threat. More sharply differentiated villages, such as those in Cochinchina or Lower Burma, lacked this economic elasticity. Village patterns of reciprocity and redistribution did far less to shield marginal tenants and wage laborers from the full blast of most economic dislocations. Thus, for the least protected lower strata of such villages, a given increase in taxes or a rise in rents would more often present a direct and unmediated subsistence threat.

In view of these contradictory tendencies, any general statement relating peasant social structures to the potential for rebellion would be questionable. While the communitarian village has a more shared class perspective and a readily available structure of action, more socially fragmented villages are both more vulnerable to market forces and less able internally to soften their impact on poorer inhabitants. The difference in those two structures seems, to me at least, to lie less in their explosiveness per se than in the nature of the explosion once it takes place—a subject far afield from our main concern.[14]

## Nonrevolt, Self-help, or *Sauve qui peut*

To speak of rebellion is to focus on those extraordinary moments when peasants seek to restore or remake their world by force. It is to forget both how rare these moments are and how historically exceptional it is for them to lead to a successful revolution. It is to forget that the peasant is more often a helpless victim of violence than its initiator.

---

14. Some of these differences are reflected in the contrasts between the Nghe-Tinh soviets, a revolt in a more communalist area, and the Saya San rebellion, a revolt in a more highly differentiated setting. Communalist villages, as one would expect, seem more prone to *levées en masse* and, because there are few internal enemies, aim frequently at separatism, withdrawal, and autonomy (i.e., more often resistance in the defensive sense of that word). Themes of countryside vs. the city or the countryside vs. the state seem to predominate over more strictly defined class issues, again because *internal* class divisions are secondary. Revolts where local class distinctions are more obvious often split the village (again, not surprisingly) with the wealthier peasants and landlords either not participating or perhaps actively opposing. Because the village is divided, outside leadership is more likely to play a role in mobilizing the local participation. As a consequence, the revolt is likely to be more outward-looking (i.e., more often an effort to overthrow the state than to retreat)—even if traditionalist and millennial. However, these schematic conclusions are not definitive, since it is clear that even communitarian villages may reach a point where quite modest class differences have explosive consequences (Java) and that certain shocks can produce a striking degree of unity even in stratified villages.

We have ignored here other facets of social structure that might be linked to both the proclivity to rebellion and the form it takes. For a convincing attempt to link the nature of rural economic organization with the nature of political and economic conflict, see Arthur Stinchcombe, "Agricultural Enterprise and Rural Class Relations," *American Journal of Sociology* 67 (1961–62), 165–76.

Most important, it is to forget that aside from these "moments of madness"[15] (and even during them!), much of the day-to-day reality of peasant life is the effort of the family to assure itself an adequate food supply. As a cultivator with a set of vital and pressing needs rather than an ideologue with a long view, the peasant inevitably seizes the opportunities that are available to him—even though many of them may be disagreeable. "Opportunities" is too positive a word for the survival strategies I have in mind. The choices may include putting all of the family to work, eliminating valued ceremonial obligations, emigrating, sharing, poverty, seeking charity, or serving in a landlord's gang against one's own fellow-villagers; and, as this list suggests, they usually entail great human costs.

It is not easy to bring conceptual order to this welter of patchwork solutions, most of which have two features in common. They represent a ransacking of the economic and social environment for those sidelines and connections that will stabilize subsistence. In the course of this process a peasantry develops that is less firmly oriented to its holding in the village. The enormous consequences of such patterns for local social structure and solidarity make it perhaps the key element in the creation of a "post-peasant society."[16] Another feature of this patchwork local economy is its effect on the potential for revolt. To the degree that the marginal opportunities open to the peasantry do in fact alleviate short-run subsistence needs, to that degree they tend to reduce the likelihood of more direct and violent solutions.

From the large array of adaptations or strategies open to peasants, one can roughly distinguish four typical patterns that differ sharply in the resources that they tap and in the social links that they create. In brief, they are: (1) reliance on local forms of self-help; (2) reliance on the nonpeasant sector of the economy; (3) reliance on state-supported forms of patronage and assistance; and (4) reliance on religious or oppositionist structures of protection and assistance. It is obvious that these four patterns are not mutually exclusive. While their importance may vary over time, an individual peasant may well make use of all four simultaneously. Each of the four, however, has different consequences for the nature of peasant politics and the potential for rebellion. Each is viable under different conditions. Each represents a different scenario

15. Term taken from an excellent article by Aristide Zolberg, "Moments of Madness," *Politics and Society* 2:2 (Winter 1972), 183–207.

16. A term employed by Alex Weingrod and Emma Morin in "Post Peasants: The Character of Contemporary Sardinian Society," *Comparative Studies in Society and History* 13 (July 1971), 301–24. See also, in this connection, Colin Leys, "Politics in Kenya: The Development of Peasant Society," *British Journal of Political Science* 1 (1973), 301–37.

of "development." In the absence of much research on "post-peasant" society, the discussion below is frankly speculative and is intended to suggest the lines along which such an analysis might proceed.

### Local Forms of Self-Help

For much of the rural population, the absence of alternatives and the difficulty of revolt tragically conspire to force a large measure of passive adaptation. Whole villages may gradually shift from the cultivation of rice to maize and then to starchy roots in order to increase their caloric supply at the cost of other, often disabling, nutritional losses. Where land is particularly scarce, passive adaptation may include the technical features of "agricultural involution"—the shift to more labor intensive techniques in return for minute, but vital, increments in yield per unit of land.[17] Many of these adaptations are a known part of the peasantry's economic repertoire, but where they had been characteristic only of the village poor or of that hungry time before harvest, they may become a permanent fact of life. The resulting pattern, while it may accommodate a growing population for a time, amounts to "water-treading" based on the "self-exploitation" of labor. In the long run, if population grows and agricultural techniques (that is, the production functions) remain unchanged, involution is a kind of ecological cul de sac that exacts a toll on social structure and eventually forces migration or starvation. East and Central Java and contemporary Burma represent the most striking examples of this pattern in the region. The average caloric intake of the Javanese has declined from 1,946 calories in 1960 (200 short of the United Nations' recommended minimum) to 1,730 in 1967 and, with it, the consumption of protein has also fallen to dangerous levels.[18] No reliable figures exist for Burma, but it is abundantly clear that the standard of consumption of the rural population has declined since independence.[19]

Occasionally, the effort to wrest a livelihood from a plot of land that cannot sustain a family with subsistence crops may entail a switch from edible crops to cash crops, especially those which are labor intensive. Hard-pressed Russian smallholders, as Chayanov described, would often switch from food crops to flax if it seemed the only way to make

17. The term and its dynamics are described convincingly in Geertz, *Agricultural Involution.* The cutting down of ceremonial expenses is another oft-noted adaptation. For recent parallels in Burma, see Lawrence Stifel, "Burmese Socialism: Economic Problems of the First Decade," *Pacific Affairs* 45:1 (Spring 1972), 60–74. Some of the same tendencies are apparent in Kenya as well; see Leys, "Politics in Kenya."

18. Richard W. Franke, "Miracle Seeds and Shattered Dreams in Java," *Natural History* 83:1 (January 1974), 11.

19. Stifel, "Burmese Socialism."

ends meet.[20] Similarly, owners of marginal riceland in Kelantan, Malaysia, have recently shifted from rice to tobacco as the only means of avoiding migration as harvest laborers.[21] The disadvantage of these crops from the peasant's perspective is that they are far more labor intensive and, more important, they expose him to new market risks (in the case of tobacco, they expose him to higher production costs as well). Cash crops as a *supplement* to subsistence crops are one thing, but pure cash cropping is a risk the marginal smallholder or tenant takes only when there is virtually no other course open to him in the context of the village economy.

Beyond squeezing the physical environment for what it can yield, the process of local adaptation to subsistence problems is complemented by various forms of mutual assistance. The growth of local burial associations, social welfare groups, rotating credit associations, and local efforts to spread the work and food resources as widely as possible are typical of such mutual help in the more communal areas of Southeast Asia.[22]

Local self-help and mutual help tend to be both initial responses to subsistence problems and lasting residual alternatives when other courses fail. The combination of labor intensification and mutual reciprocity among the poor, though it may meet critical short term needs, is untenable in the long run outside the isolated subsistence sector. It is a "retreatist" strategy inasmuch as it involves "making-do" with the resources at hand rather than recapturing the surplus taken in taxes and rents by the state and landowners. A large share of the community's land and its product, after all, is now controlled by outsiders. Most of the opportunities for employment, education, and assistance are no longer in the hands of villagers and even the effort to minimize external demands for taxes and rents requires connections, directly or indirectly, with the external world. Shared poverty and self-exploitation may be inevitable, but they offer no long run solution to the local dilemmas of subsistence and economic security.

20. Chayanov, *Theory of Peasant Economy*, p. 115.

21. Von Liebenstein and Gunawan, "Poverty in Kelantan."

22. A great many of these arrangements represent ways of providing poor families with the lump-sum cash that would otherwise be difficult to accumulate for major expenditures such as a marriage or funeral, school fees, the expenses of an illness, or the sum needed to keep creditors at bay. This is often accomplished throughout Southeast Asia by rotating credit associations in which perhaps ten persons each regularly contribute a small amount to a general pool which is then, by various means of selection, given to one of the ten. Week by week or month by month the process goes on, theoretically until all have received one pool. Toward the end, of course, the motivation to contribute is reduced if one has already been paid and such associations have a tenuous life. The main point is that subsistence difficulties, particularly where there is something of a communal tradition, are likely to give rise to new initiatives of informal organization to meet day-to-day problems.

Although lower class communitarianism is hardly a viable strategy in itself, even false starts and failures along these lines may be significant in other respects. They may well help build and reinforce horizontal bonds between peasants. They represent initiatives from below to organize local charity and ritual which in the past had often been organized by elites. In this sense the development of absentee ownership may be particularly important inasmuch as the departure of landowners leaves the village structure in the hands of smallholders, tenants, and laborers. Even the residue of local initiatives may form the potential nodes of class leadership and organization in later periods.[23]

## The Wider Economy: Capitalist Development or Scavenging?

As the limits of local resources are reached, villagers are increasingly obliged to seek all or a portion of their income from outside sources. Temporary or permanent migration, like internal self-help, is a more or less private initiative but, unlike self-help, is directed at external resources.

A GREEN REVOLUTION?: One variant of this adaptation is shorthand for what might be called the capitalist route to agrarian development. It conjures up the essential features of the English model of development in the eighteenth and nineteenth centuries. To oversimplify, that pattern involved at least three components. First, the smallholding peasantry was destroyed as a class, mainly by means of the enclosures that eliminated the economic basis of the older rural community. The economic hardship and social dislocation that this process entailed generated a good deal of peasant resistance and violence which, ironically, contributed to the ascendance of the bourgeoisie. The absence of a full-blown peasant revolution, however, may be ascribed, following Moore, to two other characteristics of English development:[24] the growth of a commercializing, landholding class whose rising production gave them an alternative to simply squeezing more and more from a static peasant society; and, more important, a pace of commercial and industrial growth that absorbed a critical fraction of the surplus rural labor that the agricultural revolution had ground out. What is notable

23. In the West there was often great continuity between local and seemingly apolitical self-help efforts and later political initiatives. Perhaps tracing the local lineage of peasant unions and radical political parties in Southeast Asia would reveal a similar continuity with earlier self-help activities. For a case from England, see Hobsbawm and Rudé's discussion of the relationship between annual village feasts (and other rituals) and the organization of rural protest movements. *Captain Swing*, pp. 66–68.

24. Moore, *Social Origins of Dictatorship and Democracy*, chap. 1. See also Moore's appendix on conservative historiography, particularly his critique of Mingay, *English Landed Society in the Eighteenth Century*.

for our purposes is that while absorption into the modern sector and local parish relief often reduced the violence of the transformation, a great deal of coercion and bloodshed nonetheless accompanied the destruction of the English peasantry.

Under favorable conditions, a comparable transformation is not inconceivable in underdeveloped countries today. The shift to high yielding varieties of wheat in the Ludhiana region of India's Punjab, as described by Francine Frankel, appears to be a case in point.[25] There the preexisting concentration of landholdings, the planting of high-yielding varieties of wheat, and costly inputs of fertilizer and machinery have given rise to huge increases in yields and a powerful new class of rural capitalists.[26] As in England, the transition has not been peaceful. The lower 20 percent of the labor force is perhaps worse off than before and open conflict between landowners' and laborers' factions is common. Tenancy shares have moved from 50–50 to 70–30 in favor of the landowner and, although the actual amount of wheat received by the tenant has risen slightly, almost all the new profits have gone to those who control land and capital. Nonetheless, the structure of growth, as in England, has been such as to reduce the explosiveness of the new situation. A portion of the tenants and smallholders forced off the land have been absorbed into the agrarian labor force, another portion into the secondary industries of processing, transport, and marketing created by the agricultural boom, and still another substantial portion into the growing industrial sector of the region. It would seem, thus far at least, that the Punjab has experienced a successful shift to productive, capitalist agriculture. The "success" has eliminated many of the traditional securities for the rural poor and has particularly damaged those at the very bottom of the social structure, but it has provided enough economic safety-valves to absorb much of the peasantry.

To what extent is a similar transformation likely in Southeast Asia? This is an important and complex question to which I can hardly do justice here. It will suffice to outline the reasons for believing that, with few exceptions, agrarian development via the green revolution is unlikely to provide a relatively peaceful path to agrarian development.[27]

25. Frankel, *India's Green Revolution: Economic Gains and Political Costs*, chap. 2.

26. The entire process has been assisted by the government which subsidizes imports of machinery, provides cheap credit, and maintains an artificially high domestic price for wheat.

27. See, in this context, the Report of the Southeast Asia Development Advisory Group, *Agricultural Revolution in Southeast Asia*, vols. 1 and 2 (New York: The Asia Society, 1970); William Collier, "*Tebasan*, High Yielding Varieties, and Rural Change: An Example in Java"; and Widya Utami and John Ihalaw, "Farm Size: Its Consequences on Production,

The first consideration is the limits of the green revolution itself. High-yielding varieties of rice and corn are enormously sensitive to variations and timing in water supply and for this reason are confined to areas where irrigation can provide water reliably. In India, roughly 20 percent of the cultivated surface falls within this definition,[28] and the figure is unlikely to be larger in Southeast Asia. Ecologically, then, the green revolution is applicable to only a minority of the region's peasantry.

The central question is whether the economic and social dislocation generated by such agricultural modernization will be largely mitigated by the new opportunities created both within and outside the agricultural sector. In gross terms, this involves asking both how disruptive is the transformation likely to be and how abaundant are the safety valves for absorbing this disruption.

Where the new technology is simple, divisible, and labor-using rather than labor-saving, where the pattern of landholding is not highly skewed, and where access to credit and inputs is available on equal terms to smallholders and tenants, the possibility for wide participation in the benefits of high-yielding varieties is greatest.[29] Unfortunately, these conditions are not typical of the new technology, nor of the main rice-growing areas of Southeast Asia.

The disruptive consequences of the new varieties stem largely from their effect on employment and from the further commercialization of agrarian class relations. The bulk of the new income created by the green revolution clearly goes to the owners of the scarce factors of production, land and capital. Production inputs (for example, tubewells, pumps, labor costs, and even fertilizer) are sufficiently "lumpy" to create certain thresholds of landholding and access to credit, below which innovation is unlikely.[30] This is partly an institutional question, too, since the provision of credit is highly skewed in favor of those owners whose assets inspire the confidence of lenders. The effect is a comparative and

Land Tenure, Marketing and Social Relationships in Kabupaten Klaten, Central Java." The last two are papers submitted to the International Rice Research Institute's Rice Farming Research Project, September 1972.

28. Conversation with Alice Thorner, December 20, 1973. Since these figures refer to land areas that are particularly rich, it is likely that they contain perhaps as much as 50 percent of the agrarian population.

29. Carl H. Goetsch, "Technical Change and the Distribution of Income in Rural Areas," *American Journal of Agricultural Economics* 54:2 (May 1972), 326–41.

30. Fertilizer is, of course, physically divisible but the returns to applications of fertilizer increase disproportionately for larger amounts. Thus, the landowner who can use optimum amounts will reap more than twice the return per acre as a poorer smallholder who can apply only half the optimum amount per acre.

cumulative advantage of medium to large owners as compared with marginal smallholders and tenants. Nor is this advantage related to efficiency, for as Goetsch notes, "the availability of savings for the acquisition of additional assets is a function of the absolute surplus of the larger farmers and not of their relative position."[31] A concentration of land is likely to result, in which small peasants whose plots are below the threshold are pushed out. Furthermore, owners of larger tracts are sorely tempted to revoke tenancy contracts and to resume cultivation themselves (or perhaps through an agent) with the aid of hired labor and/or machines. In Central Luzon provinces like Nueva Ecija in the late 1960s, this process was under way, as many tenancies on the best land had been canceled.[32]

It follows that in those regions where the smallholding and tenant classes are a large share of the rural population, as they are in most rice areas in Southeast Asia, the social effects of the green revolution will be enormously painful. There are first the insecurities that flow from the recomposition of the class structure. Many tenants and smallholders are likely to be precipitated into the wage labor class. This involves "an agonizing change from [relative] security in the midst of poverty to growing insecurity along with poverty."[33] There is some evidence as well that the security of the wage labor class itself is undermined in the process. Owners tend to move from payment in kind to payment in cash and often resort to hiring outsiders in peak labor periods, partly to break the traditional payment formulas at the local level.

> Paradoxically, their main hope of sharing equally in the benefits of the new technology is to maintain the traditional system of proportional payments in kind for major agricultural operations. Yet the landowners, calculating that their own economic interests lie in converting all payments to cash, are denouncing the traditional system as exploitive and moving to introduce a cash wage for all kinds of farm work.[34]

The need for quick harvesting and the double or triple cropping that the new varieties make possible may actually increase the daily wage rate

31. Goetsch, "Technical Change and the Distribution of Income," p. 330.

32. Benedict Kerkvliet, "Aftermath of Peasant Rebellion in the Philippines: A Microcosmic Look," mimeographed. The talk of land reform had also given landowners an incentive to remove tenants who might otherwise later be able to claim ownership rights. Occasionally, as well, sugar was replanted expressly because sugar land was to be exempt from land reform.

33. P. C. Joshi, "A Review Article," *Seminar* (May 1970), p. 32; quoted in Frankel, *India's Green Revolution*, p. 197.

34. Frankel, *India's Green Revolution*, p. 198.

during periods of peak labor demand. But this is short-term employment and the labor force is increasingly an agrarian proletariat par excellence, without any of the marginal securities it could once invoke.

What about employment itself? Presumably, if the total volume of wage labor were substantially increased, the insecurities created by the change in class structure would be somewhat reduced. The fragmentary evidence on this score is also discouraging. In parts of Central Luzon and in Thailand's Central Plain the new profits of landowners and the easy supply of credit have made possible the introduction of tractors and machine threshing which may have actually reduced total labor demand.

Even among the lilliputian holdings of Central Java, where the limits of mechanization are correspondingly narrow, the labor consequences of the new varieties seem disastrous. The data from one meticulous survey of villages where the new strains have been adapted are particularly sobering. Collier, Soentoro, Gunawan, Wiradi, and Makali describe how a new harvesting system has been introduced on the heels of the green revolution.[35] The new varieties, it appears, shatter more easily than traditional strains and cannot be easily harvested in the traditional, labor-intensive way with the *ani-ani* (knife). Previously, the owner of a .2 hectare plot might find as many as 150 harvesters and gleaners assembled at the edge of his paddyland at harvest time, all exercising their traditional rights—those of the harvesters to a fixed share (*bawon*) of what they cut and those of the gleaners to whatever was left. With this traditional system and the new, easily shattered heads, the landowner stood to lose much more rice than before. Rather than look on as his profits evaporated, he increasingly resorted to what is known as *tebasan*. This involved selling his standing crop to a broker, usually from another village, who then arrived with his own harvesters (generally from the broker's village) to cut the crop with sickles and thresh it in the field. The result was a larger profit for broker, owner, and the lucky harvesters, but a large overall reduction in the labor force (20–50 percent) and, of course, in the cost of harvesting. The broker's labor gang, in the meantime, did double duty as an armed band, protecting the broker and owner from the rage of would-be harvesters and gleaners who had lost one of their few remaining subsistence rights. While the new system creates a small and privileged labor force, it eliminates the main source of food for a greater number of landless Javanese. The potential for class polarization and conflict here is ominous.

35. William L. Collier, Soentoro, Gunawan, Wiradi, and Makali, "Agricultural Technology and Institutional Change in Java," *Food Research Institute Studies* 8:2 (1974), 169–94. See also Franke, "Miracle Seeds and Shattered Dreams."

It would appear that the prospects for a relatively peaceful agrarian transformation through high-yielding varieties are dim. In terms of both economic security and employment, the evidence points to a serious subsistence threat for at least the poorer sections of the peasantry. Given the high unemployment rates in the labor-choked cities of Southeast Asia and the low rates of urban job formation, it is hardly likely that the redundant labor force will be absorbed successfully into the urban sector. In rare cases, like that of Malaysia, overall economic growth, a land frontier, and buoyant export prices may create enough compensating opportunities elsewhere in the economy to lessen tension. For most of the region, however, the green revolution is more likely to aggravate class conflict than to provide a peaceful path to development. Although this is not necessarily a recipe for rebellion, it does imply that, far from easing rural class tensions, the social and economic consequences of the green revolution may provoke higher levels of coercion and repression.

RAIDING THE CASH ECONOMY.    Assuming that the coercive powers of the state prevent those pressures from assuming the form of revolt, what does this mean for village society? One likely consequence is a semipermanent pattern of short-term migration, or what might be termed "raiding the cash economy."

The distinguishing feature of this pattern is the growing dependency of villagers on the marginal or scavenging possibilities in the extra-village economy. Rather than outright migration and full absorption into the modern sector, it represents a largely individual attempt to make up the deficit in local subsistence resources. Essential elements of this process have for some time existed in certain areas. The steady seasonal stream of migrants from Northeast Thailand coming to Bangkok to drive pedicabs or filter into other marginal positions in what is called the "tertiary sector" by economists is a case in point.[36] For many villages in Jakarta's hinterland, short-term work as *betcak* (pedicab) drivers or in small-scale trade serves the same function.[37] One writer, describing this pattern in Central Luzon, calls it "circommuting."[38] Similar networks of migration exist linking most provincial towns and port cities of Southeast Asia with the villages of the surrounding region. Demo-

36. Robert Textor, *From Peasant to Pedicab Driver* (New Haven: Yale University Southeast Asian Studies, 1961).

37. See Richard Critchfield, *Hello, Mister! Where Are You Going?* (New York: The Alicia Patterson Funds, n.d.).

38. Otto D. van den Muijzenberg, *Horizontal Mobility in Central Luzon, Characteristics and Background* (Publication 19 of the Department of South and Southeast Asia, Center for Anthropological and Sociological Studies, University of Amsterdam, 1973, in Dutch), pp. 151–236 and 341–414.

graphic pressures and structural change in agriculture are likely to make of this pattern not simply a prelude to industrialization and urbanization but rather a fairly permanent feature of the village response to subsistence problems.

There has been, to my knowledge, virtually no field work in Southeast Asia which has analyzed the effects of such major adjustments in village society and politics, but we can look for help to the studies of, say, southern Italy, western Ireland, and northern Mexico where migration of this kind has transformed rural society.[39] Some fairly obvious consequences deserve mention. Clearly, the growing role of migratory labor works against economic and political cooperation at the village level. Financially, the most significant links are now external and the nexus of local social pressures and economic imperatives that held the subsistence-oriented village together are bound to weaken. The resulting social disorganization is likely to rule out the mutuality and shared poverty that typify involution and to produce, instead, a pattern of mutual hostility and social Darwinism. What Banfield has called "amoral familism" and others "the culture of poverty" is perhaps the social residue of a village economy that has become economically marginal in this fashion.[40]

Demographically, the withdrawal of a substantial fraction of young adult males from the village is likely to deprive it of much of its potential lower class leadership. Culturally as well, the pattern of migration tends to dilute the distinctiveness and autonomy of the village's "little tradition." Along each of these dimensions of change, then, the social and economic content of "peasantness" is gradually stripped away so that rural life, and hence rural politics, qualifies less and less as a special category.

Looked at from another angle, as peasant politics loses its distinctiveness, it is at the same time integrated increasingly into national politics. The economic and social ties that bind the village to the urban sector give rise to political linkages as well. Organizationally and ideologically these linkages foster a rural politics that is more a provincial variant of the national political pattern than a sharply delineated sphere unto itself. In the case of Northeast Thailand, the tradition of migration to

39. E.g., Edward Banfield, *The Moral Basis of a Backward Society* (Glencoe, Ill.: The Free Press, 1958); Sidney Tarrow, *Peasant Communism in Southern Italy* (New Haven: Yale University Press, 1967); Oscar Lewis, *Pedro Martinez* (New York: Vintage Books, 1964); and Mart Bax, *Harpstrings and Confessions* (forthcoming, Oxford University Press). The work of van den Muijzenberg on Central Luzon, cited above, is the only work that has come to my attention on this subject in Southeast Asia.

40. Banfield, *The Moral Basis of a Backward Society*, p. 1.

and from Bangkok has helped to create a regional sense of political identity and to integrate regional grievances into a larger left-wing opposition.[41] This homogenization of rural politics with urban politics can of course proceed along conservative as well as radical lines, as the strength of the Christian Democrats in rural southern Italy illustrates. In fact, factionalism within the village is probably more common as external political alignments reflect the diverse connections of employment, assistance, and friendships that villagers have managed to forge with the outside world.

"Makeshift migration" ties the economic as well as the political fortunes of the village to the urban economy. The situation of such villages can perhaps be likened to the situation of a growing number of Mediterranean nations which provide much of the manual labor force for industrialized Europe. By exporting laborers, the unemployment situation at home is eased and the remittances of workers abroad become a vital part of local revenue and foreign exchange. The "labor-exporting village" in Southeast Asia, in the same sense, eases the pressure on land and/or labor competition by sending workers away and gains the income they remit or bring back. By the same token, this village (or nation) is exceptionally vulnerable to an economic slump in the urban sector that would slash its income and force a return of its surplus labor force. The major source of collective economic shocks for such villages is thus not harvests or crop prices but rather the commercial wage-labor sector. Like the urban poor, the village is now dependent on the crumbs of the labor market, and its dependence is especially marked since its migrants typically hold marginal positions that are the first to be affected by a slump. At this point, it does not seem justifiable any longer to speak of peasant politics, for the political and economic life of such villages has more in common with that of the proletariat, or rather the lumpen-proletariat, than with that of the peasantry.

What is important here is not so much this speculation about the politics of villages where makeshift migration is substantial, but rather the importance of the category itself. There is every reason to believe that, given demographic pressures and the unlikely prospects for rapid industrialization, this pattern of parasitic and tenuous dependence on the leavings of the modern sector will become far more prevalent. The village thus produced cannot be understood as simply part rural and

41. To a great extent these political links were built through concrete acts of patronage as Thai MPs from the Northeast looked after the interests of many of their constituents who had migrated to Bangkok, and as the Christian Democrats used the development funds for the South to create a vast patronage machine of employment and contracts that would pay off at election time.

part urban, or part peasant and part worker, but must be studied as a hybrid species with its own unique characteristics.

*Reliance on State-Supported Forms of Patronage and Assistance*

The public sector itself, particularly after independence, has come to represent a second major pool of subsistence resources for many peasants. Here I do not have in mind basic structural reforms such as land redistribution, ceilings on tenancy rates, or cheap credit to smallholders and tenants that might offer more lasting remedies. Such efforts have been both rare and limited and, with few exceptions, ineffective. I refer rather to a whole range of public sector activity which may add something to peasant income or help stabilize it. Such marginal and usually short-term assistance may come in the form of employment on public works, in road-building, or in a variety of menial jobs in the public sector. Subsidized resettlement and military service represent slightly more elaborate (if more dangerous) economic opportunities. In a more fragmentary way, food subsidies, famine relief, or nutritional programs for children may mean a great deal for the subsistence security of peasants close to the margin.[42] This array of welfare and employment programs would of course have a legitimate place even within a larger context of structural change. But, taken alone, it comes fairly close to representing the stock-in-trade of conservative regimes that hope both to avoid a redistribution of land or wealth *and* to forestall any possibility of a rural insurrection.

To the extent that this structure of marginal opportunities generated by the state actually helps provide a modest, if risky, subsistence to many peasant families, its practical effect may well be to defuse the explosive potential of agrarian unrest. Its demobilizing potential is both economic and social. Economically, of course, it may offer a short-run solution to subsistence requirements and thus keep many peasants from the acts of desperation that characterize most peasant uprisings. Socially, these opportunities, like migration, represent an individual rather than a collective route to protection and security. A great many of these benefits, moreover, are not distributed at random but come instead through connections with politicians, officials, and local power brokers who use their positions to develop local followings. Such ties, while they may be new, are often stylistically simply a replication of traditional links of patron-client deference. When the bonds of deference have eroded,

---

42. A full discussion here would also have to include public spending for collective benefits such as water supply, public health, price supports, education, and roads, which may also raise and/or stabilize the income of peasants.

these new connections forged with state funds may come to represent the basis of the regime's following in the countryside. The peasant may regard these connections with a healthy skepticism, but their vital function for his family's subsistence will nevertheless constrain his behavior.

When financial conditions have permitted, the level of government-sponsored patronage has tended to rise in post-colonial Southeast Asia. I believe this is due in part to the fact that earlier forms of economic insurance were eroding or had all but disappeared, leaving a peasantry whose need for minimal economic security was glaringly obvious. The need was heightened further by the absence in most countries of an industrial expansion that might have accommodated more of the marginal peasantry. Within this context, however, the greatest incentive for the expansion of public patronage has been the pressure of electoral competition when it existed. Before the permanent military regime of Ne Win in Burma, factions of the divided ruling party competed for peasant votes by the distribution of loans, subsidies, and cash in the villages.[43] The prodigious road-building activity of the ruling Alliance Party in Malaysia has been similarly connected to the electoral impact of the rural employment it created. Multiparty competition in Indonesia prior to 1960 stimulated comparable rural patronage.[44] Philippine politicians, under electoral pressure, brought this system of public patronage to a level of technical perfection rarely equaled even by American urban machines. In each case, the existence on the one hand of a large marginal peasantry for whom small favors were of enormous value and, on the other, of politicians who needed votes to remain in power provided the natural formula for rural machine politics.

For the most part, such rural patronage represents an alternative to structural change rather than a complement to it. The character of Filipino parties in the countryside is a striking example of how state patronage can often neutralize incipient class demands.[45] Throughout the 1930s, the needs and grievances of thousands of Filipino peasants fueled the careers of politicians, most of whom built and maintained followings by helping peasants individually with jobs, loans, and legal matters and absorbed them into existing party networks. It was precisely the capacity of the party system to provide marginal help for some

43. See Manning Nash, "Party-Building in Upper Burma," *Asian Survey* 3:4 (April 1963), 190–202.

44. Herbert Feith, *The Decline of Constitutional Democracy in Indonesia* (Ithaca: Cornell University Press, 1962), and *The Indonesian Elections of 1955* (Ithaca: Cornell University Southeast Asian Program, 1961).

45. The definitive analysis of party electoral dynamics in the Philippines is Lande's, *Leaders, Factions, and Parties.*

peasants—and, of course, to use the constabulary against those who turned to more direct action—that allowed the Filipino elite narrowly to skirt a revolutionary situation.[46] President Magsaysay's policy toward an insurrectionary peasantry in the 1950s followed much the same pattern.[47] Despite his early enthusiasm for land reform he avoided the key issue of structural change, which would have pitted him against entrenched landowning interests, by emphasizing immediate material benefits. Ex-rebels were lured by promises of loans and newly cleared land; villagers were promised roads, jobs, and schools. Though this policy met a few critical peasant needs, it ignored the broader issues of land ownership and the conditions of tenancy. By 1970 these issues could no longer be ignored.

In broader terms, what are the preconditions for such a conservative stabilization of agrarian subsistence problems? Given the fact that government-sponsored opportunities for income and mobility derive from the financial means of the state, our attention is directed to what might be called the state's "carrying capacity." Just as the supply of opportunities in the commercial sector depends on a buoyant economy, so does the supply of state patronage depend on the fiscal health of the state. It is surely no coincidence that the heyday of state patronage and electoral politics occurred in the early 1950s when the Korean War boom for primary exports fueled rapidly growing state revenues. Nor is it coincidence that, in the late 1950s, the sharp reduction in export earnings made fiscal extravagance far more costly and undermined the capacity of elites to meet these needs through patronage.

The possibility for such stop-gap state management of the explosive potential of the peasant economy is contingent, then, on fiscal muscle. Conservative elites can avoid facing the issues of basic structural change or repression only to the extent that the economy provides them with the financial resources to meet a wide range of immediate needs through patronage.[48] However, the fiscal burden of this strategy is likely to grow faster than the state resources which make it possible. So long as the structural issues remain unresolved, so long as population growth

46. Not, however, without the Sakdalista rebellion that was in some respects the Philippine counterpart to the Saya San and Nghe-An/Ha-Tinh rebellions in Burma and Vietnam.

47. See, for example, Francis Starner, *Magsaysay and the Philippine Peasantry: The Agrarian Impact on Philippine Politics, 1953–1956* (Berkeley and Los Angeles: University of California Press, 1961).

48. Since a large share of state revenue in Southeast Asia, as in most poor countries, comes from import or export duties, the health of this sector of the economy is more decisive than the domestic sector.

creates new demographic pressures, and so long as the urban sector absorbs only a small fraction of the rural displaced, the volume of subsistence problems is likely to outstrip the financial capacity of the state. The fiscal problem for conservative regimes in Southeast Asia is a more serious version of what James O'Connor has described as "The Fiscal Crisis of the State" for capitalist countries.[49] On the one hand, the absence of structural change serves to exacerbate welfare problems and increase the need for social spending. On the other hand, the revenue to fund such programs can only come from the sectors of the economy that conservative elites, for obvious reasons, are unwilling to tax more heavily. The result, barring an export boom or the discovery of oil, is likely to be a growing disparity between the level of welfare needs and the revenue available to meet them. In rare instances, as in Malaysia, where demographic pressures are more modest and where both the modern sector and the revenue of the state are on sounder footing, such a conservative passage through the crisis may be negotiable. Elsewhere in the region, even with self-interested assistance from governments of the United States and Japan, the prospects would seem far less bright.

The collision course between agrarian discontent and state resources is painfully evident in the recent history of the Philippines. Before each postwar election there had been a characteristic deficit in government accounts as the ruling party sought, usually without success, to organize the rural vote through the patronage of the public purse.[50] More important, however, is the fact that the deficits became more and more profound with each election, while the postelection recoveries became more shallow. This reflects the greater virtuoso efforts of public spending that were required, in the face of mounting demographic pressure and welfare needs and in the absence of land reform, to capitalize the operation of an increasingly shaky electoral system. By 1970, with a decline in government revenue, the financial limits of conflict management by patronage had been definitely reached. This is hardly the only explanation for the declaration of martial law by President Marcos, but it seems clear that the classical Filipino system of electoral patronage had become, quite literally, bankrupt. It was no longer possible to avoid the

49. James O'Connor, *The Fiscal Crisis of the State* (New York: St. Martin's Press, 1973).

50. For the actual figures, see H. A. Averich, F. H. Denton, and J. E. Koehler, *A Crisis of Ambiguity: Political and Economic Development in the Philippines*, Rand Study R-473-AID (Santa Monica: Rand Corporation, 1970), p. 161. I should add that this report is, on the whole, simplemindedly optimistic about the chances of the traditional party system to weather the crisis. See also the excellent article by Thomas Nowak and Key Snyder, "Clientelist Politics in the Philippines: Integration or Instability," *American Political Science Review* 68:3 (September 1974), 1147–70.

issues of land reform or repression, particularly in Central Luzon and in the Muslim south where the settlement of peasants from other islands was meeting violent resistance. The political costs to the regime of a thoroughgoing land reform appeared to be such as to make repression (which was much in evidence even during the electoral period) the most likely course.

In brief, the chances that reliance on state patronage can constitute a stable, long-run adaptation to peasant subsistence crises would seem small. On the demand side, population growth, neglect of structural change, and even the green revolution steadily augment the fiscal costs of this strategy. On the supply side, neither the rate of growth of government revenue, nor its stability, offer much assurance that the state can cover these costs. Politically as well, the electoral forms that once provided a strong incentive to pursue such a strategy and to avoid large-scale coercion have largely been abandoned. Effective as conservative patronage may be over the short run, it is therefore not much more likely that it will constitute a reliable formula for agrarian peace than local self-help or makeshift migration.

The effects of state patronage will nevertheless probably continue to demobilize a portion of the peasantry in most of Southeast Asia. From the perspective of what a mobilized peasantry might mean for politics and structural change, this surely constitutes a tragedy. But from the perspective of the subsistence needs of peasants themselves, we would do well to understand as well as condemn. As R. C. Cobb said of the demobilized peasantry in Napoleonic France,

> Historians, few of whom have ever experienced hunger, have no business blaming poor people for accepting, even gratefully, the products of bourgeois charity. And it would be indecent to upbraid the *affamé* of the past for allowing themselves to be bought out of what historians have decreed were "forward looking" movements by the grant of relief.[51]

## Encapsulation of Religious or Oppositionist Structures of Protection and Assistance

A final and paradoxical pattern of (nonrebellious) adaptation to subsistence crises involves reliance on religious or oppositionist structures of protection and assistance. Among others, the Hoa Hao and Cao Dai sects in southern Vietnam, the Iglesia Ni Cristo in the Philippines, and perhaps even the Communist Party of Indonesia (PKI) before 1965

51. Cobb, *The Police and the People*, p. 320.

might fall into this category. The category is, however, ambiguous. Such sects and parties can as often be a prelude and stimulus to revolt as an alternative to it. Thus, the Colorums in the Philippines could, by turns, launch all-out assaults on the state or retreat into local autonomy and quietism. The Sakdalista Party in Luzon in the late 1930s could likewise veer suddenly from the familiar scenario of reform politics into armed rebellion. Just as frequently, however, such movements that begin by giving expression to class-based peasant grievances can become more or less encapsulated or sidetracked. This occurs especially when these movements are able to provide the physical security, employment, and material assistance that constitute the most pressing of peasant needs. At that point they may become an enduring part of the local structure—attempting to hold their own or even joining in coalition with conservative forces at the regional or national level. The history of Christian sects among peasants in the West, of course, offers many parallels. Given the typically localist outlook of peasants, it is not surprising that, once having devised something of a solution to their short-run problems, they should seek to defend it rather than risking everything in extending it.[52] Their ideology and local structure, like that of the Javanese Saminists, may remain at sharp symbolic odds with the larger society, but they pose no direct threat.

A brief description of the Cao Dai and Iglesia Ni Cristo sects will serve to illustrate this pattern of adaptation.[53] Founded early in the twentieth century in southern Vietnam, the Cao Dai sect came to embrace a following of anywhere from 300,000 to 500,000 and was notably strong in Tay Ninh province near the Cambodian border. Its doctrine is strikingly syncretist with Victor Hugo, Jesus Christ, and Confucius numbered among its many saints. Although it includes many peasants and workers among its adherents, its leadership was recruited disproportionately from the Vietnamese middle class—petty officials, interpreters, clerks in private firms, teachers, students, and small merchants and landowners.

52. Sects appear to court rebellion especially when their vision of local economic needs and their moral rectitude lead them to defy the state by, say, refusing to pay taxes that will ruin them or by insisting on their right to take fuel from restricted forests—as the Saminists in Java did. A great many rebellions are "backed into" in this fashion.

53. For the Cao Dai see, for example, Francis R. Hill, "Millennarian Machines in South Vietnam," *Comparative Studies in Society and History* 13 (July 1971), 325–50, and Nguyen Tran Huan, "Histoire d'une secte religieuse au Vietnam: Le Caodaisme," chap. 7 in Jean Chesneaux, *Tradition et revolution au Vietnam* (Paris: Editions Anthropos, n.d.). For the Iglesia Ni Cristo, see Hirofumi Ando, "A Study of the Iglesia Ni Cristo: A Politico-Religious Sect in the Philippines," *Pacific Affairs* 42:3 (Fall 1969), 334–45. The details that follow are from these sources.

For our purposes, its local organization and finances are of particular interest. The Cao Dai Charity Corps aided indigent members and, as in the case of many other sects, "organized mutual assistance in case of illness, aid in paying taxes and meeting corvée labor requirements, helped settle village disputes, and ran a variety of commercial undertakings."[54] On the basis of the commercial interests it controlled (timber, light industry, and a few small plantations, not to mention the opium and piastre traffic its leaders had a hand in), it was able to provide material as well as spiritual security for many believers. Its local military units helped insure its administrative monopoly and both landowners and the French helped subsidize the movement financially.

For a section of the peasantry, then, the mixture of local self-help, commercial ventures, and subsidies from outside that the Cao Dai had at its disposal provided a workable structure of material and physical security. It met many of the most urgent, tangible needs of its adherents. In addition, it was from the outset an alternative to rebellion. As long as sect commanders controlled the patronage resources that cemented their local followers together, they were free to make whatever deals they saw fit with local landowners, with the French, and later with Diem.[55] With the exception of a commander in Bac-lieu province who joined forces with the revolutionary movement, the surviving Cao Dai sects became new local structures of patronage very much tied to the existing order.[56] The modest success of the Cao Dai (and that of the Hoa Hao and some Catholic bishoprics elsewhere in the country) in meeting short-run peasant needs in a context of moral solidarity has, as is often remarked, formed a barrier against communist recruitment in these areas.

The Iglesia Ni Cristo, a Christian sect on Luzon, has recruited its following especially among the poor tenant farmers, laborers, and the urban lumpenproletariat. One writer has suggested that its recent growth may be due in part to the earlier failure of more secular attempts at revolution by the Sakdalistas and later by the Huks. In this sense we might see it not so much as an alternative to rebellion as a symbolic and material shelter when rebellion has failed or is impossible. Its strength at the local level derives in large part from the way it has restored the traditional moral economy of subsistence security. Members in need are

54. Hill, "Millennarian Machines in South Vietnam," p. 328.

55. Diem later on destroyed the military units of some sect leaders and bribed many others. Hill estimates that he spent $12 million in bribes to the leaders of the Cao Dai and other sects. Ibid., p. 345.

56. The Hoa Hao movement, though rather more millennarian and anticolonial, could be analyzed in similar terms.

helped with loans, funeral expenses, medical costs and other forms of relief. The church, moreover, functions as a kind of employment agency for its members. Like the Cao Dai, then, the Iglesia Ni Cristo has organized a modest but serviceable structure of economic security that solidifies its following. By virtue of its electoral solidarity the sect has, again like the Cao Dai, become a political force to be reckoned with. It endorses candidates who, if successful, then become brokers and protectors of sect interests at provincial and national levels. The Iglesia Ni Cristo has not become simply another patron-client structure, for its membership, its doctrine, and its egalitarianism still reflect the class issues behind its growth. Nevertheless, its relative success as a sect places it at a structural and ideological fork in the road. To the extent that it can meet the economic needs of its followers by local self-help and political connections, to that extent is it likely to become a stable and nonradical religious movement.

Radical parties and peasant unions, as well as sects, are susceptible to this process of encapsulation. Their local success in catering to the welfare needs of the peasantry may undermine the more radical objectives that guided their formation. Under certain circumstances they risk becoming parallel structures of patronage rather than class movements. The history of the PKI (Communist Party) in Indonesia from roughly 1951 to 1965 illustrates some of the main features of this process. The party's "access to the peasantry seems to have been predominantly via channels of patronage, kinship, and traditional deference."[57] Leaders of the party recognized this problem—though they had created it themselves by expanding membership from cadre proportions of roughly 5,000 in 1951 to mass proportions of over one million by 1955—and regularly denounced the deviations of paternalism or *bapakism*.

The PKI, not entirely unlike more traditional parties, provided concrete services for peasants and tended to incorporate local influentials, together with their followers, into its structure. Party leaders worked hard to legalize squatter rights, provide relief for victims of flood and fire, help execute government forms, supply legal advice, and so on. Since the PKI had some influence over the disposition of public funds, it could distribute a substantial number of full or part-time jobs and could

57. Rex Mortimer, "Class, Social Cleavage, and Indonesian Communism," *Indonesia* 8 (October 1969), 6. I have also relied on the following sources for this account: Donald Hindley, *The Communist Party of Indonesia 1951–1963* (Berkeley: University of California Press, 1966); Robert Jay, *Religion and Politics in Rural Central Java* (New Haven: Yale University Southeast Asian Studies, Cultural Report Series, 1963); and W. F. Wertheim, "From Aliran to Class Struggle in the Countryside of Java," *Pacific Viewpoints* 10:3 (September 1969), 1–17.

spend large sums in the 1955 and 1957 elections. For many Javanese peasants these party activities represented an important source of assistance and influence in the absence of other alternatives.[58]

The local significance of personal dependence relations within the PKI was particularly apparent in the composition of local leadership. A large share of rural party officials were medium and (for Java) large landowners, *abangan* (that is, nominal Muslims strongly adhering to Javanese ritual and culture) traders and shopkeepers, and traditional healers and entertainers, many of whom "retained attitudes toward poor peasants typical of others of their social position."[59] As Robert Jay observed:

> This selection of the well-to-do, the respectable, and the traditionally oriented *abangan* as left wing political leaders in a rural village was not unique to Tamansari. I found it to be a consistent pattern in the left-wing dominated villages that were a part of the traditional rural society, the exceptions occurring in villages of ex-plantation workers. . . . The same figures were the normal, even traditional, links between the rest of the village and urban society. They themselves, as well-to-do villagers generally, were strongly attracted toward urban ties and patterns, and sometimes had, or had had in the past, ties of kinship with the lower rank of the town officialdom.[60]

By 1955, when peasants had become a majority of PKI membership, party leaders were actually complaining that local wealthy elements were obstructing party decisions.[61] Banking on the protection of Sukarno and the importance of a mass electoral base, the party had in many areas accommodated traditional forms of personal dependency within the village. Much of the peasantry was linked not so much to the class program or ideology of the party but personally to local leaders. The disintegration of the PKI in 1965 was not only a consequence of the force brought against it by the army and Islamic militants but also a

58. The party did, of course, make efforts to create new horizontal links between peasants at the local level. It organized labor exchanges, work brigades, rotating credit associations, cooperative public works (schools, wells, road repair), and producer cooperatives. Largely because of its rapid expansion, however, it tended to incorporate local structures rather than to change them. Where these structures were clientelistic, the party took on a clientelistic structure. Where these structures were more class-based as, for example, among plantation workers, the party took on more of a class structure.

59. Hindley, *The Communist Party of Indonesia*, p. 163.

60. Jay, *Religion and Politics in Rural Central Java*, p. 99.

61. Mortimer, "Class, Social Cleavage, and Indonesian Communism," p. 19.

reflection of the obstacles to class militance its own structure had
created.[62]

The distinction made here is a fine one and must not be carried too
far. It is normal to expect that radical parties will establish a foothold
among peasants in part by responding to concrete local and even personal needs. As the head of the PKI, Aidit, advised: "The first step to be
taken in our work among the peasants is to assist them in the struggle for
their everyday needs, for the achievement of their partial demands."[63] It
is perhaps only when such assistance is both successful and *is organized
along lines of personal patronage* that it risks becoming an end rather than a
means.[64] If the immediate subsistence needs of poor peasants, which
form the classical basis of their radicalism, are substantially alleviated in
this manner, the effect may well be their demobilization rather than
their mobilization.

Whether encapsulation of potentially radical peasant movements occurs would seem to depend heavily on the resources available to them to
actually relieve some of their members' most pressing needs and the
degree to which they are tolerated, or even aided, by the state or outside
elites. Of these two factors the latter seems paramount. Without outside
assistance a local sect or party is more or less reduced to what we have
called internal self-help, which is unlikely to prove materially adequate
as a basis for patronage. The Iglesia Ni Cristo and the PKI, for example,
operated within an electoral system (or, in the case of the PKI from 1958

62. The paradox of a nominally class-based organization operating as a patron-client
network is not simply a product of middle or upper class leadership. The "overrepresenta-
tion" of middle class elements in the National Liberation Front leadership or in the
Chinese Communist Party (prior to 1948) did not prevent them from becoming revolutionary parties. The key consideration is not the social background of leaders but the
nature of the tie between leaders and led. While any particular leadership style is necessarily a mixture, "class-based followings" and clienteles are basically distinguishable from one
another. Class-based followers tend to share a collective interest in certain policy goals and
to evaluate leaders according to how well they represent those goals and how effectively
they work to achieve them. Clients, by contrast, have individual and usually short term
goals that they hope to achieve by their personal attachment to an influential leader. See
the brilliant argument along these lines by Carl Lande, "Groups and Networks in Southeast Asia," *American Political Science Review* 67 (1972), 103–27.

63. Quoted by Justus van der Kroef, "Peasant and Land-Reform in Indonesian Communism," *Journal of Southeast Asian History* 4:1 (March 1963), 49.

64. The PKI is not unique among Communist parties in this respect. The Communist
Party of Italy (PCI), also operating under electoral pressures where peasant votes are
critical, has tended to reflect rather than to change the clientelistic structure of Southern
Italy. See the fine study of the PCI by Sidney Tarrow, *Peasant Communism in Southern Italy*
(New Haven: Yale University Press, 1967). A comparison of these two parties would be a
rewarding study.

to 1965, with presidential blessing) which provided tangible, if modest, dividends for local adherents. Despite military confrontations with Diem, many factions of the Cao Dai and Hoa Hao were able to strike lucrative bargains with the colonial and Saigon regimes. Such bargains kept their local bases intact and filled their coffers. Apparently both electoral regimes and weak regimes that have strong incentives to come to terms with independent centers of power thus favor the peaceful and even conservative encapsulation of potential dissident movements. If this analysis is correct, it suggests that if such favorable conditions are reversed, these movements may possibly return to dissidence and even to rebellion.

NONREVOLT: REPRESSION AND THE QUESTION OF FALSE CONSCIOUSNESS

Only under very special conditions can the adaptations described offer a solution to the subsistence problems brought about by exploitation and demographic pressure. Such conservative and relatively peaceful routes to a post-peasant society would seem to require a rate of economic growth, a level of fiscal strength, and a form of government that are all conspicuous by their absence in much of Southeast Asia.

If we were to reason only from the situation in the countryside, it is likely that the economic conditions that promote rebellion have remained and, in some areas, intensified. The increasingly unfavorable ratio of population to land and the strength of the state have, if anything, reinforced the hegemony of the collectors of rent and taxes. The proportion of rural landless whose position is most precarious has steadily grown. The returns to the owners of scarce factors of production—land and capital—have expanded while the returns to the abundant factor—labor—have diminished. Out of these conditions, especially where they were most severe, have come major postwar agrarian rebellions in Burma, the Philippines, and Vietnam (with the Madiun uprising in Java in 1948 a marginal case). It is instructive that each of these rebellions was initially favored by the *weakness* of the state at the close of World War II and immediately afterward. It is equally instructive that, with the exception of Vietnam, each of these rebellions was crushed, despite the fact that they were larger in scale and better in organization than their prewar antecedents.[65] The outriders of rebellion—land invasions, local attacks on landowners or officials, tenant and labor strikes—have subsequently cropped up from time to time in Central Luzon and

65. Cambodia and Laos are also exceptions, but their rebellions did not originate in the problems of tenancy and taxes as did those of the major lowland states of Southeast Asia.

Java and have with few exceptions been checked by a state increasingly confident of its power.[66]

Growing exploitation and economic insecurity may, in this context, lead to anger and moral indignation but not necessarily to rebellion. We must acknowledge the possibility that the major obstacle to agrarian rebellion in Southeast Asia is not the lack of exploitation but the deadly risks that the state and rural elites can impose on would-be rebels. As John Dunn has noted in more general terms:

> Even the most justified rebellion in the face of the modern armaments available to every modern state is a venture in desperation. The populace at large does not revolt for fun. Lacking the rationalist assurance of a better order waiting in the future to be grasped, and having invested a lifetime of often highly repressed effort in the struggle to survive at all, most men, particularly in countries in which massive rebellion is at all probable, rebel as a final gesture of misery, not as an expression of optimism about the future.[67]

In the early colonial period, rebels who had never faced modern weapons and armies could easily misjudge these risks and strike anyway. Even in the 1930s, Saya San and his followers, who knew what the colonizers had in store, could nevertheless strike in the belief that their magical and religious powers would neutralize their enemies; peasants in Nghe-An could launch a rebellion on the basis of a local success in Vinh, misjudging the overall balance of forces from their special local situation. Increasingly, however, peasants live in a world that gives them little scope for such fatal misjudgments. The weight of the army, and often the police, as major if not dominant institutions is ever more apparent to them. They have, moreover, the sobering evidence of experience from rebellions and defiance in the past.

The tangible and painful memories of repression must have a chilling effect on peasants who contemplate even minor acts of resistance. It may well be that the experience of defeat for one generation of peasants precludes another rebellion until a new generation has replaced it. For

66. Burma drops out of the comparison at this point because of the land reform of the early 1950s that seemed to remedy, if only in the short run, the problem of peasant subsistence. The land reform, in a sense, replaced the problem of exploitation with that of involution. The fiscal problems this reform created for the Burmese state and the dramatic decline of rice exports highlight the connection between the agrarian structure and the state's claim to the surplus.

67. John Dunn, *Modern Revolutions: An Introduction to the Analysis of a Political Phenomenon* (Cambridge: Cambridge University Press, 1972), p. 246.

Filipino tenants and laborers in Central Luzon there are the intimidating memories of the 1930s and the 1950s. Those whose boldness or desperation led them to join tenant unions, let alone identify themselves with the Huks, were likely to lose their tenancies and be blacklisted by landowners in the region. Beyond economic reprisals there were physical reprisals of prison sentences, beatings, and murders at the hands of the courts, the army, the constabulary, and the private forces of hacenderos.[68] For many Javanese villagers, the memories of late 1965 and early 1966 are even more sobering. Mere association with the local PKI was usually enough to mark one as a victim of the terror organized by Islamic bands (particularly the Muslim Youth Movement, ANSOR) and their military allies—a terror that may have taken as many as 300,000 lives on Java alone. The effect of this reign of terror has been to break the capacity of poor peasants to organize any resistance to the more recent changes in cultivation which threaten their security.[69] In the last extremity, of course, it may be true that resistance is blind to risks, whatever they may be. But in any situation short of that final state, it may well be that the memory of repression is one of the principal explanations for the absence of resistance and revolt.

This assumption raises a vital conceptual problem. How are we to gauge the potential for rebellion in the absence of the possibility to act? Let us assume, for example, that we can establish that a given peasantry is increasingly exploited, in the sense in which we have defined the term, and that as a result it faces a subsistence crisis. Let us assume further that we can agree that the state has the coercive force to crush any likely rebellion. At least two divergent interpretations of this situation are possible. On the one hand, one may claim that the peasantry, because of its religious or social ideology, accepts this exploitation as a normal, even justifiable, part of the social order. This explanation for the absence of revolt—for peasant passivity—assumes a fatalistic acceptance of the social order or what Marxists might call "mystification." One may claim, on the other hand, that the explanation for passivity is not to be found in peasant values, but rather in the relationships of force in the countryside.

It is probably safe to assume that no one would claim that the absence of defiance, taken by itself, is *sufficient* evidence that rural class relations are harmonious. Even the colonial officials assessing the claims of landlords in Lower Burma in the 1930s were prepared to admit that agrarian

68. Aware of this problem, the Viet Cong took every precaution to maintain the legal status of peasants who helped them so as to minimize the threat to their security.

69. See, for example, Gerrit Huizer, "Peasant Mobilization and Land Reform in Indonesia," (The Hague: Institute of Social Studies, Occasional Paper, June 1972).

peace *might* be the peace of repression rather than the peace of contentment:

> We do not feel disposed to accept the view put before us with some frequency that the relations between landlords and tenants are generally harmonious. We doubt whether this means more than that untoward incidents are unusual and we are inclined to think that the apparently satisfactory relations mean no more than that the tenant is so completely in the hands of his landlord that he is unable to assert himself in any effective way.[70]

The issues posed by these two interpretations are central to the analysis of peasant politics. Mystification is invoked as the reason for resignation particularly in societies, such as the Indian, where a venerable system of rigid stratification is reinforced by religious sanctions. Lower castes are said to accept their fate in the Hindu hierarchy.[71] The same explanation is invoked in Java where a tradition of passivity and deference is presumed to represent a cognitive obstacle to revolt. Is there an empirical solution to this thorny issue; is there a way of deciding, in any particular situation, what weight to assign to values as an obstacle to revolt and what weight to assign to repression in memory, fact, and potential? Without underestimating the problems involved, I believe there are a number of ways this problem can be attacked.

There are, first, some nearly experimental situations that provide something of a test for these competing explanations. If the threat of repression and not mystification is the main barrier to rebellion, we would expect logically that a significant reduction in the coercive pressure of the state might by itself stimulate resistance. If we can isolate instances of rebellion and resistance that occur on the heels of a lessening of repression (and where immediately prior value changes appear negligible), the case for repression as the major barrier would receive strong post hoc support. Such cases do arise since changes in repressive capacity are liable to occur more quickly than changes in values.

A case from India will illustrate what I have in mind.[72] Prior to 1969 in the Naxalbari district of West Bengal, although there had been an active peasant union and long-smoldering discontent, no actual outbursts against the local landed elites had occurred. A period of relative quies-

---

70. *Report of the Land and Agriculture Committee, 1938*, p. 12.

71. I would expect, as argued earlier, that this deference would remain more or less voluntary only so long as the elites who claimed it actually provided the subsistence security and protection for which they are seen reciprocally responsible.

72. This account is taken from an excellent graduate term paper on the Naxalbari rebellion in West Bengal in 1969 by Ronald Herring, University of Wisconsin, 1972.

cence was broken dramatically by a large-scale rebellion which began shortly after the victory of the left-wing United Front in the statewide elections of 1969. What appears to have happened is that the electoral campaign encouraged peasants to believe that a coalition favorable to their interests had taken power. The United Front talked openly of dispossessing landlords and appointed as Minister of Land and Revenue a communist from its most radical wing. Peasants moved spontaneously to occupy the land not only in Naxalbari but elsewhere in West Bengal under the assumption that, for the first time in memory, the police and administration were on their side and would support their claim to land. After a few confrontations led to peasant victories, the conflagration spread so quickly as to rule out any possibility that peasant organizers had, in the meantime, demystified the rural poor. What had changed, it seems reasonably clear, was not peasant values so much as the capacity to act. Once it became obvious to peasants that they could move somewhat more safely, that the risks had been reduced, the resistance seemed to be virtually self-generating. In cases like this it is hard to avoid the conclusion that repression rather than mystification lay behind the earlier passivity. If, in the same circumstances, resistance had not occurred, its absence would have been telling evidence *against* the repression theory.[73]

The context and development of peasant rebellions may thus often provide post hoc evidence for the repression theory. A change of regimes, the weakness of the state that may follow a military defeat, a regional success by an opposition party, are all signs that the balance of forces may have changed and are often the motivating events for peasant rebellions. From this perspective we may also appreciate how jacqueries snowball on the basis of an initial success. When one police station is overrun, when one landlord has taken to his heels, when one granary is successfully stormed, it is a signal to other watchful peasants that it may now be possible to act. Far from demonstrating the peasantry's proclivity to collective madness, as some have assumed, such conflagrations indicate how explosive any tangible evidence of weakness can be for a state or elite whose claim to the surplus has come to rest largely on coercive force. It goes without saying that a show of strength

73. In the rare event that a peasant rebellion triumphs in an area and the risks are now greater for those who would resist the rebellion, the evidence of participation is no longer convincing support for prior intimidation. In such a case, a peasant counterrevolutionary movement (e.g., the Vendée in 1793) is convincing evidence that, for those peasants, compliance was voluntary and valued. Thus, one of the best empirical tests of "consciousness," whether radical or conservative, is the willingness to risk one's life consistently on behalf of certain values.

by the state has the opposite effect. When protesting tenants are beaten and hauled off to jail, when the attempt to storm a granary is decisively crushed, it is a chilling signal to peasants that the risks of resistance are enormous and the chances of success small.[74]

In some circumstances, then, we can assess the intimidating effect of coercion by seeing what happens when this constraint is lifted. But what of the more numerous situations in which there is no collapse of repressive force to provide us with a test case and peasants with the opportunity to strike? How can we tell the difference between false deference and real deference when the relative weakness of the peasantry may make dissimulation necessary? How can we distinguish compliance under force from mystification and fatalism? Here, the empirical going is much rougher and evidence is more circumstantial.

Evidence can be sought at three levels. First, the state and landowning elites are certain to be alive to the potential consequences of growing rural exploitation and we might expect that concern to be reflected in the growth or intensification of their coercive power. We might, for example, examine the growth of military and police budgets as they apply to the policing of the countryside. If they grow proportionally faster than other claimants for state revenue, this may be an important straw in the wind. The disproportionate rise in police budgets in Vietnam between the wars, for instance, may well have indicated a mounting concern for rural law and order,[75] although we would need to know more about the rationale behind the expansion and the actual disposition of forces to strengthen the case. In less formal terms, the growth of irregular forces assembled by landlords, their agents, provincial officials, and revenue collectors may well imply that their claim to the surplus is less and less a matter of compliance than of power. The growing role of coercion should be especially visible at rent and tax collection times and in periods shortly before the harvest when peasant resources are at their lowest ebb. The signs may vary. When the landlord takes care to visit his fields only with an entourage, when the tax collector begins to appear in the company of a policeman, when the large landowner builds a wall around his house and hires nightwatchmen, the evidence accumulates.[76] These changes may occur in the relative ab-

74. We might begin with the assumption that the more severe the exploitation and the subsistence crises it provokes, the more risks peasants are willing to take to attack it and, therefore, the more repression will be required to prevent resistance.

75. Gran, *Vietnam and the Capitalist Road to Modernity*, p. 226.

76. An acquaintance of mine was invited to a picnic on the land of a large hacendero in the Philippines. When the party arrived at the site of the picnic, four bodyguards armed with machineguns stationed themselves at the periphery of the picnic area to provide

sence of concrete acts of peasant resistance but they are a sensitive barometer of the atmospheric pressure of class relations.

A second barometer of shifting class relations includes the means peasants devise for clandestinely improving their terms of exchange with landlords while avoiding open confrontations. Tenants may secretly harvest and sell a portion of their crop before the formal division of the harvest. They may pilfer from the landowner's granary or private fields when the occasion presents itself. They may flee with the owner's plow animal and with as much of the crop as they can take. The landlord may find his baskets of rice filled with as much chaff as grain. All of these devices are a violation of the tenancy or labor contract. As such, they suggest that the laborer or tenant considers the imposed terms unjust and will do whatever is in his power to circumvent them. Evidence of this kind may not be conclusive, since a certain frequency of deception is probably a normal part of the "little tradition." But when the frequency reaches epidemic proportions, as it did in the 1920s and 1930s in Lower Burma and Cochinchina, there is every reason to believe that the terms of exchange have lost much of their legitimacy. At this point, landlord complaints about the ingratitude, insubordination, and dissimulation among the tenant class are likely to be heard as well. To avoid the loss of return that such acts represent, these complaints are likely to go hand in hand with a growing investment in watchmen and overseers. That is to say, the growth of surveillance and coercion is tied to the growth of petty defiance; they both signal a loss of the normative power of the agrarian system.

Finally, if peasants feel unjustly extorted, we might expect to find strong indications of this in the one area of their life over which they do exercise some control: their culture. I believe it is possible to find clear evidence of growing symbolic withdrawal in the culture of those who are exploited but have little prospect of revolt. The values of an oppressed group, in this sense, are one of the clearest tests of their symbolic alignment or of their symbolic opposition to elite values and homilies.

The argument for mystification or false-consciousness depends, in fact, on the symbolic alignment of elite values and peasant values—on the assumption that the peasantry accepts the elite vision of the social order. What does mystification mean, if not a group's belief in the social ideology that justifies its exploitation? For Marxists the ultimate source of mystification is to be found in the control of the ruling class over the

---

security. It does not strain credulity to assume that the man was rational and had something to fear, although whether his tenantry or his political rivals were uppermost in his mind is not clear.

means of production, which includes the means of cultural production as well. For psychologists the process of false-consciousness may be sought in what is known as "identification with the oppressor" by which victims seek to escape the pain of oppression by associating themselves with the powerful other.[77] From the perspective of cognitive dissonance, the victim aligns his values to conform with the way he must behave so as to avoid a painful clash between his values and his actions. From still another vantage point, the deference of the oppressed represents the only weapon powerless individuals have to influence the conduct of their superiors.[78]

We must be very careful, however, not to infer the values of the oppressed from their behavior. Much of what passes as deference "is ritualized and habitual" or even calculating: "a great deal of this deferential behavior can be understood solely in terms of the constraints surrounding the actor that sanction any other form of behavior."[79] There may in fact be a large disparity between this constrained behavior and the behavior that would occur if constraints were lifted. The degree of this disparity would be some index of the disingenuousness of deferential acts. The very act of deferring may embody a certain mockery:

> By easily showing a regard that he does not have, the actor can feel that he is preserving a kind of inner autonomy, holding off the ceremonial order by the very act of upholding it. And of course in scrupulously observing the proper forms he may find that he is free to insinuate all kinds of disregard by carefully modifying intonation, pronunciation, pacing, and so forth.[80]

Hence, the mere observance of forms of respect can tell us little about how genuine the observance is.

If mystification is the major reason for peasant compliance and deference, it should be possible to substantiate this by reference to peasant beliefs and culture. If mystification is not the problem, however, that too should be evident from an examination of peasant culture. The evidence will seldom be cut-and-dried inasmuch as any group's culture will contain a number of diverse and even contradictory currents. Evidence

---

77. See, for example, Abram Kardiner and Lionel Ovesy, *The Mark of Oppression* (Cleveland: World Publishing Co., 1962).

78. See, for example, Richard M. Emerson, "Power-Dependence Relations," *American Sociological Review* 27:1 (February 1962), 39–41.

79. Howard Newby, "The Deferential Dialectic," *Comparative Studies in Society and History* 17:2 (April 1975), 142.

80. Erving Goffman, "The Nature of Deference and Demeanor," *American Anthropologist* 58 (June 1956), 478.

along these lines may be sought in the dissonant subculture of a subordinate group and its relationship to dominant elite values. The importance of such an analysis has been suggested by W. F. Wertheim:

> No human society is a completely integrated entity. In any community there are hidden or overt forms of protest against the prevalent hierarchical structure. In general a more or less dominant set of common values can be discerned. . . . But beneath the dominant theme there always exist different sets of values, which are, to a certain degree, adhered to among certain social groups and which function as a kind of counterpoint to the leading melody.[81]

Such deviant values may take the form of myths, jokes, songs, linguistic usage, or religion. Wertheim mentions in particular the *Tyl Üylenspiegel* tales which may be found in many cultures and which celebrate the prankster who ridicules the social hierarchy, turns established values upside down and gets away with it.[82] These counterpoints may become an institutionalized and harmless form of symbolic protest which, like the royal buffoon, strengthens the existing order. Or they may become the normative focus of religious or political movements with an insurrectionary potential.[83] It is not their existence that is notable, for they are well nigh universal, but rather the forms that they take, the values that they express, and the level of commitment that they inspire.

Despite analytic problems, it is conceivable that a careful examination of peasant culture can tell us whether it is becoming more or less harmonious with elite culture, along what dimensions it is changing, and roughly how large the gap is. A few brief illustrations will point to the kind of evidence that would be relevant.

In Central Luzon, the Tagalog term for sharecrop tenancy is *kasama*, which may be translated approximately as "partners," "equals," or "sharing together." Linguistically, it carries the favorable connotations of friendship and egalitarianism. As the *kasama* system has become more

---

81. W. F. Wertheim, "Society as a Composite of Conflicting Value Systems," *East-West Parallels* (Chicago: Quadrangle Books, 1965), p. 26. His argument is developed at greater length in his *Evolution or Revolution* (London: Pelican Books, 1973). See also Morris Opler, "Themes as Dynamic Forces in Culture," *Journal of the Washington Academy of Sciences* 36:5 (1946), 422–42, and Anton C. Zijderveld, "Jokes and Their Relation to Social Reality," *Social Research* 35:2 (Summer 1968), 286–311.

82. Wertheim, p. 30.

83. Such counterpoints may become a stable, adaptive, and negotiated version of dominant values. This is the argument that has been made with respect to English working-class culture. See, for example, Frank Parkin, "Class Inequality and Meaning Systems," in Parkin, *Class Inequality and the Political Order* (New York: Praeger, 1971), pp. 79–102, and Richard Haggart, *The Uses of Literacy* (London: Chatto and Windus, 1959).

exploitative, however, the term has become more and more dissonant with the relationship it actually embodies.[84] To cope with this social fact, peasants increasingly use the traditional term only when addressing landlords or others in authority. Among themselves they add a cynical suffix to the term which mocks its literal meaning and makes it clear that they hardly consider the tenancy relationship one of fairness or equality. In practice, then, the peasants' view of sharecropping is *demystified*; it reveals an open contempt and ridicule for the pretensions of the word *kasama*. This hardly proves that peasants are ready to revolt when the occasion presents itself, but it is surely evidence that they see the tenancy system as the unequal bargain that it is. An inquiry into agrarian class relations might well begin at this level, asking what terms peasants actually use to describe their arrangements with landowners and their relations with officials—and what connotations these terms have. It might then be possible to say something concrete about the symbolic alignment or opposition of elites and peasantry.[85]

Folksongs are yet another facet of peasant culture where a growing symbolic gap can show up. The rural folk tunes of England in the early eighteenth century, for example, were often filled with the celebration of rural life and praise for the dignity of rural work.[86]

> The mason's a man that is proud of his post
> If it wasn't for him we'd have died of the frost.
> And the tailor's a man makes an old coat like new
> But he's not half the man that follows the plough.[87]

But "toward the end of the eighteenth century and the beginning of the nineteenth, there were a great number of ballads about desperate crimes and of highwaymen, cantering on the heath; smugglers and poachers, whole communities of them, united with the village, ready to fight bloody battles against authority if need be."[88] Above all, the new relationship between rural laborers and the gentry found bitter expression.

> With broadtail coats and Quaker hats
> and whips below their arms,
> They'll hawk and call the country round
> a-seeking for their farms.

---

84. Communication from Benedict J. Kerkvliet, University of Hawaii.

85. The meaning of the term "la gabelle" (salt tax) for the French peasantry prior to the revolution is a case in point.

86. I owe this brief discussion to a fine term paper by Jan Jaffe, "English Peasants in the Nineteenth Century," University of Wisconsin, 1970.

87. A. L. Lloyd, *Singing Englishmen* (London: Workers' Music Association, 1944), p. 20.

88. Jaffe, "English Peasants in the Nineteenth Century," p. 7.

> And they'll go on some twenty miles
> Where people don't know 'em,
> And where they'll hire their harvest hand
> and bring them far from home.
>
> On cabbage cold and taters
> they'll feed you like the pigs,
> When they sit at their tea and toast
> and ride about in gigs.
> And mistress must get "Ma'am" and you
> must lift your cap to her,
> And before you gain an entrance
> the master must get "Sire."
>
> The harvest time when it comes round
> they'll grudge you sabbath rest.
> They'll let you worship
> but they like the working best.
> The dinner hour it vexes them
> and then to us they'll say,
> "Come on my lad, you'll get your rest
> when lying in the clay."[89]

This lament, mocking the deference of "Ma'am" and "Sire" and the tipping of the cap, is a sign that we can no longer take outward deference at face value. The contrast between the tea and toast of the gentry and the cold cabbage and potatoes of the workers plus the description of employers who begrudge them even the brief respite of that meal are as sharp a sign as we might wish that the landowner has become an exploitative figure. A single folksong by itself, of course, proves nothing, but when the general drift of folk culture moves in the same direction we have a reliable index to how the peasantry views the social order.

The content of peasant folksongs in Vietnam in the 1920s and 1930s reveals a comparable level of bitterness directed at rapacious notables who fleece the people and at the galling contrasts in wealth.

> All day long, they go and take anything at all from the people.
> In the evening, at the dinh, they get along fine,
> splitting up a part of what they collected that day;
> before them, a sumptuously set table
> Nandong liquor flowing into the notable's mouths.
> Our uninstructed people stand dumbfounded,

89. A. L. Lloyd, *Folksong in England* (London: Lawrence and Wishart in association with the Workers' Music Association, 1967), p. 64.

seeing the strong and powerful eat and talk.
They make the poor bear all the charges of the state.[90]

What unhappiness strikes the poor,
who wear a single worn out, torn cloth,
who tremble at the beatings of the communal drum
announcing the beginning of tax collection,
the time of every unhappiness.[91]

Oh heaven, why are you not just?
Some have abundance while others are in want.[92]

Within the popular culture, at the same time, the age-old myths of symbolic reversal, or a "world turned upside down," found a growing resonance. One song announced a time when the natural order of animals in the forest would be upset, another proclaimed that the "last would be first."

The son of the king becomes king.
The son of the temple watchman knows only how to sweep.
When the people rise up,
the son of the king, defeated, will go sweep the pagoda.[93]

The religious beliefs and practices of the peasantry offer another rich field of inquiry. Folk religion may undergo a transformation that places it in sharp opposition to the religious and social doctrines of the elite. Before a rebellion, or in the absence of rebellion, the religion of subordinate classes may bear the marks of oppression, as in the following African example. The cult of Ryangombe among the Hutu serfs of the dominant Tutsi pastoral people embodies a nearly total symbolic rejection of the values and myths that support an exploitative tribal feudalism.[94] Where the Tutsi proclaim the sacredness of herding, the central figure in the Hutu myth is a destroyer of cattle who ritually bathes his hands in the blood of cows. Where the Tutsi proclaim the justice of caste and feudal subordination, the Hutu cult rejects all hierarchy and its hero declares, "I walk behind no sovereign and no vassal follows me."[95] The cognitive structure of revolt was already firmly in place well before the opportunity to act presented itself.

90. Hong Giap Nguyen, *La Condition des paysans au Vietnam pendant la periode coloniale à travers les chansons populaires*, p. 115.

91. Ibid.

92. Ibid., p. 141.

93. Ibid., p. 169.

94. Luc de Heusch, "Mythe et société féudale: le culte de kubandwa dans le Rwanda traditionel," *Archives de sociologie des réligions* 18 (1964), 133–46.

95. Ibid., p. 141.

> Historically foreign to Tutsi culture, the cult of Ryangombe in its typical Rwandan form is the product of a popular, multi-faceted alienation. Ryangombe offers to the ensemble of castes a mystic evasion—immediate access by possession to the kingdom of force, of liberty, of the hunt and perpetual leisure, a kingdom without hierarchy where the father and son, closely allied, affirm an equal sovereignty, a kingdom without castes or cows, without links of maternal lineages nor alliance.[96]

But it is not simply as a "mystic evasion" that the cult must be understood. It provides a critique of the existing order and an alternative symbolic universe that is so potentially explosive that the practice of Ryangombe was forbidden by the Tutsi elite. While the cult may console in the present, it also nurtures among the oppressed social links and cultural dissent that lie in wait for the future.

These transformations may come in the context of a wholly new religion or they may instead represent a heretical variant of the dominant religion. The Saminists in the Rembang area of Java around the turn of the century, for example, were a sect that rejected Islam, the state, and social hierarchy itself.[97] They refused to invite Muslim functionaries to solemnize marriages and funerals and to collect their fees; they refused to pay taxes (though they might present a "gift"); and they abandoned status-laden terms of address—instead insisting on the use of low-Javanese (*ngoko*) and addressing one another as *sedular*, "brother."[98] In the course of their conflict with an intrusive colonial state, the Saminists took existing elements of folk culture and fashioned them into a coherent and socially organized religion that consciously rejected both elite values and their claims on peasant society. It is no wonder that the Saminist heartland was later receptive to communist appeals inasmuch as its religious practices had much in common with that party's doctrines.

Through much of Philippine history, religious dissent and rebellion have gone hand in hand, perhaps because the Catholic Church was so much a part of the colonial political establishment.[99] Opposition has commonly taken the form of independent sects that were offshoots of Catholicism but were denounced as heretical by the official hierarchy. As in the case of the Saminists, the basis of a sect's appeal was often its

96. Ibid., p. 145.

97. See Benda and Castles, "The Samin Movement," and The Siauw Giap, "The Samin and Samat Movement in Java."

98. The parallel between this last and the plain talk of the early Quakers and other dissenting sects in late seventeenth-century England is striking.

99. David Sturtevant, *The Last Shall Be First*, passim.

denunciation of agrarian inequality, the state, and the financial claims of the established clergy. Opposition to colonialism itself found expression in the worship of new saints, notably the nationalist hero José Rizal, who had denounced the mother church for betraying its own values.[100] Even when such sects did not turn to open rebellion, their doctrine and practices stood in stark symbolic contrast to elite visions of the social order.

The process of religious conversion may also be seen as a means by which peasants, having dissociated themselves from dominant religious and social values, choose to give social and symbolic meaning to their personal situation. For this reason, those who are least favored by a social order and its ethical rationale are most likely to be attracted to a new creed that offers them a place of dignity and a competing great tradition.[101] Christian missions thus found a more sympathetic response among the lower castes in the Hindu hierarchy and among the minority peoples in Southeast Asia, considered by the dominant groups as less than fully civilized. In contemporary Java it is reported that Buddhism has made strong inroads among *abangan* peasants in areas most decimated by the repression of late 1965. Not much is known about this religious transformation yet, but it seems likely that many peasants have chosen to formalize their opposition to the self-conscious Moslem community by leaving Islam altogether. As a symbolic expression of withdrawal and cleavage, in the wake of a political disaster, its significance cannot be overestimated. The effect of such conversions is not merely symbolic. They both contribute to the social solidarity of the believers in the new faith and seal them off more firmly from the dominant community. As the Methodist chapels of the English working class helped provide the social soil in which unionism could grow, so may the social organization of a dissident religion among peasants provide the basis for their political organization when the time is ripe.

Drawing from such illustrations, it ought to be possible to determine to what degree peasants actually accept or reject the social order by reference to their culture. Proverbs, folksongs, oral history, legends, jokes, language, ritual, and religion can each help us gauge the symbolic distance between the elite and the peasantry. Symbolic opposition is not confined to content but may assume stylistic and esthetic forms as well. Since the freedom of peasants to elaborate and define their own culture is almost always greater than their capacity to remake society, it is to their

100. Mexican peasant revolutionaries fighting under the banner of the Black Virgin of Guadeloupe are an obvious parallel.

101. And often a powerful protector as well, especially in the case of Christians in the colonies.

culture that we must look to discover how much their moral universe diverges from that of the elite.

Some elements of folk culture are naturally more relevant to this question than others. For any agrarian system one can identify a set of key values that justify the rights of an elite to the deference, land, and taxes that they claim. It is largely an empirical matter whether these key values find support or opposition within the subculture of subordinate classes. If we find that bandits are made into folk heroes, that fallen rebels are treated with reverence, that poachers are celebrated, it is good evidence that transgressions of elite codes evoke a vicarious admiration among peasants. If the forms of outward deference and homage toward elites are privately mocked, it is at least evidence that peasants are hardly in the thrall of a naturally ordained social order. If peasant sects proclaim the equal division of wealth and the right of all to land and its products in the midst of a society in which things are very much otherwise, it is, at a minimum, evidence that the peasants' notion of social justice does not correspond with the existing distribution of resources.

While answers to the question of false consciousness may be sought in the study of culture, they are not likely to be simple. We may discover, for example, that a peasantry accepts the principle of land ownership but rejects a particular set of landowners who have violated what peasants regard as the duties of landownership. Such a belief may be at least as explosive as a rejection of landownership in principle, though its implications may be less revolutionary in the classical sense. Peasant rebels in Russia were often as devoted to the Czar as they were repelled by the rapaciousness of his subordinates.[102] Rejection of elite values is seldom an across-the-board proposition and only a close study of folk culture can define the major points of friction and correspondence. Furthermore, one proverb or folk tune or legend may be suggestive but it is hardly convincing. What is important is the central tendency of peasant culture in its entirety.[103] Finally, it is obvious that any class system, no matter how legitimate, promotes a certain cultural differentiation. In this sense it is not the *existence* of cultural differences that is critical, but rather the fact that these differences center around key values in the social order and that they grow and harden.

The problem of whether peasants submit to exploitation because of mystification or because they have no other choice is, thus, not an

102. See Donald W. Treadgold, "The Peasant and Religion," in Wayne S. Vucinich, *The Peasant in Nineteenth-Century Russia* (Stanford: Stanford University Press, 1965), pp. 72–107.

103. One can expect, in this context, to find interesting disparities both between regions and between different classes within the peasantry.

analytical cul de sac. It can be resolved by asking how much coercion it takes to maintain the agrarian order and what happens when the balance of forces changes. It can be resolved by asking how common it is for peasants to circumvent the rules of tenancy or labor by petty violations that stop short of rebellion. Most important, it can be resolved by asking directly whether the values embodied in peasant culture do in fact accord with the dominant myths of the social order.

It is especially at the level of culture that a defeated or intimidated peasantry may nurture its stubborn moral dissent from an elite-created social order. This symbolic refuge is not simply a source of solace in a precarious life, not simply an escape. It represents an alternative moral universe in embryo—a dissident subculture, an existentially true and just one, which helps unite its members as a human community and as a community of values. In this sense, it is as much a beginning as an end.

# Index

Adas, Michael, ix, 68 *n*, 74
Africa, 21, 182, 236–37
Anderson, James, 37 and *n*
Annam (colonial period), 1; agriculture, 1, 22, 47, 127–28, 138, 139–40, 197; communal land, and loss of, 43, 129, 130, 131, 132; Communist Party, 139, 142, 144, 145, 147–48, 149, 150 *n*; economy, 60, 90, 92, 140–41; economy, Great Depression, 88, 127, 134, 136–41 *passim*, 201; Nghe-An/Ha-Tinh Soviets, 3, 89, 91, 120 *n*, 127–49 *passim*, 150 *n*, 154 *n*, 157, 166, 191, 192, 197, 202, 203 *n*, 226; population and growth, 82, 131; rebellion and unrest, 32, 92, 113, 128, 197, 201 (*see also* Nghe-An/Ha-Tinh Soviets *above*); secondary occupations, 14, 129, 135–36, 137; smallholders, 81, 108, 130–31, 134, 136; social structure and village life, 40, 43, 201–02; taxation, 32, 60, 88, 92, 106–10, 113, 120, 129–30, 132–37 *passim*, 139, 141–42, 144 *n*, 201; tenants and sharecroppers, 47, 48, 79, 81, 82, 83, 108, 120, 129–33, 136, 137, 141, 146, 186 and *n*; wage laborers, 81, 110, 129, 130, 131, 133, 136, 137, 141
Annam (precolonial period), 128
Annam. *See also* Vietnam

Balandier, Georges, 181 and *n*
Banfield, Edward, 213 and *n*
Baumol, William J., 24 and *n*
Binns, B. O., 56 *n*, 87–88
Blau, Peter, 164 and *n*
Bloch, Marc, viii, 184
British India. *See* Burma (colonial period); India (colonial period)
Brocheux, Pierre, 79 and *n*
Burma, 64 *n*, 205, 216, 225; land reform, 196 *n*, 226 *n*
Burma (colonial period), 36, 195; Great Depression, 87–88, 104–05, 166; millennial movements (19th and 20th cents.), 149, 150 and *n*; taxation, 52, 93, 99–108 *passim*, 110, 112, 122, 150, 156, 199
Burma, Lower (colonial period), 40, 63, 67, 198; economy, 8, 57–58, 59, 60, 84, 90, 198; economy, Great Depression, 86–90, 115–18; Indians as creditors and labor competitors, 85, 86, 89–90, 150, 151, 154; population and growth, 63 and *n*, 67–68; rebellion and unrest, 40, 58, 68, 74, 75, 76, 85, 89, 99, 198; rebellion and unrest, Saya San, 3, 76, 89, 95, 99–100, 149–57 *passim*, 166, 203 *n*, 226; smallholders, 71, 72, 74, 85, 86, 102, 118, 150, 151; social structure and village life, 40, 60, 67–76, 202, 203; taxation, 99–105, 118, 120, 150, 151; tenants and sharecroppers, 37, 47, 59, 68, 70–76 *passim*, 78, 80, 83–89 *passim*, 99, 101, 102, 118, 150–51, 173, 176, 179, 227–28, 231; wage laborers, 68, 72, 74–75, 87, 89, 90, 101, 102, 151
Burma, Upper (colonial period), 1, 14, 64 *n*, 102; economy, 87–88, 90; population and growth, 67, 71; rebellion and unrest, 32, 198; social structure and village life, 40, 67, 169, 201–02; taxation, 99, 102, 105, 120; tenants and sharecroppers, 36, 71, 72, 75, 78, 83, 102, 120

Cambodia, 195–96, 225 *n*
Chayanov, A. V., 13 and *n*, 14, 15, 19, 59, 205–06
Chesneaux, Jean, 62 and *n*
Chettiars, 85, 86, 89–90, 150, 154
China, 171, 178, 196 *n*, 200, 224 *n*
Cobb, R. C., viii, 8–9, 9 *n*, 219
Cochinchina (colonial period), 40, 57–58, 67; agriculture, 86, 88, 128; economy, 60, 84, 90, 198; economy, Great Depression, 86, 87, 88, 120, 122; population and growth, 67–68, 76; rebellion and unrest, 40, 58, 68, 78, 82–83, 88, 123–27, 142, 144; smallholders, 78, 85, 86, 122–23; social structure and village life, 40, 60, 67–68, 76–84, 202, 203; taxation, 88, 106–10, 118, 120–27 *passim*, 142; tenants and sharecroppers, 67–68, 76–85 *passim*, 88, 108, 118, 123, 124, 126–27, 131, 179; wage laborers, 68, 118, 123, 124, 131